# Prescription

*for*

# Murder

D0005494

# Prescription
## *for*
# Murder

The True Story of
Mass Murderer
Dr Harold Frederick Shipman

BRIAN WHITTLE
and
JEAN RITCHIE

WARNER BOOKS

A *Warner* Book

First published in Great Britain in 2000
by Warner Books

Copyright © 2000 by Brian Whittle and Jean Ritchie

The moral right of the authors has been asserted.

All rights reserved.
No part of this publication may be reproduced,
stored in a retrieval system, or transmitted,
in any form or by any means, without the prior
permission in writing of the publisher, nor be
otherwise circulated in any form of binding or cover
other than that in which it is published and without
a similar condition including this condition being
imposed on the subsequent purchaser.

A CIP catalogue record for this book
is available from the British Library.

ISBN: 0 7515 2998 2

Typeset in Plantin by M Rules
Printed and bound in Great Britain
by Clays Ltd, St Ives plc

Warner Books
A Division of
Little, Brown and Company (UK)
Brettenham House
Lancaster Place
London WC2E 7EN

For Maureen, Mark,
Christopher and Peter

# Contents

'[Death is] . . . the anaesthetic from which none come round.'

—PHILIP LARKIN

'The doctor is a specially dangerous man when poor.'

—GEORGE BERNARD SHAW

# Acknowledgements

This book could not have been written without the help, support and encouragement of many people, including: Clive Entwistle of Chameleon Television; Stan Egerton BEM; Sarah Dean Forrester of the Greater Manchester Police Press Office; everyone at Cavendish Press, especially Diana McCarthy, Pat Hurst and Tim Downs; Joe Gribben at the Crown in Hyde; Mike Ridley of Ridley Media; Roger Houghton at Lucas Alexander Whitley; and others too numerous to mention.

# Introduction

For an August night, the weather was atrocious. The rain was lashing down, the wind was fierce and the sky was black and moonless. Looking out of the window of the Laurel Bank Nursing Home in Gee Cross, Hyde, the night staff saw something that made their blood run cold. Across the road, in the graveyard, shadowy figures were moving about. Some lights were on, and there were men with spades. They rang the police, convinced that they were witnessing an evil black magic rite.

But the macabre truth was that the men in the cemetery were the police. They were digging up the coffin of Kathleen Grundy, an 81-year-old widow who had died five weeks earlier, suddenly, at her £200,000 home a quarter of a mile away. The detective inspector who had obtained permission to exhume the body, a bluff, genial copper with only eight months to go to retirement after thirty years' service, shared the unease of the watchers: the night was so black and the rain so unremitting that he could imagine at any moment lightning forking across the sky, illuminating a black carriage with plumed horses and bats fluttering overhead, like a scene from a Denis Wheatley novel or a Hammer horror film.

At that moment he felt a different kind of fear. Supposing he had got it all wrong? After all, the doctor who had signed Mrs Grundy's death certificate was one of the most respected, popular GPs in the town. He *couldn't* be a murderer . . . could he?

DI Stan Egerton was not just playing a hunch. He had evidence that convinced him there was something very seriously amiss with Kathleen Grundy's unexpected death. Yet, standing in that graveyard, in charge of the first exhumation ever ordered by Greater Manchester Police, he wondered whether he had made a terrible mistake. Then he remembered the strange and worrying things he had been hearing about Dr Fred Shipman, the GP who would, according to Mrs Grundy's will, inherit her entire £400,000 estate. Surely there could be no mistake.

But what Stan Egerton could never have predicted on that wild night was that, as they opened Mrs Grundy's muddied coffin, they were also opening the investigation into the biggest serial killer in British criminal history, probably in the world.

It was not until 20 August 1998 that the national newspapers in Britain caught up with what had happened in the graveyard of Hyde Chapel twenty days earlier, and by then, Stan Egerton had more idea of the enormity of the case.

'POLICE EXAMINE 19 DEATHS AFTER WIDOW CHANGES WILL FOR DOCTOR' was the headline in *The Times* on that morning. 'DOCTOR IN PROBE ON 20 DEATHS – PATIENT KATH LEAVES HIM HOME', screamed a *Sun* headline running down three-quarters of a page. 'WIDOW EXHUMED AS FAMILY CONTEST WILL', the *Telegraph* proclaimed.

'Police are probing the deaths of twenty patients of a doctor after discovering one of them changed her will to leave him a substantial amount of property. Dr Harold Shipman will be quizzed over the death of 81-year-old Kathleen Grundy, whose body has been exhumed for post-mortem following a complaint by her daughter Angela. Lawyer Angela was shocked to find neither she nor her two sons had inherited a pair of cottages owned by former mayoress Kathleen, and together worth around £250,000,' ran the *Sun* report. More or less the same details featured in every other newspaper.

Why had it taken so long for the media to wake up to what was happening in Hyde? Journalists are usually very good at picking up on sensational stories. Good news editors, like good policemen, have a nose for it: they know when some small detail in a story singles it out as potentially more exciting, more newsworthy, more likely to sell papers, than the others on the list.

But as far as the Shipman story goes, most of them had their antennae switched off. A query over the death of an elderly lady meant another 'mercy killing' doctor, or possibly a case of medical negligence. There's a predictable newspaper scale of interest in death which tails off according to how remote from Britain the victims are (hundreds killed in an earthquake on the other side of the globe may rate only a couple of paragraphs) and how old the victims are: the murder of a child or a pretty young woman rates far more inches of newsprint than the death of an old woman.

Besides, there had been a spate of euthanasia stories, and although they merited a good debate on the feature pages of the broadsheets, they did nothing to boost circulation. The press would cover the case of yet another doctor suspected of helping an elderly patient escape from a life of pain and misery, but it was not big news.

There was one journalist, though, who picked up on the same sense of unease that gripped Detective Inspector Egerton when he was first handed the case of Kathleen Grundy. Brian Whittle, one of the authors of this book, runs a well-respected independent news agency in Manchester, servicing the national press, radio and television stations with stories from what is, by any standards, a good news patch. Hyde, one of the satellite towns which has been absorbed into Greater Manchester, is just a small part of this patch, and, at first, covering the police interest in the death of Mrs Grundy was nothing more than a routine part of the agency's work.

But a combination of local knowledge and gut instinct told Brian that there was something much more important than one mercy killing, or even a possible will forgery, unfolding in Hyde. He assigned reporters and photographers to the town to cover – and uncover – every aspect of the case. Before the rest of the media world woke up, he was aware that the case of Dr Fred Shipman was going to be massive news.

The Shipman story that he filed to the news desks of every national newspaper resulted in the spate of sensational headlines on Thursday 20 August. And because he and his staff were busy in Hyde before the media circus turned up (the people of the town have faced television crews from Japan, Germany, Belgium, Scandinavia and America; there have been reporting teams from all over the world; the British press have blitzed the area), he has had better access and more insight into what has occurred, and the effect it has had on the inward-looking community of Hyde, than anyone else.

This is his story of Fred Shipman, the man who metamorphosed from a caring, committed and respected GP into the 'Doctor Death' of tabloid headlines, a mass murderer whose motives will puzzle psychiatrists and psychologists for generations to come, and whose tally of victims will never be fully known.

# 1

# Died Unexpectedly

The headstone on Kathleen Grundy's grave in the cemetery behind Hyde Chapel is tasteful, plain. 'Died Unexpectedly After a Lifetime of Helping Others' are the words etched into the pale stone, beneath her name, and above the details of her family: husband John, daughter Angela, grandsons Richard and Matthew.

The inscription on the headstone is a simple and moving tribute to a woman who, however she had died, would have deserved a place in the chronicles of Hyde; a woman who took genuine pleasure in being useful to the community. But there is a greater commendation that the people of the town owe to Kathleen Grundy, summed up here in the words of Debbie Massey, the young undertaker who twice supervised the burial of Mrs Grundy: 'She helped other people all her life, and she carried on helping them in her death, too.'

For it was Kathleen Grundy's death that brought to an end the murderous career of Dr Fred Shipman.

The papers that Chief Inspector Eileen Scarratt dropped on DI Stan Egerton's desk made interesting reading. A woman had gone into a police station in Leamington Spa,

Warwickshire, to ask the police to investigate her mother's will, which she believed had been forged. The Warwickshire police passed the case on to Greater Manchester Police, because the mother had come from Hyde. A quick reading of the notes aroused Stan Egerton's curiosity: this was not the usual will wrangle, with brothers and sisters squabbling over who should get what, and which, if it ever reached the attention of the police, would be quickly passed on to be settled between solicitors in a civil court.

For a start the woman, Angela Woodruff, was herself a solicitor. Secondly, her mother was Mrs Kathleen Grundy, an ex-Mayoress of Hyde and someone whose death had caused quite a stir in the town. Stan, who has lived in Hyde for more than thirty years, had never met her to talk to, but he knew her by sight and he had certainly heard about her: her husband John, who had died thirty years earlier, had been Mayor of the town in the 1960s, and a lecturer at Manchester University. Both he and Kathleen were born and bred in the area, and they first met when he was her history teacher at Hyde Grammar School. After his death in 1968 she continued to live at their beautiful seventeenth-century cottage in Gee Cross. She always referred to Gee Cross as 'the village' and there were few people in the village she did not know, or who did not know her. She served for many years on the local council, as Conservative member for Werneth Ward, and had been chairman of the Tameside and Glossop Community Health Council. One of the tower blocks in the town is named after her husband, and there is a plaque commemorating his service to Hyde in the Town Hall.

Kathleen Grundy was a regular member of the congregation at Hyde Chapel on Stockport Road, Gee Cross, a Unitarian chapel as big and imposing as any parish church, the first fully Gothic nonconformist chapel in England.

DI Egerton also knew, because he is a sociable man with a great many friends and contacts in the town, that her death had come as a shock to many people. She may have been just a week away from her eighty-second birthday, but she was only old in terms of years: in every other way Kathleen Grundy was fit, active, alert and a great asset to the community. Unlike the deaths of most old ladies, hers had raised comment. One resident in Gee Cross was away at the time of her death and only heard about it on return from holiday. 'I said, "Did she get knocked over?"' she recalls. 'I'd seen her jumping off a bus before it reached the stop a couple of weeks earlier, and the only way I could envisage her dying was in an accident. It was hard to believe she'd died at home.'

The first step for DI Egerton was to see Mrs Woodruff to establish why she thought her mother's will had been forged. He and Detective Constable Dave O'Brien made a 200-mile round trip to Mrs Woodruff's home, in the village of Harbury, near Leamington Spa, where she lived with her husband David, a university professor. They discovered that Mrs Woodruff had already made enough enquiries about the forged will for them to be sure there was something suspicious going on.

Kathleen Grundy was a loyal and enthusiastic patient of Dr Shipman's, feeling, as so many of the people on his list did, that he was one of the last of a dying breed: an old-fashioned family doctor with plenty of time for his patients. When he had set up a solo practice she had followed him as a patient. She was so enthusiastic about him that she had, according to a friend, considered giving £200 from a charity she was involved with to his patients' fund.

Despite her age, she had few physical problems. She loved gardening, she walked miles, she was on the committees of several local charities, and mentally alert enough to do two half-days a week working for the Age

Concern shop opposite Shipman's practice, known as 'The Surgery': she banked the takings the day before her death. Three times a week she helped prepare and serve lunches for old people at the luncheon club, held at Werneth House, a social centre for pensioners about half a mile away from her home. As the organiser of the club, she would shop for the food, help prepare and serve it, and assist with the clearing up: the other volunteers were on average twenty or thirty years younger than her, but Kathleen Grundy did not think of herself as old.

Three days before her death she went on a coach trip to Derbyshire, and is fondly remembered as having been the life and soul of the party. 'She was in such good spirits on the day of the trip,' says her friend Phyllis Howsam. 'She was a marvellous lady: she would do anything to help anyone.'

She loved watching sport on television, and had been really enjoying the summer of 1998: both Wimbledon and the football World Cup had been on in the weeks prior to her death. One of her closest friends, another ex-Mayoress, May Clarke, who lives just a quarter of a mile away from Mrs Grundy's cottage, remembers her calling round for the evening just a couple of days before she died: 'She left at 10.30pm to get home in time to watch the World Cup highlights: she loved football.'

On the day before she died, she visited her friend May again. She talked proudly about her grandsons, one of whom, 24-year-old Richard, had just got a first at university and the other, 23-year-old Matthew, had just got a job in Japan.

She told May she was expecting Dr Shipman to call the next day to take a blood sample and get her to sign some papers. She said how good it was of the doctor to come to her home, rather than expect her to go to the surgery. She also discussed buying a new car: she was certainly not ready to give up driving, although when she went to visit

Angela it was usually by train. She went three or four times a year to Warwickshire: there was no time in her busy social calendar for more visits. On her last trip, a few weeks before her death, she went walking with her daughter and son-in-law and on their return, while Angela and David recovered with a sit-down and a cup of coffee, she insisted on doing the ironing.

Geoffrey Ridgeway, a friend of hers for thirty-four years, and who lives in a cottage owned by Mrs Grundy, likened her to a March hare – always dashing about doing something for somebody. 'She loved her gardening, her sport on telly and she thought the world of her family. She had no airs and graces: she was a down-to-earth, lovely person.'

She was also wealthy: as well as her home, £200,000 Loughrigg Cottage, she owned a £90,000 terraced cottage nearby and a £60,000 flat in the Lake District. (It was while on holiday in the Lake District, where they both loved walking, that her husband John had died unexpectedly thirty years earlier.) Her total estate was worth just under £400,000.

Her death was discovered when, on Wednesday 24 June, she failed to turn up at Werneth House to help with the lunches. When telephone calls to her home went unanswered the caretaker from the pensioners' centre in Lord Derby Road, John Green, and one of the volunteers, Ronald Pickford, went to the house and, failing to get a reply to their knock, let themselves in through a door they were surprised to find unlocked. In the living room they discovered Mrs Grundy, fully clothed, curled up on the sofa as if asleep. She looked peaceful, but had a grey complexion.

Mr Pickford knew that Shipman was her GP, and knew his number. When the doctor arrived about ten minutes later he told John Green that he had seen Mrs Grundy earlier that morning but 'only for a talk'. He said she must have been well enough to get dressed, as when he saw her she was in her night clothes. He carried out what the police described as a 'cursory examination' of the body and told the two men she had had 'a cardiac arrest'.

Mrs Grundy's friends from the luncheon club asked Dr Shipman what they should do next, and he advised them to contact a firm of solicitors in the town, Hamilton's, who he said would handle everything. When they were contacted, they denied acting for Mrs Grundy, but said that they had received a will, supposedly from her, that very morning. They advised the Werneth House volunteers to contact her family. When the two men could not get hold of Mrs Grundy's daughter, Angela, the police were called. Two police constables went to Mrs Grundy's house, and spoke to Shipman by phone: he again said she had died from natural causes.

For Angela there was an enormous sense of shock and loss. She had no clue that her mother had any health problems. Angela, who was fifty-three at the time, drove with her husband David to Hyde early the next day and saw Shipman at his surgery before going to her mother's home. The GP told her that he had seen her mother the day before for a routine matter but that Mrs Grundy had complained of feeling unwell in some ill-defined way.

'He said that sometimes old people complain about feeling unwell before they die, and then they simply die. He implied it was old age, but he didn't actually say it,' said Angela.

He said it clearly enough when he filled out her death certificate because he put only one cause of death: old age. It is a perfectly legitimate medical explanation of death, but among doctors it is regarded as a last resort, to be used only with the very elderly and infirm, when so many organs and bodily functions are failing at the same time. When it is used, it is usually accompanied by some more specific medical information. For Kathleen Grundy, one of the healthiest 81-year-olds anyone could think of, it did not make sense. (Many doctors have been consulted during the research for this book, and none could think of an instance where they wrote 'old age' as the only cause of death on a death certificate.)

In the immediate aftermath of the death, there was the usual activity surrounding the organisation of a funeral: hundreds of mourners packed Hyde Chapel on 1 July to pay their tributes to Mrs Grundy. There was also the sad duty of sorting out her mother's will: as a solicitor, Angela had always handled all her mother's legal affairs, and knew from the will she had in her possession how the old lady wanted her estate disposed of, with the bulk of her money and property going to the family.

Angela was amazed, therefore, to be contacted twelve days after her mother's funeral by the solicitors in Hyde, Hamilton Ward, saying that they had Mrs Grundy's last will and testament. They were unhappy with the way in which they had been instructed to act for Mrs Grundy, and wanted to talk to Angela about it. It was as a result of this conversation with Brian Burgess, the probate and conveyancing manager at the firm, that Angela began to investigate, and quickly came up with sufficient information to make her suspicious enough to go to the police.

What DI Stan Egerton discovered was that on the day of Mrs Grundy's death, Hamilton Ward received a typewritten letter, apparently from her, dated 22 June. With it was a will, dated 9 June. The letter, purporting to come from Mrs Grundy, said: 'Dear Sir, I enclose a copy of my will. I think it is clear my intention and wish Dr Shipman to benefit by having my estate but if he dies or does not accept it, then the estate goes to my daughter.' It also said that she would call in within the next few days to verify her instructions. The will reinforced the letter: it stipulated that her entire estate be left to Dr Harold Frederick Shipman. There was nothing for her daughter or the grandsons she adored. It also requested that her body be cremated, which was completely at odds with everything Kathleen Grundy had ever expressed about her death. As this will had a later date than the one in Angela's possession, at face value it appeared as though, in the final days of her life, Mrs Grundy had acted completely out of character and without discussing the matter with her daughter or any of her many friends, had simply rewritten her will excluding everyone except Fred Shipman.

This alone was enough to make Angela – and subsequently Stan Egerton – very suspicious. There had been no family quarrel, and Mrs Grundy had shown no signs of becoming confused or demented; quite the reverse. The firm of solicitors in Hyde had also received another letter, again typed, dated 28 June (four days after Mrs Grundy's death) purporting to come from someone who signed their name S. or J. Smith, and who claimed to be a friend of Mrs Grundy's. The letter said: 'I regret to inform you that Mrs Kathleen Grundy of 79 Joel Lane died last week. I understand she lodged a will with you, as I am a friend who typed it out for her.'

The solicitors were not willing to start winding up an estate on the basis of two letters from people they had never met. It took them a few days to trace Angela Woodruff, tracking her down through a neighbour of Mrs Grundy's in Joel Lane. As soon as they did make contact they sent her photostats of all the documents. Angela's suspicions were immediately aroused by the phraseology of the will, by the fact that it referred to her mother's house, when Mrs Grundy owned two houses, and the bad typing. It did not seem at all like the handiwork of her meticulous mother, who had worked as a secretary before her marriage and was a proficient typist.

Before going to the police she tried, and failed, to track down the unknown letter-writer called Smith, who, despite claiming to be a friend, did not attend Mrs

Grundy's funeral. (There was a couple named Smith at the funeral, a former Mayor and Mayoress of Hyde, but they knew nothing of the mysterious S. or J. Smith.) But Angela did find the two people who had witnessed the 'will', Paul Spencer and Claire Hutchinson, and travelled to Hyde to see them. Talking to them confirmed her fears that the new will was a forgery. She also went to the bank which handled the Age Concern account, and compared her mother's signature on paying-in slips to that on the will. Again, the signatures did not match, and she asked the police to start an investigation. It was on Friday 31 July that Detective Inspector Stan Egerton and Detective Constable Dave O'Brien travelled to Leamington Spa to meet her.

Paul Spencer was running a pet shop in Market Street, close to The Surgery, with his girlfriend Sarah Coulthard, at the time he was asked to witness the will. He was twenty-nine, and had been a patient of Dr Shipman's from the age of eleven. He shared the popular view of the doctor, describing a visit to him as 'like chatting with a favourite uncle'.

'I genuinely thought he was a great doctor, very intelligent. I went to see him with different things, and he always had time to talk. You would expect to be kept waiting when you went to his surgery, but you accepted it because you knew he would spend time with you. You knew he would be gabbing with the little old lady who went in before you about her cats, and you just had to wait your turn. He treated you personally, using your first name, asking about your life, holidays, family. He would drop things into conversation: "I remember when you had your jab before going to Spain" or "I remember when you had measles." Of course, he had your medical records in front of him, but he made an effort: he was not just an overworked doctor who hasn't got time to talk. There was a year-long wait to get on to his list: he was the most popular doctor in Hyde.'

Paul went to The Surgery on 10 June to get a repeat prescription for antibiotics. As he expected, he waited for some time.

'I sat there reading the posters, as you do at the doctors – anything to pass the time. There was only me, a young woman with a baby in a pushchair, and the receptionist. Then Dr Shipman popped his head round the door of his consulting room and said, "Would you two mind witnessing a signature for me?" Me and the other patient, the young woman, just glanced at each other and shook our heads – we didn't mind. We followed him into his room and sitting on the patient's chair next to his desk was this old dear. He said something like, "Are you sure about this, Kath?" or "Are you positive, Kath, is it okay?" and the old lady said, "Yes." Then he said casually to me and the young woman, "Just pop your names and addresses there, print and sign it at the bottom, will you?"

'The form was A4 size, doubled over, with the back folded over to the front halfway. All I could see was the name Kathleen Grundy and her signature at one side. I signed first and went out, and a few seconds later the young woman came out. We didn't discuss it. I thought it was some sort of routine medical form, and I didn't think any more of it. It never occurred to me to ask what it was that I was witnessing: in fact, I didn't actually witness a signature, as I never saw her sign it.

'I didn't pay much attention to the old lady, and I don't remember seeing her come out of his room: I may simply not have noticed, or she may have gone out the other way, through a door to the back.'

The police now believe that what Mrs Grundy believed she was signing was a consent form to participate in the survey on ageing that Shipman claimed he was involved in, although this piece of paper has never been found.

In the months after Mrs Grundy's death, as the police investigation escalated and culminated in the conviction of Fred Shipman, Paul Spencer has been asked many times by friends who heard of his involvement why he did not question the doctor about the document he was being asked to witness, and with sad hindsight he describes what he did as 'virtually signing Mrs Grundy's death warrant'.

But he rightly guesses that the vast majority of people would have done the same. 'If a geezer comes up to you in a pub and asks you to sign something there is no way you'd do it without reading it all very carefully, and finding out what it's about. But if your own doctor, who you have known since you were a kid and who is extremely well-respected in the town, asks you to do him a favour and sign something, you don't think twice. It was all run of the mill, unimportant.

'When I finally went in to see the doctor he never mentioned the signing. Neither did I. We chatted and he gave me my prescription.'

Three weeks later Angela and David Woodruff arrived on Paul's doorstep, although he had no idea who they were.

'The woman said, "Are you Paul Spencer? Did you sign a form at Dr Shipman's surgery?" She showed me a photocopy of a document. It had my name on it, but it was not my signature. She asked me to do some specimen signatures, which I did. Mrs Woodruff seemed upset and agitated. She kept saying to her husband, "I can't believe she has done this." I had no idea she was Mrs Grundy's daughter, I assumed she was something to do with the firm of solicitors in Hyde.

'I was puzzled by the whole thing: it looked as though my signature had been forged, and not very well. I didn't know what to make of it. They thanked me and left, and I didn't hear anything else for another week.'

This time it was a policewoman, Detective Constable Sally Reid, on Paul's doorstep. As soon as Stan Egerton and Dave O'Brien saw the photocopy of the will and the original letter to Hamilton Ward, they were sure they were dealing with forgeries: even to an untrained eye it was obvious they had been typed on the same typewriter. When they subsequently collected the letter signed 'S. Smith' from the offices of Hamilton Ward, they could tell that this, too, had been typed on the same machine. DI Egerton dispatched DC Reid to interview the two witnesses to the will. When Reid asked Paul Spencer if he had signed Kathleen Grundy's will, he explained that he had signed a document, but had no idea what it was. Again, she asked for samples of his signature. A week later, he was asked to give finger- and palm-prints to check against those on the will.

Mrs Claire Hutchinson, the other witness, was also surprised and shocked when Angela Woodruff visited her.

'I felt quite upset that this lady had been to see me at my house,' she said. 'I went to see Dr Shipman and told him she was very upset, and there was some question about something we had signed. He apologised and said he was very sorry we had been bothered at home, and if he had had any idea what would come of it he wouldn't have bothered. He said he was never going to ask anybody from his surgery to be a witness again. He said he would have asked the receptionist, and he would have signed the will, but he asked the lady if there was anything in the will for the surgery and the lady said there may be a small bequest. Dr Shipman said that because of this he was not eligible to sign the will, so he asked us.

'He said normally if one of his patients left money it was a small amount to buy a picture for the surgery. He said he had known Kathleen Grundy for a long time but never saw her much as a patient because she was rarely ill, but he had sat on committees at the Community Health Council with her. He said she had just turned up and asked him to sign this will.'

Mrs Hutchinson visited the surgery a few days later to make an appointment. Dr Shipman was at the reception desk and said to her, 'Have you heard the latest? She's left it all to Age Concern.'

Mrs Hutchinson thought this was odd, and made no comment. She, too, was later visited by the police and gave samples of her signature and fingerprints.

It was instantly obvious to the police that they were dealing with a serious case of fraud. But alarm bells were ringing in DI Egerton's brain: it seemed clear, although he needed to gather more evidence, that his main suspect was Dr Harold Frederick Shipman, a well-established and busy GP with a flourishing practice in the town. This was obviously not one of the usual run of crimes that he had investigated in thirty years in the force, nor the usual run of criminal. But there was something far more important at the back of his mind: he remembered a previous police investigation, which had happened while he was away on holiday, earlier that year. The doctor at the centre of that was Dr Shipman. He spoke to DI Dave Smith, who had handled that investigation, and who confirmed that another GP had alerted the coroner to the large amount of deaths among Dr Shipman's patients. Suddenly, a case of fraud began to look like something even more sinister, especially in conjunction with Angela Woodruff's assertion that her mother's death had been totally unexpected.

Stan Egerton is an old-fashioned policeman, from a working-class Manchester background, who rose through the ranks by virtue of hard work and an instinct for the job. He really wanted to join the police force: he took the Manchester and Salford Police (later to become GMP) entrance examination several times, always failing the spelling test: his formal education had been disrupted by ill health. He persevered, turning up every six months for another go, until eventually the inspector in charge of recruitment recognised him, and recognised in him something that is not easily tested on paper. He saw the makings of a good cop, someone who was dedicated, determined and intelligent – even if he didn't know how many 'c's and 'm's there are in *accommodation*. In 1969 Stan was given his uniform and sent to work at Mill Street police station in the Ancoats area of central Manchester: as tough a patch as the city has to offer.

After moving to the Serious Crime Squad as a detective constable, he was promoted to sergeant, working in the Collyhurst area, then went to the Discipline and Complaints section (investigating other police officers). After becoming an inspector and then detective inspector he worked in Altrincham and then Stretford, had another stint in the Serious Crime Squad and then moved to Stalybridge in 1995. He was awarded the British Empire Medal in the New Year Honours List for 1989 for his voluntary work with mentally handicapped children and with the Scout movement.

A big, cheerful man with cropped grey hair, he wears two hearing aids: the legacy of a firearms training exercise. He is blunt, forthright, and makes up for any lack of educational refinement with what northerners call nous (common sense). He's TV's Dalziel, Wexford or Frost rather than Pascoe, Morse or Dalgleish.

His career has naturally included its share of big investigations, although nothing on the scale of the Shipman case. But apart from this one, which has impacted hard on him because he is part of the community that has been so devastated by it, the one he is most proud of is bringing to justice a rapist whose victim was a nine-year-old girl. One of his most treasured possessions is a commemorative Greater Manchester Police plate, which she bought for him out of her pocket money when the case was over. The GMP motto, 'To Serve and Protect', is printed on the plate: an appropriate accolade for his handling of a difficult and delicate case. A family man, with three grown-up children and several grandchildren, he has never been brutalised by his work, and remains very aware of the feelings of victims. At the same time, he is very much a man's man, at home with other policemen and with a well-developed black humour about the job.

Stan Egerton could see that the only way he was going to satisfy his fears about Mrs Grundy's death was by the radical step of exhuming her body. Exhumations of the recently dead are rare in Britain: most exhumations are of old graves being cleared to release land for road or housing developments. Greater Manchester Police had never before carried out an exhumation. Stan Egerton rang Detective Superintendent Bernard Postles, who was based in Oldham but in charge of CID for both Oldham and Tameside divisions, and the two of them met to discuss it. Det. Supt. Postles agreed that an exhumation should be the next step, and after discussing it with V Command (the section responsible for CID policy decisions) he authorised Stan to apply to the coroner for authority. The whole area of exhumation was unknown territory, and there was even confusion about who would fund it: it was agreed the police would pay half and the coroner half. Stan applied to the coroner, John Pollard, for the go-ahead. He went to the coroner's office in Stockport, and gave a résumé of the evidence the police had, on oath. The coroner, too, remembered the name of the GP.

'The police kept me informed, because they knew of my interest in Dr Shipman because of the previous investigation, but my first official involvement was when they applied for an exhumation order,' says John Pollard. 'I had to take into account everything the police had ascertained in their investigations, the fact that Mrs Grundy's daughter wasn't happy about her mother's death, and the fact that I knew questions had been raised previously about the same doctor. I had to balance all those factors against any distress, not just to the family but to the community. Exhuming bodies always causes distress, and I was aware of that. In the end, I took the view that the interests of justice required me to make an order for the exhumation. I regarded it purely as a one-off.'

So did Stan Egerton. Even knowing of the worries of the other GP, who had originally contacted the coroner four months before Mrs Grundy's death, he confined himself to the one case which was before him. It was unusual enough to be organising one exhumation: he did not think ahead to any more.

Most policemen (like most members of the public) are under the impression that exhumations have to take place at night: there is a popular myth among police officers that there are prescribed times, between midnight and six in the morning, for bodies to be unearthed. In fact, as Stan Egerton soon discovered, there is no such law: the decision to exhume at night is taken purely on the grounds of causing the least distress to the bereaved family and the general public. The mechanics of carrying out an exhumation were something Stan had never had to think about before. He quickly discovered that the acknowledged specialist in the field is a company called UK Exhumation Services, based in Sheffield. The boss of the company, Paul Needes, is an undertaker by trade who has branched into exhumation work, and who is used to clearing cemeteries for land development. He and Stan Egerton came to know each other well over the next few months, because his company carried out all the exhumations ordered for the Shipman investigation.

It was exactly one month after Mrs Grundy was buried that a small team of police officers and staff from UK Exhumation Services met at Hyde Chapel, in the early hours of Saturday 1 August. Although the previous day had been fine, the weather had changed and it was cold, windy and very wet. They started work at 2am, unsure of how long the job would take, and not wanting to upset the local community, most of whom would instantly realise whose grave was being excavated.

Although access to the cemetery was relatively easy (some of the later ones would be more difficult), the driving rain bogged down the small mechanical digger which the exhumation company brought, and the neat lawn in front of the row of graves where Mrs Grundy had been laid to rest was churned up. There were three staff from the exhumation company, DI Egerton, DC O'Brien, three scene-of-crime officers (SOCOs), and a police photographer. They were joined by Alan Massey and his daughter Debbie, and Debbie's husband David Bambroffe, who run Hyde's oldest established firm of undertakers. They were the funeral directors who had buried Mrs Grundy, and their role at the exhumation was to confirm that the right coffin had been brought up: they were shown the brass nameplate, which was unscrewed and placed in a plastic bag by one of the SOCOs.

Soil samples were meticulously taken from above the coffin, at all sides, and eventually from beneath it, so that any possible contamination from the soil could be eliminated. The bulk of the soil was placed on boards, in order not to make a mess of the cemetery or in any way disturb the adjoining graves.

The men from the exhumation company worked quietly and as rapidly as they could in the appalling conditions, while the police stood at a respectful distance, all of them aware that this was the strangest duty that their career had ever called them to. They were going into the unknown, both in terms of procedure and results. For the two young undertakers it was equally strange: neither of them had ever been present at an exhumation before, and although they were used to dealing with death, there was, as Debbie's father Alan Massey says, 'a feeling that it was all wrong. We put bodies into the ground, we don't take them out.' He, at least, had attended an exhumation before: he had gone as an observer to see an old grave being opened years before, purely out of professional interest.

As they struggled against the rain and the mud, Stan Egerton's radio crackled into life to tell him that the staff at the Laurel Bank Nursing Home, whose upper storey looks across the graveyard, had dialled 999 to report intruders in the cemetery. They had been reassured that the police knew what was going on.

DI Egerton glanced across at the windows where the watchers were observing the bizarre events below. He understood their unease: it was a terrible night, and digging up the body of a much-loved old lady was a terrible thing to be doing.

The post-mortem on Mrs Grundy was carried out the same morning, at Tameside General Hospital. The forensic pathologist, Dr John Rutherford, would, like the exhumation specialist Paul Needes, become familiar with Stan Egerton's cheerful face over the ensuing months: Stan was at every post-mortem. Rutherford, one of two forensic pathologists who carry out post-mortems for Greater Manchester Police, was able to tell Stan immediately that there was no obvious physical cause for a sudden death: Mrs Grundy's heart was sound, there was no embolism and there was no damage to any of her other organs. The only remarkable thing about her body was how good its condition was, for an 81-year-old.

Tissue samples were then sent off for testing to the North-West Forensic Science Laboratories at Chorley, Lancashire: the scientist in charge of analysing the samples had no guidance as to what she was looking for, and it would be some weeks before she was able to give the police her results.

In the meantime, important things were happening in

Hyde. Up to this point, the police had given Dr Shipman no clue as to their interest in the death of Mrs Grundy. But on the same day that the exhumation took place they raided both the doctor's surgery and his home: they knew they could not delay, because word of the exhumation was bound to get out and alert him. There was nothing over-dramatic about the exercise, no doors kicked in or suspects arrested. Detectives simply waited in unmarked cars outside The Surgery until his Saturday morning patients had all been dealt with, and approached the doctor as he was locking up. They took him back inside the building.

He did not register any surprise at seeing the plain-clothes officers: he spoke to them arrogantly, setting a precedent for his future dealings with the police. He offered to assist them in any way they required, and gave a faintly contemptuous smile as they read out the search warrant. The warrant specifically mentioned a typewriter, and Shipman went to a cupboard and produced a Brother portable, asking if this was what they were looking for.

'Mrs Grundy borrows it from time to time,' he said, tacitly admitting that he knew what they wanted it for.

The typewriter was taken away and the forensic laboratory was later able to tell the police team that it was indeed the machine on which both letters to Hamilton Ward, and the will, had been typed. Shipman's fingerprints were found on the typewriter, and a print from his left-hand little finger was found on the will: but not Mrs Grundy's or those of the two 'witnesses'.

While the detectives were there on that first search of his premises, Shipman asked for permission to ring a solicitor, and was allowed to contact the Medical Defence Union (the organisation which provides legal insurance cover for doctors). He was not questioned by the detectives.

At the same time, more police officers were visiting

the Shipmans' house in Roe Cross Green: it was important to do both searches simultaneously, to prevent Fred
destroying any evidence. The officers who carried out the
search were shocked. Policemen and women spend a
great deal of their working lives dealing with poor people,
criminals and low-life families: you don't have to be in the
force long before you are expected to walk into the kind of
home where the smell catches in your throat and makes
your eyes water, squalid places where poverty, apathy and
addiction drag conditions down to a sordid, sub-human
level. They are used to it but they are, nonetheless, still
disgusted by it. They also, based on experience more than
prejudice, expect it on certain cases: when they are called
in to help social workers remove children from unsuitable
homes, or when they raid premises where drugs or alcohol have reduced the residents' ability to cope, or when
they are dealing with the mentally ill or the educationally
sub-normal.

They do not expect it in tidy working-class terraces, in
council houses with neat flowerbeds, in well-maintained
middle-class enclaves with two cars on every drive. It is
always more of a shock when, behind the painted doors of
suburbia, they find families living in filth and mess. That's
what they found at the Shipman home. One WPC later
described it as the sort of place where you wipe your feet
on the way out. There were piles of newspapers, other
papers and dirty clothes in every room. The mess was not
just untidiness, it was filthy: another policewoman wore
rubber gloves to sift through it. Yet another cop joked
that the doctor was growing his own penicillin on the grill
pan.

Although the search did not produce anything relevant
to the forgery of Mrs Grundy's will, there were some surprising finds at this and subsequent searches. There was a
great deal of jewellery, rings that would obviously never fit
round his wife Primrose's chubby fingers, brooches of

little worth but no doubt of sentimental value to their owners: the sort of cheap bits and bobs that every old lady in Britain has.

There were also medical records: a carrier bag in the garage was found to be full of records of patients, and a large cardboard box in the house contained even more.

Fred Shipman remained cool, calm and appeared unsurprised by the police invasion of his premises. He was superficially co-operative, although he established the ground rules by which he would always attempt to deal with the police: he treated them with condescension and superciliousness.

It was not until 2 September that the toxicologist at the forensic laboratory, Julie Evans, came up with a cause of death for Mrs Grundy. The police were notified that the morphine level found in the old lady's body was consistent with that found in cases of overdose, and that death would have occurred within three hours of the fatal dose. Even though the police were now convinced they were dealing with a major crime, it still came as a shock. This was the first tangible evidence of anything more than a forgery: from this moment on, it became a murder inquiry. Now they knew the drug used was morphine, it would be easier to know what to look for in future cases – because by now they suspected that there would be more deaths to investigate, and that they were on the brink of something much, much bigger than a forged will and the murder of one old lady.

Perhaps one of the most bizarre corollaries to the police investigation of Mrs Grundy's death was Fred Shipman's assertion, during police questioning about the level of morphine in her body, that she was a drug addict. (He'd hinted at it, perhaps rehearsing his defence, when he talked to Nurse Marion Gilchrist before his arrest.) The police officers present when he made this outlandish

allegation had to suppress smiles. As one of them said, a
picture flashed into his mind of the immaculate, smartly
dressed 81-year-old ex-Mayoress of Hyde, trotting down
to Moss Side to score some smack. It was an allegation
that was as unkind as it was untrue, but prior to his arrest
Shipman had made some efforts to substantiate it by
adding false entries to Mrs Grundy's medical records,
trying to establish a pattern of drug dependence.

He had squeezed extra entries on to the ends and mar-
gins of her handwritten medical notes: a GP called in by
Greater Manchester Police as an expert witness was able
to state that in his opinion they had been written later
than the rest of the notes, and a nurse, familiar with deci-
phering the scrawl of doctors, was employed to put the
notes in order (she spread them out on her kitchen table:
they were a mess).

A pattern of fake entries emerged. On 12 October
1996 there was an entry about irritable bowel syndrome,
and a comment that her pupils were small. 'Drug abuse at
her age!' he had written. A year before her death he had
noted: 'Should I do blood tests/urine? Denies everything.
Not an IV user.'

He also made four phoney entries on to the computer
records of Mrs Grundy, two of them supporting the idea
that she was a drug user. Needless to say, the police found
no evidence of morphine-based drugs or drug-taking
paraphernalia in the neat home of the ex-Mayoress.

Even more tellingly, when the police trawled through
his Visa credit card statements they discovered that he
was not working on one of the days he claimed to have
been treating Mrs Grundy for her 'addiction' problem.
He had, on the day in question, been in York, spending
money at Waterstone's bookshop and later buying himself
a £140 fountain pen and some ink in a specialist pen
shop. The salesman in the shop remembers him clearly:
typically, he insisted on trying many different nibs before

settling on one that was not standard with the pen (probably because he needs a left-handed nib). When police interviewed the locum who was brought in to work in The Surgery for that week, he was able to tell them that Shipman may have popped in, but certainly did not see any patients. There is no mention of Mrs Grundy in the list of surgery appointments for that day, nor was there any reference to seeing the doctor in Mrs Grundy's personal diary: and she was meticulous about noting down her appointments and the names of any drugs prescribed for her.

Not content with murdering her, and attempting to defraud her family of all her wealth, Fred Shipman also tried to slur the good name of Kathleen Grundy, a woman whose life was exemplary and who leaves behind her so many good memories for the people of Hyde. The ultimate justice is that she, in death, vanquished him: it may be simplistic, but it is possible to see the conviction and imprisonment of Fred Shipman in terms of the goodness of Kathleen Grundy triumphing over his evil.

But what was the genesis of that evil?

# 2
# Morphine Eases the Pain

The streets of Nottingham were quiet. It was the early hours of a wet Saturday morning, but even the drunks had found their way home. A short, thickset youth wearing shorts and a red singlet pounded around a playing field, running doggedly through the heavy rain with his head down. His strongly muscled legs and his level breathing showed that he was physically comfortable: the pain he was feeling was not from exhausted limbs, but from the thoughts and memories he was struggling to suppress.

Only hours earlier, Fred Shipman had been at the bedside of his mother, watching her die. He was only seventeen, and although for weeks and months he had known her death was inevitable, even longed for it as her world shrunk to the boundaries of her own pain, it was hard now that it had come.

Sleep was impossible that night: his mother had achieved rest and peace, but he could not. Perhaps he never would again. An accomplished athlete, happier on a sports field than anywhere else, he put on his school PE kit and went out for a run. He ran and ran, through the night, arriving home long after dawn, as the glistening streets began to come alive with newspaper and milk deliveries, and shift workers making their way to and from factories.

In the last, painful months of her life, Vera Shipman spent the afternoons sitting at the window of her red-brick council house in Longmead Drive, Nottingham, waiting for her son Fred to arrive home from school. Fred, the middle of her three children, was the apple of her eye. He was the clever one, the one she had plans for, the one who was going to make all the scrimping and saving to send him to grammar school worthwhile. Some dying people cling to the past; to old, happy memories: for Vera, only forty-three years old, her life-raft was the dream of Fred's future, a dream of his achievements, success, and wealth enough to put council estate life behind him.

The Shipmans were no better or worse off financially than their neighbours on the Edwards Lane estate. Vera's husband Harold, after whom their first son, Harold Frederick, was named, was a lorry driver. The boy was always known as Fred, to avoid confusion in the immediate family. (Surprisingly, Vera tolerated 'Freddie' and 'Fred' for her son: her husband, also known in his childhood as Fred, had changed to Harold at her insistence when they married, because she preferred it.) From the day her first child, Fred's older sister Pauline, was born, Vera had been determined that her children would have a better life. The Shipmans, though polite enough, were regarded as standoffish by some of their neighbours, although plenty of others approved the tight control Vera exerted over her well-mannered children.

For Fred, seventeen years old and in the first year of the sixth form at High Pavement Grammar School, it was a terrible time. He had never made friends easily, and he confided in nobody as he watched his beloved mother wasting away. Vera had lung cancer, and in 1963, before chemotherapy and radiotherapy made a dent in the mortality statistics, she was under sentence of a slow, agonising death.

There were only two bright points in the dark cloud of pain that hung over her. One was the arrival home each afternoon of Fred, her favourite child. Her face would visibly brighten when he came up the front path, wearing his school blazer and with a heavy rucksack slung over one shoulder. He would make her a cup of tea and sit with her, telling her about his day. The other relief, and a sweet one, was the doctor's visit, when an injection of morphine would dull the sharp edges of her pain, and make what life she had left more bearable.

For Fred, so acutely aware of her suffering, the injections achieved a mythic importance. He, too, lived from one to the next, watching as her pain ebbed away when the opiate flooded her system. When, finally, on 21 June 1963, Vera died, it was as peaceful a passing as could be hoped for, with the morphine soothing the physical suffering, and with her husband and children by her side. But while friends and family murmured the usual platitudes about a blessed release, and while her husband Harold, daughter Pauline and youngest son Clive all began to come to terms with their grief, nobody realised the profound and ultimately devastating effect of his mother's death on seventeen-year-old Fred Shipman.

It would be another thirty-four years before his twin obsessions with death and morphine would come to light. And by then, who knows how many other old ladies had unwittingly played out the scene that dominated his formative years: sitting peacefully in an armchair, a cup of tea beside them, and a shot of morphine percolating through their bloodstream to take away pains and worries they didn't know they had?

The Edwards Lane council estate is in the Sherwood area

of Nottingham, a district which takes its name from, but has no obvious connection with, the famous forest where legend says Robin Hood robbed the rich to give to the poor. A latter-day Robin Hood would find worthier recipients for his generosity than the inhabitants of the Edwards Lane estate: they are not wealthy, but the estate is quiet, respectable, with most houses and gardens well maintained. The residents were up in arms when, a few years ago, the local TV news used a clip of boys playing football in one of the local streets to illustrate inner-city deprivation. Although it is only three miles from the centre of the city, it is hardly a depressed and needy area, and some of the residents felt angry enough at the aspersions cast on their decent lives to protest to the TV station. The estate is five minutes' walk away from Nottingham City Hospital, there are playing fields and a swimming pool nearby and work to be had in local factories.

Unlike many other Victorian cities, Nottingham diversified early in the twentieth century, and relied not just on traditional trades (in Nottingham's case, machine-made lace and frame knitting) but also had 'new' industries like bicycles, tobacco, and the massive Boots the Chemist to provide employment.

What's more, compared to the soulless, massive developments thrown up after the war, there is an intimacy about the Edwards Lane estate, which is no more than a couple of dozen roads of 1930s red-brick houses, more solid and individual-looking than their post-war counterparts. It was livelier and noisier back in the immediate post-war years, when Fred was little: the average age of residents was younger, but they were still difficult times for young couples trying to establish a normal family life after the strange hiatus of wartime. There were occasional drunken brawls between young men, odd incidents of name-calling between wives: nothing serious, nothing that would even raise an eyebrow on the estates of big cities today.

Harold Frederick Shipman, born on 14 January 1946, was a celebration baby whose birth, eight months after VE Day, came at the beginning of a huge boom in the population. Young couples rushed headlong into starting a family, making up for the lost time of the war years, when many of them were separated for long periods. For a great many of these husbands and wives, the end of the war marked the beginning of their lives together; but for Harold and Vera Shipman, married three days before the end of 1937, and with their first child, Pauline, born in March 1938, it was a matter of picking up where they had left off, before Harold went off on war service with the Sherwood Foresters regiment. Vera was eighteen when she married; Harold, who was five years older, was working at that time as a printer's assistant. They were both of solid working-class stock: Vera's father was a bricklayer's labourer, and Harold's was a hosiery warehouseman. Vera's mother worked in another traditional local trade: she was a lace clipper. The birth of Fred, followed just over four years later by their third child Clive, gave them the family they had planned, and for whom they both had high hopes.

Harold, one of a large poor family of eight children, was a quiet, unassuming chap, conscientious both at work and at home, but not ambitious. He left that to Vera, whose own humble origins (her father's name does not appear on her birth certificate) gave her a quiet determination that her children would do well and better themselves. For Harold, after a day's work driving his Bedford tipper lorry, moving stones and broken tarmac for local building firms, the garden was relaxation, and a trip to Notts County home matches on Saturday afternoons was pleasure. He smoked a pipe and wore a trilby hat over his thinning, grey hair. Vera, a small, slim woman with the same dark eyes and hair that Fred had as a boy, had a clear idea about what she required from her children in terms of behaviour, and enforced her standards by expectation rather than by shouting and smacking. None of her children ever wanted to disappoint her, least of all her favourite, Fred. The family were the epitome of working-class respectability: a hard-working father, a mother who ran a neat home and brought up children who were described by the other wives on the estate as 'a credit to her'.

Number 163 Longmead Drive, where Harold and Fred's sister Pauline lived until after Harold's death in 1985, is the middle of a terrace of three houses. In those early days, when all the family lived at home, it had three bedrooms, with a bathroom downstairs; more than twenty years later, after Vera's death, Harold bought the house from the council, and had the small bedroom upstairs converted into a bathroom and the kitchen extended into the old bathroom area. There is a small front garden and a larger back garden, both of which were kept immaculately in the days that Harold Shipman ruled them; they have now been sadly neglected for some years, to the dismay of older residents on the estate, who remark that Harold would be horrified to see all his hard work gone to rack and ruin.

Vera was a good housekeeper, staying at home (only one woman in five worked in those days) to bring up her children and keep the house spotless. Although she doted on her family, especially Fred, there were no obvious signs of spoiling: she believed in discipline, and there was no spare money for treats or expensive presents. Having a sister seven years older than him brought Fred even more attention – Pauline, too, was fond of both her little brothers, and was old enough to help her mother. The Shipmans were not a demonstrative family, but there was a tight bond between them and it would, by any account, be deemed a happy, functional family. In years to come, when psychiatrists, psychologists and others would pore over the early life of a man who would go so bizarrely off the rails, they would find few clues at 163 Longmead Drive.

Hannah Cutler, an elderly neighbour whose deceased husband was a friend of Harold's, says: 'The family were rather insular, but I knew them well because I lived opposite. I've known the children since they were little. They never mixed with other kids, they didn't play in the street and when they came home from school they stayed in the house. I think Harold and Vera wanted them to be different: they didn't want them to be like other kids on the estate, they wanted something better for them. In a way, they were investing in their children.'

This was one element of life in that neat council house that may have laid down a crucial aspect of Fred's adult personality, and an aspect that may have contributed to his later behaviour: Vera brought her children up to believe that they were better than those around them. They were not completely shut off from contact with other kids on the estate – in the 1950s playing outside was the normal occupation of children after school and during school holidays. There was not the endless taking and collecting of children to pre-arranged teas at schoolmates' houses or the ordering of a schedule of after-school activities that children today enjoy; and the long summer break was not punctuated by a fortnight somewhere hot. On sunny evenings, weekends and school holidays, small tides of children ebbed and flowed through the streets of the Edwards Lane estate, their numbers not fixed, their games spontaneous: balls were kicked around roads where cars were a novelty; skipping ropes, conkers, jacks and marbles enjoyed phases of popularity.

The Shipman children were occasionally allowed to join in, but they were never completely initiated into the

gangs. If Fred played outside he tagged along with others.
They never came calling for him to play, because he was
such an irregular member of their group. Another boy, a
couple of years older, remembers Fred on the edge of the
gang.

'He was sometimes with the lads, but not one of the
lads. We used to all go down to the pictures every weekend. We were mad for the latest Roy Rogers, or Tarzan or
Robin Hood films. Fred would come out of his house
and tag along with us. Afterwards, we'd all be full of it,
and we'd be ready to act out the adventures we'd seen.
But Fred would always have to go straight home.

'Sometimes we'd play cards, squatting down on the
kerb. Or we'd go pinching apples from someone's garden.
But Fred was never with us. Like the rest of the family, he
kept himself to himself. He was clever, so I always
assumed he was reading books while we were playing.'

Alan Goddard spent his childhood and early years five
houses away from the Shipmans, at 175 Longmead Drive.
Just six months younger than Fred, Alan was in the same
class in infant school, junior school and grammar school
as Fred, and knew him better than any of the other boys
on the estate – there were only three boys from the
Edwards Lane estate who went on to High Pavement
Grammar School, a prestigious state school which was
the first choice for the parents of any boys who passed
their eleven-plus.

The two boys first met at Burford Infants School, a
short walk from Longmead Drive, where all the small
children from the estate arrived holding the hands of their
mums or older brothers and sisters. In a photograph of
eight six-year-old boys sitting round a table on a sunny
day outside the school building, Fred wears a bow tie,
while the others are tieless. It was Vera's idea of being
smart, a bow tie, and it has stayed with Fred Shipman
throughout his life.

Because of an idiosyncracy of planning, the junior school closest to the estate was not big enough to accommodate the burgeoning numbers of post-war children, and the Edwards Lane estate kids had to make a two-mile bus journey every day to and from Whitemoor Junior School. They started there at the age of eight, joining Whitemoor in what was then called the second year of junior school education: in other words, they stayed at Burford for an extra year, and joined Whitemoor pupils who had already been in the school for one year. It was a compromise arrangement made by the education authority for Nottingham which, like every other big city in Britain, was under extreme pressure from the population explosion.

For Fred, who struggled with the problems of left-handedness as he learned to read and write, and his classmate Alan, it meant boarding a double-decker bus which travelled from the estate every morning and returned at lunchtime, and then repeated the run in the afternoon. There were enough children picked up en route to fill two buses: one strictly for boys and one for girls. As most children stayed for dinner at school, there was only one bus on the lunchtime run.

'We were outsiders when we first arrived at Whitemoor, but there were a lot of us, so we settled quickly,' recalls Alan.

The school was built in the mid-1930s, celebrating its twenty-first anniversary with a church service during the years that Fred was there. Fred was not in the football team for his year, but he played for the Whitemoor stool ball team. Stool ball is unique to Nottinghamshire, a cross between rounders and cricket played with a large paddle which looks like an oversized table-tennis bat. Whitemoor topped the local schools' league, and Fred was photographed, dark-haired and dark-eyed, proud in the school T-shirts issued to the team.

'I didn't see much of him out of school,' says Alan Goddard. 'The rest of us would play in the street. There was a playing field attached to Burford Infants which was locked up after school hours, and we'd go round there and find ways in.

'Freddie was never part of all that. There would often be scuffles between different boys on the school bus, but he never joined in. He would never say boo to a goose – he was quiet and kept out of the way of rougher kids. I think the family was quite disciplined, and he stayed at home. It was a feather in our caps to get into High Pavement at eleven. My older brother was there, so I was pleased to emulate his achievement. The Shipmans were pleased for Freddie: all parents were pleased if their sons got into High Pavement.'

Today, under a comprehensive education system, High Pavement is a sixth-form college open to all. But in 1957, when Fred Shipman first went there, it was an elite, traditional grammar school with an interesting history. Its unusual name derives from its original address: in the centre of Nottingham is a street which has existed since the Middle Ages, leading from the castle to the middle of the city, and changing its name from Castle Gate to Low Pavement, Middle Pavement and then High Pavement. On High Pavement, in the building that is now the Lace Hall, was the Unitarian Chapel, or 'Chapel of the Society of Protestant Dissenters Assembling at the High Pavement'. It was a place of worship for nonconformist, Christian intellectuals who challenged some of the orthodox teachings of the established church. Lord Byron's mother, Catherine Gordon, a Scottish heiress from Gight near Aberdeen, worshipped at the chapel while her son, aged ten, was being treated for his deformed foot at the hospital. More than a century later, D. H. Lawrence used the chapel as the meeting place for his fictional characters Paul Morrell and Miriam Leivers in *Sons and Lovers*.

High Pavement school, founded in 1788, was originally open to children of all denominations, the first non-sectarian school in England. It achieved another notable first a hundred years later, when it became the first school in the country to teach practical science.

By the Second World War it had become a boys-only school, with a separate establishment, Manning School, for girls, and was outgrowing its second set of buildings. By the time Fred Shipman went there in September 1957, the school had been established for two years in brand-new purpose-built premises in Bestwood, less than a mile away from the Shipman home. Not only was it the best state grammar school in Nottingham, it was also the nearest to his home. Among the school's old boys are actors Peter Bowles and John Bird, and former England and Nottinghamshire batsman Tim Robinson. (Now, of course, the most famous ex-pupil is Fred Shipman.)

When Fred went there, 60 per cent of High Pavement pupils were working-class. The head teacher at the time, Harry Davies, who went on to become Director of the Institute of Education at Nottingham University, wrote two books, *The Boys' Grammar School* and *Culture and the Grammar School*, defending grammar schools against accusations that they were middle-class institutions and extolling the opportunities they offered to working-class pupils: 'The grammar school . . . stands for important values which our society badly needs, and it has shown that it is well able to accommodate children who come to it, in ever-increasing numbers, from under-educated homes,' he wrote in *Culture and the Grammar School*. He dedicated the book 'to many boys and masters of High Pavement School, past and present'. When the book was published in 1965, Fred Shipman was about to become a past pupil, after eight years at the school.

His career at High Pavement was largely unspectacular.

Like so many other grammar school entrants, he went from being one of the bright kids at junior school to being run-of-the-mill among so many other clever boys. He and Alan Goddard used to walk to school together, Alan pushing his bike. They wore brown blazers trimmed with brown and yellow braid, brown caps, ties striped in brown, yellow and blue, school socks and, for the first year, short grey trousers. Not wearing a tie meant automatic detention: at times of very hot weather there might be a ruling that shirts could be worn open-necked, but this happened rarely. After the first three years, caps could be abandoned. The school motto was in Latin, *Virtus Sola Nobilita* (virtue is the only nobility) and at speech days and ends of term the boys sang the school song, Una Voce Concanemus Omnes Paviores' (with one voice we Paviorians all sing together). Bulky satchels full of text books and exercise books were hauled to and from home every day.

In his first year, in form 1C, Fred had a story published in the school magazine, *The Pavior*:

When Uncle Ted visited us last year he brought along his little puppy, Soot, who was of course black. While he was here we had a budgie given to us and Soot grew very jealous of him when we tried to make the bird talk. One day he knocked over the cage and broke Joey's wing so we took him to a vet and he put a splint on the wing. One day Joey went and had a bath in Soot's water and pecked at his bone. Now Soot's fond of Joey and lets him ride on his back and pull his tail and have a bath in his water. Joey says 'Naughty Soot, naughty naughty Soot' and Soot goes and barks at Joey as if to say 'Naughty Joey, naughty naughty Joey.' Wherever Joey goes, Soot goes. How's that for being friends.

This early success did not presage a talent for writing: English was one of his weakest subjects.

There was a four-class entry into the school, and the boys were streamed by ability. Fred was in the C stream, and never rose above it. The school day was completely structured, with bells ringing at the end of lessons, desks arranged in rows, strict no-talking rules in class, and masters flitting about wearing black gowns.

Harry Davies was a Cambridge-educated historian, himself coming from a working-class background in Todmorden, West Yorkshire, a place which would become very significant in Fred Shipman's later life. He was an inspirational head, a Liberal who consumed the *Guardian* (or *Manchester Guardian* as it was) daily and who attracted a staff of young, dedicated teachers.

Although corporal punishment existed, Davies was not keen on it. He was not, according to one member of staff, 'a beater', although as a proficient tennis player he could 'give a good stroke with the cane'. Bob Studholme, who was a contemporary of Fred's from the third form onwards, remembers being caned by Davies for throwing stones at the groundsman's tractor. Afterwards, the headmaster shook hands with him.

Davies was a progressive within the strictures of the academic education he believed in passionately. Although there was a nominal service held every day (by law), he did not believe in ramming orthodox religious teaching down the throats of his boys – his idea of a good morning assembly was to have a rousing hymn 'to wake the boys up', and his favourite prayer was pragmatic rather than dogmatic: the short invocation written by one of the Royalist generals before the battle of Edgehill: 'O Lord! Thou knowest how busy I must be this day; if I forget thee, do not thou forget me.'

One distinguished member of staff who taught Fred was Stanley Middleton, who was joint winner of the

Booker Prize in 1974 for his novel *Holiday*. He has written over thirty books – gentle, accomplished novels of modern manners which ex-pupils read to find thinly disguised descriptions of the staff they knew. It is a measure of how insignificant Fred Shipman was at school that there was nothing about him to make him stand out among the hundreds of boys who passed through Stan Middleton's English classes: the long retired teacher has no particular memory of him.

For many new boys at the school in the late 1950s, like Alan Goddard, there was still time after classes to join the other estate boys playing outside. Fred was not missed: he had never been part of the gang, and it was assumed, without rancour, that he was at home studying hard. Certainly, Vera made sure that he had peace and quiet to do his homework – Fred's schoolwork was the most important thing in the household. His sister Pauline left school at fifteen and was working in the shipping department of a company manufacturing knitted garments, and his younger brother Clive did not follow him to High Pavement, so it was Fred's achievements of which Vera was most proud.

Occasionally Fred would go with his father to watch Notts County at their Meadow Lane ground, and Alan Goddard would be invited along.

'It was a great treat. After the match we'd walk a couple of miles to Trinity Square to get the bus home, stopping in the central market for a bowl of hot peas.' Conversation centred around the match.

On Bonfire Nights the Shipmans had a bonfire in their garden, and Alan would be invited along. It was not open to lots of local kids – in his memory, Alan is the only guest. Vera would serve treacle toffee and baked potatoes to the boys, and afterwards they would play blow football on the dining table. Although teenagers did not move between each other's homes in the 1950s and '60s as they do today, Alan felt welcome and comfortable in the Shipman household.

The two boys followed roughly the same course through school, until Alan left at sixteen, having taken his GCEs, while Fred went on to the sixth form – as did 60 per cent of all High Pavement boys. Fred passed five GCEs. It was a mediocre total for a High Pavement boy, but enough to get him a place in the sixth form, where he added another two GCE passes to his total.

Although he was no academic star, throughout his school career he was a model pupil. Just as Alan Goddard knows he was not one of the 'gang' on the estate, Bob Studholme remembers that he was never one of the 'wags' in class.

'His school career was marked by his quietness. We'd all be swearing, making rude bodily noises, getting into mischief. A couple of the lads had berets, and would do silly skits pretending to be French before the French teacher arrived. If you got caught being too silly, you got a detention, but I don't remember ever seeing Fred in detention.

'Once, when we were in the fourth room, I can remember a boy called Pete Jackson telling a dirty joke in the changing rooms. We all belly-laughed: we were at the age when dirty jokes were our favourite pastime. I looked in the mirror on the wall and glimpsed Fred, sitting on a bench a little way off and smiling. But he was not grinning at the joke: it was a faintly condescending smile, as if he was looking at a gang of kids and thinking "you'll grow up one day". It was an almost affectionate smile, as if he liked us but thought we were fools. I saw him more than once with a wry smile on his face, as though he tolerated us but felt we were all rather immature.'

It was in the school sports department that Fred made his greatest contribution, and sports played a very strong part in the High Pavement ethic. Rugby was new to the working-class kids who got into High Pavement, and for the first three or four years the teams were soundly beaten by the local public school, Nottingham Boys High School, whose pupils had been playing since prep school. By the fifth year, however, High Pavement prided itself on always winning. Fred took to the game instantly, playing fly-half at first, and later as centre or wing. He also excelled as a distance runner, and was vice-captain of the athletics team in his final year. He merits various accolades in *The Pavior* magazine for his contributions to school and house teams for both rugby and athletics.

He played for the Nottinghamshire Schools Under-15s team in the winter of 1959–60, and when he reached the sixth form had become an important member of the rugby squad. He was stocky and tough, with an aggression and determination that was well hidden off the pitch. Contemporary Phil Pallant, now a headmaster of a Nottinghamshire prep school, did not know Fred well at High Pavement, but vividly remembers one rugby match.

'Fred carried out the most horrendous tackle I've ever seen. It was not unfair, but he just cleaned this lad out, taking him round the waist. I remember everyone wincing and I was glad that I was not on the receiving end of it.'

Bob Studholme, who also went into teaching as a career, says: 'I was very surprised that he didn't carry on with his rugby after school. He would definitely have been good enough to play for Leeds University. He might even have made it into a minor county side. I can see him now, running hard with the ball in his hands, a curving run down the pitch. He could rattle people's teeth: he was an aggressive player. He was definitely not the same person off the pitch as he was on.'

In the spring of 1963 Fred went away with the rest of the sixth-form rugby players, thirty-two of them in all, on a trip to the north-east, staying at Saltburn-by-the-Sea near Redcar. The trip was organised by maths teacher

Jack Barratt, a keen rugby player who had connections in the area, and who had arranged four matches against other grammar school teams. The trip lasted five days, starting at Glasshouse Street in the centre of the city – a meeting-point which always caused a lot of schoolboy sniggers, as the coach depot was next door to the VD clinic. The most popular song on the coach was The Beatles' latest hit, 'From Me To You'. In the coffee bars of Saltburn, it was the first selection from the jukebox every evening.

'Fred wasn't an outsider, he knew how to join in. But he was quiet, never a ringleader and never a trouble-maker,' says Bob Studholme. 'He wasn't part of the in-crowd. If we went for a few beers after a match, he'd tag along – but I don't remember him ever drinking. He was pally, but not an essential part of the group.'

On cross-country runs, away from the watchful eyes of the games staff, boys would stop off for cups of tea at the home of Michael Heath, who now works in the pharma-ceutical industry, and who regularly walked home from school with Fred when they were in the sixth form.

'He'd come in for a cup of tea at my folks' house, but he'd never stay very long. He was always aware that we'd be in trouble if we were caught. That would have been a pretty black crime to Fred, and he always took off quickly. He never put a foot out of line,' recalls Heath, who really only got to know Fred in the sixth form.

'I liked him a lot and had great respect for him – he was a bit of a role model, because he was so good at sports and worked so hard. He wasn't one of the bright ones – being in the C stream, it was unusual to go on into the sixth, so he achieved everything by hard work. He would have started in the sixth form behind the rest of us, and it must have been tough. He was very serious, a bit of a loner. He'd smile occasionally, but he took life very seri-ously.'

Life in the sixth form at High Pavement was more relaxed than in the lower school. Although the boys still wore blazers, they were allowed to wear waistcoats of any style or colour (although there was an unwritten acceptance that nothing too outlandish would be worn). Fred is remembered for a bright mustard yellow waistcoat, which gave him a dandified air, and which was strangely at odds with his quiet personality.

There were organised trips, apart from the sports fixtures; the staff were consciously trying to raise the expectations and increase the experience of their charges. On one trip the sixth form flew down to Gatwick on an old Dakota from Birmingham, for many of them their first trip on a plane. They then travelled to Heathrow, another new experience, crossing London. There, they watched planes coming and going before travelling back to Nottingham by coach up the M1: again, for many of them, it was a first, the motorway having only recently opened.

Sixth-formers had more contact with the girls from Manning, inviting them to join the sixth-form society meetings, uniting for drama productions and going on occasional outings together (although the boys lived in terror of the Manning headmistress, commonly known as Fag-ash Lil, a formidable woman who always wore net gloves, reputedly to cover her nicotine-stained fingers). The greatest achievement and badge of rank was to have a Manning girlfriend. But Fred never achieved this: he was shy and awkward with girls. Although he was not tall, he had filled out before many of his contemporaries – he matured early, and was envied by other boys for having to start shaving as early as fourteen, and for his embryonic sideburns: rock 'n' roll hit the British charts in the months before Fred started at grammar school, and although High Pavement boys tended to look down on Elvis Presley, it was the main ambition of many of them to be

Buddy Holly lookalikes ('We regarded Buddy Holly as the thinking man's rocker,' says Bob Studholme). But Fred never capitalised on what other boys would have seen as an advantage: he appeared to have no interest in music or clothes.

At school dances he turned up with his sister Pauline who, being seven years older, seemed strangely out of place among the gauche sixth-formers who were jiving with the Manning girls.

'At school dances you either turned up with a girl-friend or you went with your mates and got drunk,' says Michael Heath. 'I think we would have laughed at anyone else who turned up with their sister, especially as she was quite a bit taller than him and they looked odd dancing together. They did a really strange dance, a sort of jive, that looked as though they practised it together. Because it was Fred we just felt it was a bit sad.'

It may have been socially more relaxed, but the sixth form was an academic hothouse. Boys were expected to study more than just their A-level subjects (Fred chose Biology, Physics and Chemistry as his subjects). Harry Davies prided himself on turning out well-rounded pupils, so there were extra classes in English for the sci-entists, and lessons on politics, world history, practical subjects like woodwork and metalwork, and discussions of topical affairs (as Stan Middleton points out, the Shipman trial would have provoked an interesting sixth-form debate). Boys were expected to take part in debates, in drama and public speaking, but Fred never did. He lis-tened to the others, rarely joining in.

Vera Shipman's death came towards the end of Fred's first year in the sixth form, when he was seventeen and a half. It was a difficult time for all the family: she had always assumed the traditional role of housekeeper so that, as well as the emotional trauma of losing her, there were a lot of readjustments needed in the running of the household.

'It was heartbreaking for all of them,' says neighbour Mrs Cutler, 'but it seemed to make a very deep impression on Fred particularly. She was dying over a lengthy period of time.'

The family's GP, Dr Andrew Campbell, visited the house regularly in the weeks before Vera's death, giving her welcome injections of morphine in ever-increasing dosages. Dr Campbell's wife Angela, also a GP and in partnership with him, occasionally made the trip to Longmead Drive from the local surgery.

'I remember going to the house once or twice, although my late husband made most of the visits. They were a decent, hard-working, working-class family, and her slow death from cancer must have been devastating for them all," says Dr Angela Campbell.

Vera's death came before the hospice movement, Macmillan nurses and syringe drivers for delivering morphine made the terminal stages of cancer at home a more comfortable, manageable experience. The active, house-proud woman whose quiet determination had shaped the characters of all her children, but particularly Fred, was reduced over time to a mere shadow of herself. Always slim, she became emaciated, gaunt, and debilitated, putting all her energies into coping with her pain. Seeing Fred at the end of his school day rallied her, but as the weeks went by she could hardly raise the energy to sit up any more, and spent all her time in bed. As Pauline, then twenty-five years old, and her husband were at work, and Clive was only thirteen, it was Fred who cared for her from the moment he arrived home from school.

Finally, on a Friday afternoon, she died, living until both her sons were home to say their final goodbyes to her. It was a harrowing weekend for Fred, and he ran around the playing field at night, wearing his school house colours, to dull his emotions with sheer physical exhaustion.

In the way of the Shipman family (and the times they were living in) he kept his feelings in check, and was back at school on the Monday. He met Michael Heath on the way to school that day, and Michael (known as Mick to his schoolmates) asked him what he'd been doing over the weekend. The shockingly simple reply was, 'My mum died.'

'I can't remember what I said – I'd had no idea that his mother was even ill, so it came completely out of the blue,' says Michael. 'I don't suppose I was much comfort. At that age, boys aren't very good with feelings. I don't think we talked about it much, except that he told me about going out running in the rain. It wasn't mentioned again.'

Fred didn't mention it directly to anyone else, but he wore a black armband over his blazer on the day of the funeral, and inevitably word got around.

'I was flabbergasted when I heard his mother had died,' says Bob Studholme. 'We weren't discouraged from talking about our families, parents were always welcomed at the school. I was closely associated with Fred, playing with him in the rugby team, but he said nothing to me. Other boys would talk about their mothers – moan about being made to go shopping or whatever, and I'm sure I'd have known if anyone else's mother had died. He never mentioned his family at all. It wasn't because he was ashamed of his working-class background, because there were so many of us with the same kind of roots.'

Ursula Oldknow, who still lives next door to the old Shipman home, moved there shortly before Vera Shipman died. She too had cancer. Ursula was twenty-four at the time, and moved in with her mother Phyllis who nursed her back to health after a hysterectomy made necessary by cervical cancer. Because of her illness neither she nor her mother, who worked split shifts as a bus conductress, was able to go to Vera's funeral.

'Freddy was only seventeen, and very shy. You could hardly get two words out of him. But they were all very polite, and quiet. Pauline had to take on the role of looking after her brothers, but Mr Shipman, Harold, more than did his bit. It was him who kept the house clean.'

It was Fred's mother's death, and the close contact it brought him with the medical profession, that inspired him to want to be a doctor. He had already opted for the right A-levels for a medical career, but a clear picture of what he wanted to do only emerged as he watched at her bedside as morphine was injected into her. Whether it was the skill of the doctor, the respect in which doctors were held in working-class communities, or the lure of working with the drug that offered his mother so much relief, is impossible to say, perhaps not even by him. But it was in his mother's death that his careers were born: two careers, one as a caring and much-valued GP, the other as the exact antithesis, a doctor who murdered some of the people he was supposed to be looking after.

Fred Shipman failed to get the grades for Leeds University Medical School at his first attempt in the summer term of 1964. Perhaps his mother's death the previous year had seriously disrupted his studies, more than he showed to his school friends. Or perhaps he simply found three science A-levels heavy going – he was not alone among the medical students at Leeds in having to resit some papers. His academic achievements at school, both at O- and A-level, were sound rather than spectacular; this would be entirely irrelevant were it not for the fact that in later life Fred Shipman has made a point of stressing his intellectual superiority. His ultimate condemnation of anyone is to describe them as 'stupid': not a word that could ever be attached to him, but it is important not to lose sight of the fact that he was no intellectual high-flyer, either.

He took A-level resits in November 1964, and then took the rest of the year off school, waiting to start at Leeds in September 1965. Because his lorry-driver father was not earning a high wage, he qualified for a full student grant from his local authority. This came to £340, the equivalent of £3,730 in 1999, the year his trial began. Although not generous, it was enough to live on. All tuition fees were paid for British students in those days, so the maintenance grant had to cover his rent, food, books and entertainment. Money was tight for all students on grants, but there were many of them in the same boat, and university life was geared to living as cheaply as possible.

Medicine was a popular choice of career: there were strenuous government efforts in the mid-1960s to attract more students to it, because of an acute shortage of family doctors since the establishment of the NHS. The shortage of doctors reached its nadir in 1965, just as Fred left home to go to medical school, with many GPs across the country having more than the permitted limit of 3,500 patients on their list. By the time he qualified the worst of the crisis was over, but there would always be work available for doctors. His family were proud of his choice, and they enjoyed the status of having a potential doctor in the house.

For Fred, leaving home was a time of mixed feelings. Without his mother, things at home were not the same. His sister Pauline was efficient to the point of being brusque: a keen netball player, she shared his love of sports and was proud of his success, but was busy with a full-time job and the need to help their father run the home. Clive was training as a health inspector; Harold was barely over the grief of his wife's death. It had never been a home full of hugs and laughter; it was now a joyless place.

Leeds, too, offered a new beginning. Fred, the quiet schoolboy, always on the edge of the group but always watching what the others were doing, was aware of the changing world around him. It was the middle of the 1960s, The Beatles were the biggest thing going (more popular than Jesus, as John Lennon was to claim only a few months later), The Who released the youth anthem 'My Generation', and minis – both mini-skirts and Morris Mini cars – defined the times. Fred, who had taken his older sister to a school dance, who had never joined in the dirty joke routines of his contemporaries, who stood at a bar with the others without drinking alcohol, who never had a detention and was wary of bunking off a cross-country run for a cup of tea, was beginning to tire of always being on the sidelines of life.

At Leeds he would start again, and he would be a participator, not an observer.

# 3
# A Girl Called Primrose

As Fred Shipman was struggling with the trauma of his mother's death and the heavy workload of his A-levels, eighty miles further north a gauche-looking schoolgirl with a pudding-basin haircut was also nearing the end of her school career. The life of Fred Shipman is inextricably intertwined with that of Primrose Oxtoby, the girl who at seventeen became his wife and who has remained steadfastly by his side ever since. Both working-class kids, both uncomfortable with the youth culture of the 1960s, their early lives have many parallels – but also some significant differences.

An ill-omened star must have crossed the heavens on the day that Edna Constable came into the world. Born in 1910, to a society without phones, fridges or television, and where cars and radio were rareties, she has been witness to almost a whole century of change, a restless century in which technology and social mores slipped more gears than at any time in the millennium.

Living through two world wars, going from life in service through marriage and motherhood into frail old age, Edna Constable, who became Edna Oxtoby at the age of twenty-four when she married farmworker George Oxtoby, has had to cope with more than her fair share of problems. She does not have the support and comfort of her children and grandchildren in her lonely widowhood; Edna's two daughters have both, in entirely different ways, brought her problems and worries.

The elder, Mary, has battled multiple sclerosis for many years and is confined to a wheelchair, needing full-time nursing home care. The younger by thirteen years, the one on whom so much hope and expectation was pinned, has through her marriage brought to the family a terrible notoriety, lessened only by the fact that for many years she and her mother have not spoken to each other. If nothing else, old Mrs Oxtoby can say, 'I told you so.' She never liked her son-in-law, Fred Shipman, whom she first met when he was a medical student. In good music-hall tradition, many mothers-in-law are unhappy with their daughters' choices: Edna's disquiet has, more than thirty years later, turned out to be entirely justified.

Edna's husband George was five years older than her, and shared her simple, upright values. Both Methodists, they met when she worked as what was described on their wedding certificate as a 'general servant' and he was a labourer on the same farm at Upper Poppleton, three miles from York. Servants were common enough in the ordered society of the pre-war years: wages were low and there were no labour-saving washing machines and vacuum cleaners, so most middle-class families employed at least one young woman to tackle the housework. Although the servant class was increasingly dying out by the 1930s, it remained entrenched in farming areas, where the farmer's wife was often expected to supervise the dairy as well as run the home, and needed the general hard-working assistance of a girl like Edna. Edna's own father was also a farm labourer, so it was a life she was bred to.

Marriage gave the couple a tied cottage, which Edna maintained as scrupulously as she had been expected to work in the farmhouse. She had absorbed the traditional Yorkshire values of thrift, caution and cleanliness. The place sparkled, the food put before George when he finished a hard day on the farm was plain but well-cooked and satisfying. Edna was, by all accounts, a 'good wife', one who budgeted the housekeeping perfectly and ran the place – and her man – like clockwork. She was determined to better herself and her family, and that determination has made her single-minded, proud and tough.

George's toughness, on the other hand, was all physical. Although small, he was strong, and he delivered more than an honest day's work for his masters. To the end of his life he worked hard in his immaculate garden, growing his own vegetables and fruit. He had a ready smile and a softer personality than his wife, but he accepted the regime she imposed on the family, and supported her standards. He wanted a quiet life, and he was content to let Edna run it for him.

Their first daughter was born in May 1936, when George was working for a farm in the small North Yorkshire hamlet of Wilstrop. Thirteen years later, when Primrose was born, he had risen to become the foreman at a farm at Hutton's Ambo, near Malton. Whatever the reason for the long delay between the two births, it is clear that Primrose was a wanted child. The names they chose for her – Primrose May – are rare expressions of exuberant delight from the strait-laced Oxtobys, who christened their first daughter with the sensible, biblical name of Mary. Born in April, when primroses lined the steep Yorkshire lanes, and may blossom was beginning to froth the hedgerows with white, their new baby was given names of spring, of hope, of new beginnings, of renewed life. Many years later Primrose would tell casual acquaintances that her mother did not want another girl, and that the age gap between her and her sister caused her to be a lonely child; but the Oxtobys showed no outward sign of disappointment in their new, and cherished, baby.

Edna and George were already, at thirty-nine and forty-four, relatively old parents, both in terms of their ages and in their habits and old-fashioned values. Primrose, like Fred, was part of the population explosion in the immediate post-war years, and Edna must have felt curiously out of step with this new generation of mothers, as she queued with them for free orange juice and cod liver oil at the clinic.

By the time Primrose reached school age, the family had moved to the tiny hamlet of East Rigton, between Leeds and Wetherby, where George was again working as a farm foreman. They lived in a small tied cottage at the bottom of a lane, and every day George walked up the hill, past the straggle of twelve or fifteen houses that make up the whole community, to the farm. Today, he would not recognise East Rigton: the tied cottages have gone; new, modern farm buildings have been erected; the houses are the tarted-up desirable residences of wealthy Leeds commuters.

What remains the same now as then is the main road, the A58. Although the traffic today whizzes past with alarming speed and density, it was busy enough in 1954, when Edna first took her youngest daughter by the hand to cross it on their mile walk to Bardsey Primary School. The village of Bardsey is bigger than East Rigton, straddling both sides of the road that links Leeds and Wetherby, but just as picture-postcard pretty. The village pub, The Bingley Arms, is one of several which claim to be Britain's oldest pub.

In 1952, a new primary school was built in Bardsey to absorb the children from the surrounding villages. The building, still in use today, is a grey-brick flat-roofed construction. It was here that the young Primrose Oxtoby learned to read, write – and play.

Play did not come easily to the little girl brought up with the austere standards that Edna Oxtoby set. Play was frivolous and unnecessary, and Edna's philosophy did not encompass anything frivolous and unnecessary, or anything that involved getting dirty. Primrose was not allowed to go to tea at other children's houses, nor could she play in their gardens. It was as if Edna, wanting so much for her daughter, feared she would be contaminated by other people's relaxed attitudes. If children wanted to play with Primrose, it had to be near her home, and they had to be children of whom Edna approved. But Primrose had inherited Edna's resourcefulness and strength of character: she soon found that she could manipulate other children into playing on her terms, using her formidable mother as a weapon.

'We would have to play with her – or else,' said one primary school friend. 'She would threaten us with her mother, and we were all wary of Mrs Oxtoby. If we were playing with Primrose and making too much noise, her mother would come out and we would all run off home instantly. With other mothers, we'd take a bit of a telling-off and then carry on playing, but with Mrs Oxtoby, we wouldn't wait around.'

By this time, Primrose's sister Mary, who was eighteen when Primrose started school, was training as a nurse at a local hospital in Thorp Arch, near Wetherby. Like her mother, the young Mary had a forbidding exterior: always very smartly dressed, she had an efficiency of manner and sternness of expression that inspired confidence in her nursing skills but did not invite friendly overtures. It was only a façade: nurses who worked alongside her soon came to realise that she was a pleasant and reliable colleague. After her training she moved to Leeds, where she worked at one of the large teaching hospitals. With such an age difference, her relationship with Primrose was never that of a playmate, but the two got on well enough, Mary being fond (in the undemonstrative way of the Oxtobys) of her little sister.

At the age of eleven, when they grew beyond primary school, the children from East Rigton and Bardsey were bussed to the nearby town of Wetherby to attend Wetherby County Secondary Modern. It was a journey Primrose would never have to make, because just before her transfer to secondary school the Oxtobys' lives changed radically when her parents moved the family from their tiny tied cottage to a substantial stone-built semi-detached house in Wetherby itself, the house where Edna Oxtoby still lives. A family inheritance allowed them to buy the three-bedroomed house, set on a hillside overlooking the town centre. Prospect Villas are a row of four matching pairs of houses, built in 1876 (at a cost of £300) by a man called Jackson, whose unmarried daughter Fanny lived at number 1 throughout Primrose's years there. At the time they were built, the houses were part of the mushrooming development of the western side of the town, and were given the grandiloquent title of 'villas' to attract professional, middle-class people, who for the first time could commute to Leeds on the newly opened railway line.

Today, the railway line has gone, but the market town of Wetherby thrives. It wears a prosperous air, genteel clothes shops rubbing shoulders with farm machinery suppliers, broad Yorkshire vowels butting against clipped county tones. There are over 20,000 people living there, a huge increase on the 6,000 residents when the Oxtoby family arrived. Yet the expansion has not spoilt the attractive centre of the town, with its traditional marketplace surrounded by grey stone buildings. With the River Wharfe forming a natural southern boundary for the town, and the nearby racecourse, Wetherby today has become a magnet for tourists on the Yorkshire Dales trail.

The new house must have seemed vast to the Oxtobys after the succession of farm cottages in which they had lived. The rooms are large, with eleven-feet-high ceilings and very solid walls. There is an upstairs bathroom at the front of the house, installed some time during the early years of the century; downstairs are two living rooms, a large kitchen and a cellar. The back yard is small, with an outhouse, but the front garden is long, and George Oxtoby soon had it planted with vegetables and fruit bushes.

His new job, now that the family had left the farm, was as a road labourer for the council. His wage in the early 1960s was £11 11s a week (£11.55), less than a white-collar worker but enough to keep his family comfortably. It was more than the going rate for a farm labourer or foreman, and, besides, work on the land was becoming scarce and precarious as mechanisation reduced staff levels.

Primrose transferred smoothly to her new school in Crossley Street, a five-minute walk away from her new home. All her old classmates from Bardsey were there, so the disruption for her was no bigger than for anyone else. It may have been daunting for a few days, going from a single-stream primary into the three streams of the secondary modern, but by today's standards it was a modest school. The third stream was remedial, and very small, so effectively the school operated with A and B streams with about thirty-five children in each.

A select few youngsters who passed their eleven-plus went to Tadcaster Grammar School, making the same life-shift that Fred did when he went to High Pavement. But although Primrose was a bright child with a chance of passing, she failed to make the grade and, in the words of the headmaster of the secondary modern, Harry Fitton,

'In those days, if you failed that one exam at eleven the wall came down in front of you.'

Fitton, who took over the school in Primrose's third year there, was an advocate of the comprehensive system (which came to Wetherby in 1967, three years too late for Primrose) because, as he says, few expectations were put on the children who went to a secondary modern. They left at fifteen, without taking any GCEs or CSEs (which were yet to be invented), although in theory they could transfer to the technical colleges in Harrogate, Leeds or York. In practice, less than 5 per cent continued in education, and most of these were girls doing short-hand and typing courses. An ex-pupil who became an optician is the apogee of Wetherby Secondary Modern's old pupils, in Harry Fitton's recollection.

Not only did he, as head, face the daunting task of motivating staff and pupils for four years of education that would lead to no specific qualifications, he also faced a battle to get better facilities. When Primrose joined the school in 1960, there was already an agreed plan for a new building to be erected on the site of some old Admiralty buildings a quarter of a mile to the east of the existing school.

For the first two and a half years of Primrose's time at the school, some classes were held at the old naval building, with teachers squiring gaggles of rowdy kids across the busy A1 trunk road. But with the arrival of Harry Fitton they retrenched on to the original premises in Crossley Street, with the promise that work would start on the new school imminently. Harry Fitton noted in his log that 'it is necessary to occupy one class outside doing Rural Studies at all times to keep the school running on available accommodation'.

It was early in 1964, as Primrose was nearing the end of her four years at the school, that the bulldozers finally moved in to demolish the old building. Harry Fitton hoisted the Union Jack over the Crossley Street school in celebration and watched, with some of his pupils, as the first walls were knocked down.

From an early age, Primrose was familiar with the town of Wetherby. It was here that she came every Sunday, sometimes three times, to the Methodist church in Bank Street, with her mother Edna and sister Mary. George was also a regular member of the congregation, but never with the unswerving constancy of his wife. The family were there at 10am prompt for a service, with Primrose and the rest of the children being led out at 11 for their own, less formal worship in the church hall. Here they would listen to parables and sing cheerful hymns, accompanied on a piano, while their parents sang sterner tunes to the organ in the church, and heard stronger messages of Methodist morality. In the afternoon, she and the other children would attend Sunday School, sitting in a circle round their teacher to discuss the meaning of Bible stories. In the evening, there was another service.

By the time she was eleven Primrose was also attending the Tuesday evening Methodist Fellowship meeting, where she heard more Bible stories, was tested on them, and took part in discussions about her religion: unsurprisingly, to this day, she is steeped in the simple tenets of Methodist Christianity, and has an impressive knowledge of the Bible.

The Fellowship meeting was not fun: fun wasn't part of Edna's agenda for her daughter. She loved Primrose, but wanted to imbue in her the formidable work ethic her own hard life had taught her. Edna, like so many other women of her generation, cared greatly about appearances, about respectability, about doing things right. She wanted her two children to have fulfilling lives, but in her lexicon 'fulfilling' was not synonymous with 'happy'. It was important to be good, to be proper, to be decent. Fun was self-indulgent, wasteful, ungodly; fun was for other people, and more fool them.

Yet 1960, the year that Primrose Oxtoby started at Wetherby Secondary Modern, was the year from which many observers of modern manners date the beginning of fun. It was the start of the decade that took that invention of the 1950s, teenagers, and exalted them. It was the decade that finally threw off wartime austerity and made frivolity an art form. It was a decade that Edna and George Oxtoby would have preferred not to happen and one which they tried, as best they could, to ignore.

It was not so easy for Primrose to ignore, however, as she began to grow up. She was not allowed to go with her friends to the two local youth clubs, one held not a hundred yards away from her home, where they played table tennis and crowded round a record player to listen to the Everly Brothers and Cliff Richard, and practise jiving and the twist. She was not allowed to go to the Rodney cinema, just down the hill. She was certainly not allowed out to meet her friends on the playing fields, chatting to boys until the dusk curfew sent them giggling home. She showed little outward sign of chafing at these restrictions, but as adolescence crept up on her she felt more and more resentful of her mother's strict discipline.

At Sunday School she met her closest friend from this period, Una Ripley. Una had to walk past the Oxtoby house on her way to school, and would call every morning for her friend Prim. Sometimes Edna would invite her in, and she would sit round the scrubbed kitchen table while Primrose finished getting ready. From the age of thirteen Primrose did a paper round for a shop in the town centre, and would occasionally be so delayed that Una would be told not to wait: Primrose would run panting after her down the hill. The girls, both quiet among their rowdier school friends, enjoyed each other's company, chatting about the stories they read in *Bunty*, the one comic that Primrose was allowed to have.

Una, like other friends who were invited in to number

4 Prospect Villas, describes it as dark and formal, with heavy mahogany furniture (at a time when most families were outgrowing their utility furniture and replacing it with G-plan teak, bought on hire purchase). There was a piano, which Primrose played without any aptitude or enthusiasm, at Edna's insistence. George was usually outside tending his disciplined rows of vegetables, a flat cap on his head and a roll-up cigarette in his mouth. Too many of Edna's home-made pies and cakes left their mark: as they grew older both George and Edna became rounder.

'Both her parents were friendly, but her father was shy, and said very little. Her mother would chat, asking me about homework and things to do with the church,' says Una. 'I never went round much after school, except to call for Prim if we were going to Guides. I don't know what she did in the evenings, when the rest of us went to the youth club or at weekends to dances. I know she was a member of the library, so I suppose she sat with her parents reading or doing needlework. She had pet rabbits in a hutch in the garden, and there was always a small black poodle – I think they replaced it with another identical one when it died.'

Girl Guide meetings were Primrose's only real escape from the domestic regime. She loved the meetings, and best of all the occasional days out and weekend camps. Pauline Elson, another friend, says: 'My mental picture of Prim is in her navy-blue sweater, slacks and wellies, lugging a large piece of wood for the camp fire. She joined in, got on with things. She loved it.'

Pauline only went to the Oxtoby home a few times, and remembers it as 'an old house with old furniture and old-fashioned people. They were very strict: you just knew you had to mind your p's and q's. It wasn't as if they were unfriendly, but you never felt comfortable or welcome.'

It would be simplistic to blame the repressed morality

of the Oxtobys on their strict religious background, and it would be unfair. Wetherby was far removed from 'swinging' London, where Carnaby Street was becoming the centre of the universe and the intelligentsia were queuing to defend Lady Chatterley's uninhibited sex life against obscenity charges at the Old Bailey. The local paper was still full of stories about the Methodist young wives' group; the brides whose smiling portraits crammed the weddings page wore satin, tulle, organza – fairytale-princess clothes for a time when marriage and motherhood were still the chief goals for the girls at Wetherby Secondary Modern.

Yet, even by the standards of the time and the place, the Oxtobys were strait-laced, proud and difficult. To Edna, 'keeping yourself to yourself' was a virtue. She would smile and pass the time of day with neighbours, but never invite closeness. If anyone upset her, she was unforgiving, as the family which lived next door to the Oxtobys for twenty-six years discovered. The Wilsons moved in to Prospect Villas in 1961, and for the first five years relations between the two households were pleasant and polite, if not cordial. But in 1966 that changed completely after the birth of Paul Wilson. He was a sickly baby, and his father was in hospital with pneumonia. His mother, coping alone with Paul and his toddler sister, politely asked the Oxtobys to stop banging on the wall at midnight: they were removing a fireplace from the adjoining house, and the noise was keeping the baby awake.

The next morning, a handwritten note from Edna Oxtoby was pushed through the Wilsons' letterbox, informing them in stilted, formal terms that from henceforth they would have nothing further to do with them.

And that, as Paul Wilson says, was the end of the Wilsons and Oxtobys speaking to each other. Now running his own successful glass company, Paul Wilson remembers as a child being warned not to go near the reclusive,

old-fashioned couple next door. With a hedge of trees sep-
arating the long front gardens, and outhouses forming a
complete barrier in the backyards, it was not too difficult.
He saw George regularly, working in his vegetable patch,
but Edna was, to the young Paul, only an upright little
woman who walked past with her eyes averted. He knows
how houseproud she was, both from his mother (who,
prior to the rift, had been inside the Oxtoby home) and
from his observation that they were the first residents in the
row to have their window frames replaced and double-
glazed, a fact of professional interest to him.

The dispute between the Wilsons and Oxtobys was a
cold war – there was no outright hostility, no name-calling. If Paul's ball went into the garden next door he could
quickly retrieve it. Silence and disapproval were Edna's
main weapons, and ones she was practised at using.

Una Ripley also came from a strongly Methodist
family, but her parents were not living at war with the
times. Una and the other girls at school listened to Radio
Luxembourg and the pirate radio station Caroline (which
started broadcasting a few months before they left
school), saved up for Beatles singles, back-combed their
hair, caked their eyelashes with mascara and went to
dances in local village halls, walking home at night giggling and chattering. Drugs and casual sex were not a
problem: it was an innocent age when the boys walked
miles out of their way to see the girls safely to their front
doors, and when trying to thumb a lift from a police car
was the most daring thing any of them did.

'I was her best pal but she wasn't mine, because she
could never go out with us,' says Una. 'My mother
thought it was terrible the way her parents controlled her.
But she never complained. She never talked about clothes
or make-up – she seemed to accept that she couldn't have
them. If she resented not being allowed to be like the rest
of us, she kept it to herself.'

She did confide her unhappiness about her appearance to another friend, Julie Goddard. Julie knew Primrose from early childhood: they were at the same junior school as well as the secondary modern. 'She was a real plain Jane, and she knew it. She wasn't happy about it, but I kept telling her it would change as she grew up. It never did.'

The boys at school took little notice of Primrose. Their eyes were on the pretty girls, like Susan Crook, Susan Massey, Barbara Swann and Maria Dukes. Maria, who married her childhood sweetheart Jim Swales, remembers Primrose as rather butch-looking, with a pudding-basin hairstyle and a scrubbed face, wearing twinsets and pleated skirts when the other girls were folding the waistbands of their skirts over to make them into minis, clamouring for patterned tights and hipster jeans.

For Jim Swales, who was 'going around' with Maria from the age of twelve, Primrose was a barely noticed face, a frumpy, unobtrusive girl who 'wasn't so odd that she was ridiculed, but was a nothing really. Definitely not one of those who the boys fancied.'

The words 'unobtrusive', 'quiet', 'plain' and 'forgettable' come up time and again when school friends dredge up their memories of her. Even at thirty years or more distance, some old classmates stand out in everyone's memory. Primrose was the opposite, a nonentity, a girl who made little impression, good or bad, on anyone. Headmaster Harry Fitton remembers her, but admits that it is only because of her name: Oxtoby is rare, and he has never encountered another Primrose.

For Una Ripley, who knew her better than most, there was the glimpse of something else beneath the quiet, repressed exterior. She saw a sense of humour that occasionally bubbled to the surface, and the odd moment of stubbornness. 'There would be a glint in her eyes. And you could never get her to do anything she didn't want to do.'

By the time she reached her final year at school, Primrose was as tall as she is today – five feet four inches – and sturdily built, but not fat. Beneath the unflattering haircut her face was pleasant, almost pretty, and she was gaining in confidence. She was vice-captain of Fleming House (named after Sir Alexander Fleming) to Una's captain. They wore yellow badges of seniority, and were in charge of organising teams for inter-house sports days. Primrose proved to be a natural organiser.

She was also still a keen member of the Guides, and her Guide training proved a great asset when a small bunch of girls persuaded one of their teachers, Esther Barnes, to take them on a hiking trip in the Yorkshire Dales during the final half-term of their school lives. Miss Barnes enjoyed walking, and with her sister to help out, she took six girls youth-hostelling for four days. All of those who went on the trip have fond memories of it, a last rite of fun and innocent companionship before they started work and the serious business of life. Unlike contemporary youth, these girls were expected to grow up at fifteen, to get jobs, find boyfriends, marry and bring up families – yet, in so many ways, they were also immature and innocent compared with today's streetwise teenagers.

'Primrose was the sensible one, the one who organised us all,' recalls Esther Barnes. 'I did not know her well before the trip. I taught the remedial class, and Primrose was far from being remedial. She was a jolly, sensible girl with short hair. Tomboyish in her appearance. The others all chattered about boys all the time, but I don't remember her joining in. She was more into games. And she took over organising the food for us all, which was a relief for me. When we returned to school it was only for a few more weeks, and then they all went their separate ways and I never saw them again.'

The girls all begged, borrowed or bought hiking boots and rucksacks for the trip. The weather was good, and they giggled and sang 'Can't Buy Me Love' as they tramped through some stunning scenery. At one stage they bumped into a group of police cadets, who were lost. It was a flirtatious encounter, the girls crowding round the map that the young men were struggling to follow. Primrose's Guide training came in useful as she showed the cadets where they were and how to get to their destination.

'She cadged a ciggie off them as a thank-you,' says Una. 'She only took a couple of puffs at it – I never saw her smoke.'

The solitary cigarette was a trophy for Primrose, a memento of her first brief encounter with the thrill of innocent flirting; her first taste of the apprenticeship the other girls were getting in life and relationships.

If Edna Oxtoby had let her daughter join in, grow up naturally, find her own feet with boys and clothes and pop music and all the other trappings of teenage life, would things have turned out differently for Primrose? Possibly, but it is unfair to lay all the blame at the feet of her parents. The 1960s were a time of great social upheaval, and Edna and George were not the only parents who found it hard to cope and who clung desperately to their traditional lifestyle. They were well into their fifties in those heady days of 1964, the year that Primrose and her friends went their separate ways when they left Wetherby County Secondary Modern. The Beatles had filled the air with 'I Want To Hold Your Hand' and 'Can't Buy Me Love' for weeks, Cilla Black was enjoying her first taste of stardom with 'You're My World', the Rolling Stones were emerging to inflame their fans and incite the wrath of the establishment. None of this meant anything at the Bank Street Methodist Church, the touchstone in Edna's life. But as Primrose walked slowly home from school for the final time, she was beginning to be acutely aware of the gulf between her life and that of her contemporaries.

The studied indifference she had shown to Una, affecting not to care that her clothes were outmoded and so obviously chosen for her by her mother, was starting to crack. The unobtrusive, quiet, plain Primrose of the classroom had made up her mind: she was not going to spend the rest of her life under Edna's thumb. The times they were a-changin', even at number 4 Prospect Villas, and it would not be long before Edna and George would find that, as Bob Dylan predicted, their younger daughter was beyond their command.

# 4
# Marriage and Medical School

The Wetherby girls filled the front seats of the Number 38 red double-decker bus heading towards Leeds. Every morning, a whole clutch of them, bound for jobs and colleges in the big city, scrambled to their favourite seats for the forty-minute journey, gossiping and giggling all the way.

In September 1964 Primrose joined the regular group who met at the bus station at twenty-five past seven each day, and jostled their way to their customary places. There were always between six and ten of them, girls who knew each other from school and Guides and a lifetime of living in the area. They talked about clothes, make-up, music and boys. Other passengers, faces buried in their morning newspapers, would often ignore the day's national news in favour of eavesdropping on the chattering teenagers. They were never allowed to be too silly: Christine Snape, a few years older than the others and their Guide Captain from the 1st Wetherby Girl Guides, was among them and would shoot a look of disapproval at any girl who was talking too much, or revealing too many details about her latest boyfriend.

For Primrose, the bus journey was the start of a new

life. She had never been independent before: even her secondary school was only five minutes' walk away from Edna's disapproval. Yet here she was, fifteen and a half, and on her way to start a college course in Leeds. Primrose was one of the few secondary school pupils from Wetherby who went on to any kind of further education – she had won herself a place on an art and design course.

'She did a painting of hats not long before the end of term,' says her classmate and friend Julie Goddard. 'It was really good, I can remember it to this day. It was striking.'

Although Edna Oxtoby was disappointed that her younger daughter did not want to follow her sister Mary into nursing, she was prepared to let her go to college with one proviso: that she should learn something useful, something from which she could make a living. Art was combined with catering. Her artistic skills were not wasted – she learned to decorate cakes to a professional standard, even being commissioned to make wedding cakes for friends and family.

She was excited to be embarking on this whole new way of life. Just to be on a bus heading out of Wetherby was intoxicating; to be part of this cheerful crowd of girls made it even more exhilarating. She no longer felt defensive because there was no record player, no transistor radios for listening to the prattle of disc jockeys on Radio Caroline, no amused tolerance of mini-skirts, hair lacquer and pale pink lipstick at home. No, she was no longer defensive: she was resentful. Edna's regime, based on the belief that everything had to be sensible, economic and worthy, had finally turned her younger daughter against her. The grip in which she held Primrose loosened with every mile the bus clattered along the A58. Leeds was going to be different, Primrose was sure of that.

To the other girls she did not appear to have changed. She still had her plain, unflattering short hairstyle, while the others sported sleek imitation Mary Quant bobs, or long straight styles which they ironed under sheets of brown paper to remove any kinks. She still had scrubbed apple cheeks, without a scrap of make-up enlarging her eyes or giving a pout to her lips. But inside, she was changing all the time, watching the others and envying them their casual familiarity with pop music and fashion and the mysterious arts of flirtation.

The year at college helped. She became more independent of Edna and George, more determined that life offered something more exciting than the Methodist Fellowship, piano lessons in the dark living room of number 4, and homilies from Edna. Although she was always injuncted to catch the first bus back to Wetherby, she occasionally defied her mother by visiting coffee bars and even, once or twice, a pub. When her behaviour was met with nothing more than stern silence and implicit disapproval, it began to dawn on Primrose that she really was beginning to be mistress of her own life, and that life did not have to be the one chosen for her by Edna.

With her college certificate, she set about finding a job. Determined that she would, at all costs, not work in Wetherby, she found herself a job as a window dresser. Edna was not delighted, but was at least relieved that her daughter was not just a shop girl.

And now Primrose had not only physical freedom, but some money of her own. She handed over much of her wage to Edna for her keep, and the bus fares cost her another chunk, but even so, there was a couple of pounds a week left to spend at a time when that was enough to buy a new blouse or a pair of shoes. She would never indulge herself with clothes and make-up; Edna had ingrained some values deep into her soul, and vanity would never be part of Primrose's character. But she could choose to go to the cinema, or even to a dance. And as her options opened up, the other girls on the Wetherby bus began to notice the changes. She seemed more relaxed, more cheerful, a practical girl who gave the impression that nothing could bother her.

But something was bothering Primrose, and as the Number 38 neared the ring-road around Leeds, she would find herself looking anxiously at the bus stop, keen to see who else was going to board the bus that day. Because it was on the Number 38 West Yorkshire Road Car red double-decker that Primrose Oxtoby first set eyes on the young man who would become her first and only boyfriend, and who would dominate the rest of her life: Fred Shipman.

For Fred, too, Leeds was an exciting place. The bluff Yorkshire city, home in its Victorian heyday to more than a hundred woollen mills, was described by historian Asa Briggs as 'a study in civic pride', a boom town of the Industrial Revolution where vastly expensive municipal buildings were erected at the same time that street upon street of dingy hovels were being thrown up for the working classes. It is, in appearance and culture, not dissimilar to Nottingham, although the latter would probably win any beauty contest organised by the tourist trade.

It was in the early years of the twentieth century that Leeds rose above its woollen-industry past and expanded to become a great and diverse city. The ready-made clothing trade flourished, the well-established engineering industry brought wealth and employment, and the emergent middle class moved into large houses in leafy suburbs. Headingley cricket ground was built and Leeds University received its charter; by the time Fred enrolled in 1965 it was one of the five largest in Britain, and had been voted the most popular university in the country in a national newspaper survey. The medical school has an even longer history, going back to the foundation of Leeds School of Medicine in 1831. The city itself, as Fred first saw it, was largely the same as it had been before the war: Leeds was not a target for Hitler's bombs, and therefore did not need wholesale post-war redevelopment.

For Fred, like Primrose, the excitement owed little to the architectural and industrial history of the city. What they both cherished about Leeds was the opportunity to be away from home, to explore for the first time their independence, to find the heady 1960s mix of freedom and fun which, until Leeds, had passed them both by. They were two of a kind: repressed working-class kids who yearned for something more, who glimpsed a lifestyle to which other teenagers seemed to have the passport, and yet which was as exotic and alien to them as a foreign country. They both stood on the sidelines of the times, watching a parade of mini-skirted girls and long-haired boys pass by.

As a result of the mushrooming student population, Leeds, like many other red-brick universities, found itself short of halls of residence. Traditionally, all first-year students were given a place in a hall so that they could be loosely supervised by staff during what was, for most of them, their first experience away from home. There were no mixed halls in 1965: it was strictly male or female and, astonishingly, in those far-off days there was a hall exclusively for public school boys, where they dressed in dinner jackets for their evening meal.

Faced with a crisis of accommodation, Leeds instituted a system of 'approved digs'. Families across the city were encouraged to take in students for that crucial first year. University staff checked out the digs, and handed out addresses to the bewildered new arrivals.

The address Fred was given was 164 Wetherby Road, and the instructions he received to get there were to take the Wetherby bus and get off just beyond the A6120 ring-road around Leeds, in an area known as Wellington Hill, about twenty minutes' ride from the centre of the city. If he was disappointed to be billeted so far out, away from the student social haunts, he must have felt a sense of relief, and slight awe, at his first glimpse of the house that was to be his home for the next twelve months.

Despite its unexpectedly pretentious name (a previous owner had called it Harewood House, a strange choice as it lies less than ten miles from the eighteenth-century stately home of the same name), the house is the apotheosis of suburbia, a 1930s brick-built and rendered detached house with mock timbers, large bay windows and an arched front door. John Betjeman would have approved: it is as solid and respectable as it could be, a whole world of aspirations away from the council estate in Nottingham. As he walked down the long front drive, past the well-kept lawn, did Fred feel slightly nervous, out of place, unsure of himself? If he did, the couple who owned the house, Mr and Mrs Copley, did their best to put him at ease. Taking in students was a sideline for them, supplementing the takings of their greengrocery business, but Mrs Copley was a kindly person who wanted the youngsters who came to her to feel at home.

It must have helped, too, that he was not the only student sent there, and that his companion for the next year was another first-year medic, Peter Congdon. The two young men settled in well together, both quiet and studious, both having worked hard to get the necessary A-levels for the course. They were comfortable at the Copleys', even if they laughed together at Mrs Copley's limited menus: cold beef and baked potatoes figured a lot as evening meals.

Together they also boarded the bus for the city centre every morning, usually getting on the same one as the excitable, giggly Wetherby girls. Sitting several rows back from Pauline North, Christine Snape, Primrose Oxtoby and the others, the two young men, smart by the standards of the '60s in the sports jackets, ties and flannel trousers that were standard for the earnest youths of the medical school, were amused by the ebb and flow of gossip and daydreaming that they heard from the girls.

It was Primrose who caught Fred's eye, perhaps because she had already fixed hers on him. It took several journeys, over a few weeks, before they plucked up the courage to speak to each other, at first exchanging shy smiles, graduating to nods, and eventually to banter and chat, and a date. The other girls noticed the burgeoning friendship with amusement and pleasure, happy for Primrose, who was popular, that she had found herself a boyfriend at last. The others, some of them already sporting diamond engagement rings, knew about the rituals of courtship and naïvely assumed that she did too. It never occurred to any of them that Prim needed advice, a confidante, support: they all had mothers and sisters and friends with whom they could share their worries about boys 'going too far' or 'wanting only one thing'.

It was, compared with today, an innocent age. As Maria Dukes, who married her boyfriend Jim Swales soon after they left school, explains, even those who started their sexual apprenticeship much earlier than Primrose were restrained and prudish by the standards of modern teenagers. 'You let them kiss you, but that was all. We didn't get anything in the way of sex education at school, but we all knew that we couldn't let our boyfriends go too far. And they knew it, too, and didn't try.'

A great many of the Wetherby girls were still virgins when they joined the brides on the weddings page of the *Wetherby News*, in yards of tulle and satin and net and lace. Their parents expected it of them, as did their future husbands. Girls who 'did it' were given 'a bad name', they were popularly thought to have failed at one of the first, and biggest, hurdles of adult life. Some of them might be reading Edna O'Brien, and thrilling to her daring exploration of female sexuality, but they were still keeping their legs together in real-life encounters with the opposite sex. Despite a few media scare stories about the growing numbers of unmarried mothers, the reality was that less than 8 per cent of all babies were born out of wedlock, compared to five times as many today.

The stage and cinema may have been overwhelmed by kitchen sink dramas, many of them set in Yorkshire (*Room at the Top, Billy Liar, A Kind of Loving, This Sporting Life*), but with a few honourable exceptions (*A Taste of Honey, The L-Shaped Room*) the gritty realism on the screen was presented from a male perspective. Women were victims, or an obstacle course that the heroes (or anti-heroes) had to run. There were few clues there for Primrose, a girl who had never been encouraged at home, school or anywhere to accept her sexuality, or to value herself. The rest of the cinema output was fantasy stuff: in the year she left school, Cliff Richard's *Summer Holiday* was playing at the Rodney Cinema in Wetherby.

For Fred, too, coming from Nottingham where the defining *Saturday Night and Sunday Morning* was set, the images on screen bore little resemblance to his own working-class background. Both he and Primrose came from families which would easily have fitted into the definition of working-class, but which shared the values of the middle classes – both cared about appearances, decency, getting on in life. Saturday nights of drink and sex and hungover Sunday mornings were not part of their experience.

They were both nervous of the changing world around them, the newspapers full of pictures of big-eyed, long-legged models like Jean Shrimpton, the streets full of Beatles and Rolling Stones lookalikes, the air full of vibrant music from 'boutiques', small shops that for the first time ever catered just for the fast-changing styles of youth. The '60s were swinging, and although most of the outlandish behaviour that defined the decade took place within a small radius of the King's Road in Chelsea, there was a mood across the land of restlessness and new freedoms for young people. Post-war austerity was finally banished, old values were questioned, hedonism and protest were the two conflicting calls of youth. In France, Daniel Cohn Bendit, 'Danny the Red', would soon lead student riots, and there were real fears that chaos and violence would be disseminated across British campuses. Students sat late into the night in smoky bedsits, listening to Bob Dylan and planning a world that their parents would not recognise.

But the social upheaval, although seminal, was limited. While newspaper headlines shrieked of drugs problems and 'free love' leading to unmarried pregnancies, the actual numbers involved in either drugs or unprotected sex would put a wry smile on the face of any Home Office minister of the 1990s. Most kids, while dancing to the Mersey Sound in coffee bars and dingy cellar clubs and espousing the rhetoric of protest, still clung to the personal and family values drilled into them by their parents.

The common denominator for Fred and Primrose was that they were both lonely and sexually frustrated, and the secret glances between them on the top deck of the Wetherby bus, interpreted so easily as falling in love, were founded on a recognition of their own need in each other.

Within a few months of arriving in Leeds, Fred had acquired the status he craved: he had a girlfriend. Primrose, too, revelled in the same achievement. They wore each other like badges to allow entry into their own generation. They delighted in their own sensuality, tentatively exploring each other. They were intensely happy, high on first love, proud of sexual success, and as confused as many others at the time about just how much of the new freedom to enjoy. Not knowing the rules of how far to go, not having the self-confidence to use condoms, not frightened of the risks they were running (because they both felt, in the heat of that first love, that they would be together for ever), they had unprotected sex, and Primrose, to the astonishment of everyone who knew her, became pregnant.

And so they were together for ever, and always will be: bound now, not just by the normal ties of family life, but by the enormity of what lay ahead for them.

It was towards the end of Fred's first year at Leeds Medical School that he 'got Primrose into trouble', as it was still described at the time. His relationship with his new and only girlfriend dominated that first year, yet there was plenty else to occupy him. Leeds University may have been a hotbed of student radicalism (Jack Straw was there at the same time, taking a year out from his law studies to serve as President of the NUS) but, as with everything else in the 1960s, it was a minority making waves – the majority of students were happy to get their degrees, drink cheap beer, listen to records in their bedsits and have endless drink-fuelled discussions about the need for change in society; then, armed with their qualifications, go out to take their places in that same society.

Medical students, particularly, had little time for banner-waving, and would have been given short shrift by the traditional medical establishment who taught them if they had. It was then (and is now) the toughest course for any student: five years in university, followed by one compulsory year in hospital as a junior doctor. There was very little free time, and the burden of work was so great that evenings and weekends were needed to keep up with it. When Fred was not with Primrose he was studying – it was the only way that he, or any of the others, could hope to get through.

Lectures started at 8.30am and went on until 4pm without any free time, apart from a short lunch break.

Wednesday afternoons were free, traditionally so that the students could take part in sports, although most of them used the time to catch up with their academic work. For Fred, the free afternoon dovetailed with half-day closing in the shops of Leeds, giving Primrose a precious few hours off work, and the couple a chance to spend some time together. To make up for this rare tranche of free time, the medical students had to attend lectures again on Saturday mornings. Every student had a tutorial in physiology every week and was expected to revise the theme for the week: nerves, veins, blood vessels or whatever. Twice a year there were *viva voces*: verbal interrogations of terrifying thoroughness, dreaded by all the students.

The Medical School in those days was in Great George Street, at the side of Leeds General Infirmary, and quite separate from the rest of the university, giving the medics a feeling of not quite belonging to the main student body. Beyond the main school was the pathology and biochemistry building, where the dogs used for dissection were kept in kennels on the roof – it was disconcerting for new students to hear the howls and barks as they approached the building, and even more disconcerting when they faced cutting up one of the animals.

In those days Fred Shipman was thin, small and dapper: one fellow student describes him as looking 'rather spivvy, wiry and dark'. Another describes him as 'just one of the crowd – there was nothing about him that stood out. He certainly wasn't flamboyant. Although he had a blunt, northern manner and said what he thought, he didn't seem to be arrogant or have any need to be the centre of attention.'

Dr Susan Pearson, a retired GP who trained with Fred, says, 'He was quiet. He liked to be part of the group, he wasn't reclusive or isolated. But he wasn't one of the noisy ones. Somehow he seemed more mature than the rest of us, he didn't seem to be as worried about the amount of work we had to do. It was such a gruelling course that a lot of people dropped out, and others seemed to be permanently exhausted. Freddie seemed to cope better than most.'

As part of their physiology coursework, the students carried out experiments on themselves, usually working in pairs. They measured each other's oxygen consumption, there were unpleasant experiments which involved swallowing tubes to measure gastric juices, one which entailed drinking gallons of water to see whether it had an intoxicating effect, another in which blood was taken from earlobes.

It was while doing these experiments that Fred again encountered morphine, when the students did double blind tests (some taking it, some taking placebos) to monitor its effects. Nobody remembers him taking any particular interest in it, but Fred was already expert at keeping a lid on his reactions.

The other students soon knew about Primrose the girl-friend – mainly remembering her, as her old headmaster had, because of her unusual name. Those who met her give descriptions very much in line with those provided by her old classmates: nondescript, plain, nothing memorable about her. If she felt out of her depth with these young people who had achieved a much higher educational level than she had, she did not show it. She was cheerful and friendly, but eminently forgettable.

On one occasion, with her parents away on holiday, she and Fred invited two other medical students, boyfriend and girlfriend, back to Prospect Villas, where Primrose cooked them all a traditional Sunday lunch, serving Yorkshire pudding with gravy as a starter. The others found the house depressing but the meal very good.

The other students, as well as all the Wetherby girls, were genuinely shocked to hear of Primrose's pregnancy. Many years later Fred told a nurse with whom he was working that getting Primrose pregnant was a mistake. 'I was a bright boy, I should have known better, shouldn't I?' he said, but he said it without rancour. The nurse got the impression, as many of his colleagues and acquaintances have over the years, that Primrose is not the girl he would have married had he been given time to explore other options. But a pregnant girlfriend offered few options in 1966: a year later, and legal abortions and free contraception would be possible on the NHS (although not abortion on demand), but in 1966 – unless you were very wealthy or were prepared to risk a back-street abortionist – there was no choice but to have the baby. Adoption was a possibility, but for Primrose the baby offered a wonderful opportunity to escape completely from Prospect Villas and Edna's regime. For Fred, too, it added a comforting permanence to the relationship, and it did not take a great deal of pressure by Primrose to persuade him to marry her.

Primrose first shared the news of her pregnancy with Pauline North, one of the Wetherby girls from the bus, and a friend Primrose had known from first joining the Guides. Pauline, two years older than Prim, had not been close to her at school, but got to know her well when she joined the bus gang.

'I don't remember her having a boyfriend until she met up with Fred. She wasn't the boyfriend type, she didn't seem interested. I saw Fred on the bus with her, and sometimes in Leeds. I'd never have put them together, they were an odd couple. He was quite good-looking, although you didn't eye up each other's boyfriends so I didn't take too much notice. Prim came round to my flat a few times, and it was there that she told me she was pregnant. I think I was the first person, apart from Fred, to know. I can remember the scene clearly – it was such a shock. She was leaning against the worktop in the kitchen while I made a sandwich and she came right out with it:

"I'm pregnant." Out of the blue, no build up – I nearly dropped everything.

'I can't remember if she told me where it happened. My first and main thought was about her mother and father, because they were so old-fashioned and prim and proper. I asked her what her mother would say: she hadn't told her parents at this stage. She didn't seem worried, but she should have been. I would have been. I don't imagine they took it easily. Perhaps she was just putting a brave front on it for me, but she genuinely seemed very relaxed about it.'

Unsurprisingly, both families were horrified. Harold Shipman even felt a brief relief that his wife was dead, and had not lived to see her favourite child make such a mess of things. Fred's sister Pauline, who was proud to have a medical student in the family, did not talk about it. As for the Oxtobys, Edna and George were shaken to the core, and to this day friends and neighbours refer to it as 'the thing that broke Edna's heart'. To a woman so immersed in duty and respectability, an unmarried pregnant daughter was just about the worst thing imaginable. Even when Fred and Primrose arranged a wedding, she was mortified, and insisted they did not get married in Wetherby, with Primrose's bump evident for all to see.

When they met Fred, the Oxtobys did not like him. Was it instinct, or was he the blustering, arrogant Fred that he could be with people he despised? Despite the unpropitious circumstances, for their teenage daughter to bring home a medical student, a young man with every likelihood of becoming a doctor, ought to have been a coup. Most working-class mothers with ambitions for their girls would have been delighted, but Edna was not. She disliked Fred from the word go, and nothing she has learned about him since, even before his crimes, has given her any reason to change her mind.

As far as the wedding was concerned, she and George

were prepared to stand by their daughter and do their duty. It was a joyless occasion: a quick, legalising ceremony in a register office at Barkston Ash, ten miles from Wetherby, on 5 November 1966, with the bride six months pregnant. The two fathers were witnesses at the ceremony, which was not attended by any of the young couple's friends. Fred used the Copleys' address in Wetherby Road, which gave him the required residential qualifications for a ceremony in a register office away from both Wetherby and Leeds.

The same day that they married, the *Wetherby News* recorded joyful milestones in other young people's lives: 'Given away by her father, the bride wore a white satin dress with embroidered motifs, a bouffant veil and camellia headdress. Her bouquet was of pale lemon rose and white heather . . .' For ever after that day of grim duty in a small register office, would Edna turn hurriedly away from the page of smiling brides and proud parents? Would George regret never walking either of his daughters to a Christian sanctification of marriage? For Mary never married at all, and may already have been experiencing the first symptoms of the disease which would eventually blight her career and confine her to a wheelchair.

On the evening of Primrose's wedding, Bank Street Methodist Fellowship celebrated its union with the other Methodist group in the town, North Street Methodists, with a firework display followed by a supper of beans, sausages, parkin – a traditional north country Bonfire Night treacle cake – treacle toffee and cheese scones. Did Edna, such a stalwart supporter of church events, attend? If she did, it is hard to believe that her heart was in it.

Less than two months into his second year as a medical student, Fred was a married man. What's more, on 14 February 1967 at Harrogate General Hospital, Primrose presented him with a baby daughter, Sarah Rosemary. For the final weeks of her pregnancy and the first months of motherhood she lived at her parents' home in Wetherby. Both Edna and George melted towards their beautiful little baby granddaughter, but relations with Fred and Primrose remained strained, and before long the young couple had found a flat near Blackman Lane, in the Woodhouse district of Leeds. The area was, and still is, classic student territory: a warren of narrow streets with two- and three-storey houses split into flats and bed-sits. The flat was barely half a mile from the medical school and not isolated then, as it is now, by the fast-moving traffic of the inner ring-road.

It cannot have been easy for Fred. His student grant of £340 a year was enough, just, for a student to live on, but hardly adequate for a wife and baby as well. Primrose had to give up her job soon after the wedding, when she became too big to clamber in and out of shop windows, and without the support of the Oxtobys they would have been in serious financial trouble.

While his fellow students could relax over a pint in the evenings at The Vic, the medics' favourite pub, only a few hundred yards from the medical school, or go to see groups like The Hollies appearing at the union, or use the discounts given to students for theatre and cinema seats, Fred went home to a flat full of damp nappies and the demands of a tiny baby. With a heavy workload for his course, finding time to put in enough study must have been hard, and no doubt there were times when he resented the way his life had changed. He was just twenty-one the month before his daughter Sarah was born, but instead of celebrating in time-honoured tradition with lashings of alcohol, he typically said nothing to his fellow students. Family celebrations back in Nottingham would also be muted: any spare money from presents was needed for the baby.

For Primrose, not yet eighteen, it was even tougher, although in some ways she revelled in her new life. She had learned, as Edna's apprentice, the mechanics of running a home: she knew about cleaning and cooking, and she enjoyed baking cakes and pies. Being tied by a baby would mean a huge loss of freedom for most teenage girls, but for Primrose, so accustomed to the restrictive regime of the Oxtoby household, the tiny flat in Leeds was a release.

She made it a welcoming place; two friends of Fred's, who visited the flat entirely independently of each other, both described it as 'homely'. Even though they were aware of all the trappings of a baby in such a small space, they both came away with the unarticulated feeling that it was a happy household.

Dr Susan Pearson, who also married and had a baby during the course, remembers getting off the bus in Woodhouse Lane with Fred and a couple of other students after they had all been on a placement at Seacroft Hospital, north-east of the city. Fred invited them all in for tea. Whether or not Primrose was expecting them – it seems unlikely as it appeared to have been an impromptu invitation – she had cakes freshly baked and the kettle boiling.

Although the flat was in a run-down area and the furniture was the usual spartan standard of student lets, Dr Pearson remembers it as very welcoming. Sarah was toddling by this stage, and there were toys scattered about the room, which was clean and well cared for. 'It was much more appealing than the usual student flat, because of the baby's things. It was a relief to go there, you felt cosy and welcome. Primrose said very little, but she looked after everybody.'

At the end of their second year the students crowded on to the steps of the medical school to hear the results of their exams being read out by the Dean. It was a moment of great tension, made more so by the quaint ritual. Some of them had fortified themselves with a trip to the nearest pub, The George, just across the road. The Dean, an elderly orthopaedic surgeon called Paine, read them out slowly, to cries of relief and delight from the majority and quiet despair from those few who faced taking resits. Fred was through: he never achieved any academic distinctions during his time at university, but his work was always solid and reliable, and he had his second MB (Bachelor of Medicine: the first component is the right A-levels, the second comes after two years at medical school, and the third on completion of three years of clinical work).

For clinical work the students were put into groups, usually of four, and the constitution of these was changed every two months or so, so that students got to work with a cross-section of their contemporaries. Again, those who worked with Fred remember him as diligent, hard-working, amenable and no problem. He was not one of the popular members of the course, partly because he was unable to spend time socialising, but neither was he unpopular.

For three years the students split their time between various local hospitals. Most teaching was done at the Leeds General Infirmary, but they also went on visits to St James's, Menston and Highroyds Hospitals, and even as far away as Wakefield, where they went to see an iron lung.

The climax of the three years was a month of finals, the examinations which would allow them, if they passed, to be provisionally registered as doctors. Again, the results were read out from the steps of the medical school by the Dean, this time Professor Wood, a professor of pharmacology. Most of the students were too tired to celebrate: they received the good news in a daze of exhaustion, knowing that within a week or two they would start their final year of hard slog, as junior hospital registrars.

The majority of them found placements in hospitals in Leeds, mostly at the Leeds General Infirmary or St James's, now famous as 'Jimmy's' from the long-running fly-on-the-wall television series. But for the married students, like Fred Shipman, the trick was to get a junior housemanship in one of the satellite hospitals, where there was a greater provision of accommodation for doctors' families.

For that reason, Fred chose to take Primrose and Sarah, now an energetic three-year-old, to Pontefract.

# 5
# Practice and Pethidine

**T**he hard work expected of him at Leeds medical school stood Fred Shipman in good stead for the next three and a half years of his career, at Pontefract General Infirmary. The life of a junior houseman is notoriously hard: they work unremitting shifts, coping with all sorts of medical emergencies and procedures. Many years later, when he was in Strangeways Prison, Shipman would joke to a doctor friend that if you could cope with the junior houseman regime, then prison life was certainly no worse. A one-year hospital appointment is compulsory; at the beginning of it a young doctor only has a provisional registration with the General Medical Council, made up into a full registration at the end of the year. The year is divided into two: six months' medical work and six months' surgical work, under a 'firm' of consultants who are responsible for the supervision and training of the houseman. Fred Shipman stayed on in Pontefract for another two years and nine months after he was fully qualified, doing a senior housemanship, during which time he acquired a diploma in child health and a diploma in obstetrics and gynaecology.

It was during his first year in Pontefract, almost exactly

nine months after passing his final exams at Leeds, that
the Shipmans' second child arrived. Christopher Fredrick
Shipman was born at Wakefield Maternity Hospital on 21
April 1971, while the family were living in a house within
the hospital grounds at Pontefract. It was the accommodation that had first attracted them to the hospital: they
lived in a solid, red-brick, 1930s part of a complex of a
dozen houses. Today the houses are shabby, looking like
part of a run-down housing estate, but for the Shipmans,
used to living on a pittance in the cramped flat in Leeds,
it was spacious – an ideal place to expand their family.
Living within the hospital was easier for Fred because of
the demanding hours he worked, and the hospital situation in a built-up area of Pontefract meant there were
plenty of shops and amenities for Primrose and her two
small children.

But working in a hospital was never Fred Shipman's
first choice: he always wanted to go into general practice.
On 1 March 1974 he joined a group practice in
Todmorden, working at the Abraham Ormerod Medical
Centre.

Todmorden is an attractive town situated in the meeting of three valleys formed by the hills of the Pennine
chain. The River Calder, which runs beneath the impressive town hall, used to form the boundary of Yorkshire
and Lancashire, leaving the town split between the two
counties, but since the latter years of the nineteenth century it has been wholly in Yorkshire. At least, it has been
administratively in Yorkshire: the postal district is still
Lancashire, the cricket teams play in the Lancashire
league and, with its history of cotton mills, it has more
affinity perhaps with Lancashire than West Yorkshire.
'Tod people are Yorkshire folk who think Lancashire,' said
one longstanding resident.

Whichever direction they choose to face, the 15,000
Tod folk can be in either Manchester or Bradford in

thirty-five minutes by train or, in a slightly longer time, by road.

Fred arrived to join a busy group practice with three full-time colleagues – Dr Michael Grieve, Dr John Dacre and Dr David Bunn – and one part-timer, Dr Brenda Lewin. The Abraham Ormerod centre, named after the local benefactor who payed for the original building, is well placed in the centre of the town, and serves the whole of Todmorden apart from a couple of outlying districts. The doctors were overstretched, and delighted to welcome such a hard worker. He was taken on for a month's trial, and then became a full member of the practice. The others gave him a warm reception; he established a good rapport with the patients, and was happy to work long hours.

'He was young, enthusiastic, full of energy and anxious to do more than he was paid for,' says Dr Michael Grieve, now retired, who was one of the senior partners. 'He taught the rest of us a lot, because he was last out of medical school and knew all the latest methods. He assisted me with centralising the sterilising service at the health centre; we went to the Royal Halifax Infirmary together to research into how we should do it. He also took sheafs of patient records home with him to summarise them so that we could streamline them. Fred was very willing to get stuck in in his own time.

'He liked to do everything himself. If he could do it, he would – he didn't even use a nurse as much as other doctors would. We were delighted with him because Brenda had not been well, and was unable to do night cover, and the doctor Fred replaced, Jim Howat, was also only working part-time because he had multiple sclerosis. It was a great relief to have another full-timer, and especially one so keen. We were at rock bottom, and we really saw him as our saviour.'

The Shipman family found a house to buy on mortgage, an attractive stone-built semi in a road with the appropriate name of Sunnyside – the road is little more than a terrace of houses set into a steep, tree-clad hillside, facing south with nothing but the hills to obscure the sun. The road twists round a scruffy low-rise British Telecom building and peters into a neglected narrow lane which rises steeply and bends under a railway bridge, emerging at the solidly built row of homes, some the traditional three-storey weavers' houses of the area, some newer bay-windowed semis. The Manchester-to-Leeds railway line runs just below the front gardens, which made the house in Sunnyside a strange choice for a family with a three-year-old and a six-year-old.

Primrose found the house, which was called Sunny Bank. She was driven around looking at properties by the wife of one of the other doctors, who was surprised by her: she was then, as she is now, not what people expect of a doctor's wife. Being a family doctor's wife is a strange position in any society, tending to distance the wives from some normal friendships, especially in a traditional community where a GP is regarded with godlike awe. Other doctors' wives (and doctors) throughout the research for this book have made the point that they are not being snobbish (a great many of them share the working-class origins of Fred and Primrose) when they say she fell short of expectations. By the time she reached Todmorden she was seriously overweight (although not as large as she is today); she appeared not to care about her dress; she was loud and slightly coarse (her 'loudness' interpreted by those who like her as ebullience and a bubbly personality, as overpowering by those who do not). As she viewed properties in Todmorden she carried Christopher, who had a piece of old nappy pinned to his clothes as a comforter: it was very dirty.

Outside surgery hours, Fred Shipman became an enthusiastic member of the Rochdale Canal Society, an organisation Dr Grieve was involved with. The group was set up within months of Fred and Primrose arriving in Todmorden, with the express aim of digging out and reopening the Rochdale Canal (which had been abandoned by the Rochdale Canal Company in 1952). Neither Fred nor Michael Grieve were at the first meeting, in June 1974, but they both joined shortly afterwards, as a flood of publicity brought offers of help from local volunteers as well as a small amount of funding from big business.

Fred was one of the 'labourers' who turned out in all weathers to spend their free weekends digging mud and sludge from the disused canal bed, and restoring the gates on just one of the ninety-one locks along the canal. It was back-breaking, dirty, wet work, but Brian Holden, chairman of the association, remembers Fred Shipman as conscientious, cheerful and reliable. Primrose helped too, mucking in with the other wives to provide sandwiches and brew tea for the 'navvies', using a Calor gas boiler sheltered behind a stone wall or inside an old van.

'She was pleasant,' says Brian Holden. 'She was well built, quite large. But she had a very cheerful personality.'

In the twenty-five years since the work started, half the canal has now been restored – and the other half has secured a grant of millennium money to make sure that it can be opened. The confirmation that the project would get £23 million was given by Deputy Prime Minister John Prescott in May 1999: the story, carried in all the serious national dailies, may have aroused Fred Shipman's interest as he whiled away the time in Strangeways Prison, waiting for his trial.

Not content with the physical labour of the canal, Fred got busy in the house – he built a garage and some walls, although his skills as a builder left a lot to be desired. His handiwork was described by a subsequent owner as 'a hotch-potch of crooked walls'. Where he did show talent – and enthusiasm – was in the garden. The front garden was formally laid out with pink and red rosebeds in a controlled and symmetrical pattern.

The back of the house led to the tree-clad hills, and there was a footpath through to the cricket field and down to the town. It was a cosy house, easy to heat in the bitter Todmorden winters.

Neighbour Eric Crossley, who has lived in Sunnyside for more than fifty years, remembers Sarah and Christopher Shipman playing outside his house. 'Their mother Primrose would come out to collect them for their tea, and would always have a friendly word. They were good, well-behaved kids who played on bikes and did all the normal things kids do. I rarely saw Fred, he was so very busy at the surgery.'

Fred's involvement with the canal association and his DIY projects in Sunny Bank ended as abruptly as his career as a GP in Todmorden. The first clue that the other partners had that anything was amiss was when he started to have blackouts. At least two of the others were called out to his home by Primrose because Fred had lost consciousness. When Michael Grieve went, it was because Fred had blacked out in the bath, but by the time he arrived Fred had come round. The partners were very concerned, and referred him to a consultant in Halifax who diagnosed epilepsy. At the time, epileptics were not allowed to drive (the regulations have changed since) and the other members of the practice were, in Michael Grieve's word, 'shattered'.

'We assumed he would have to leave his job. But then Primrose came to the rescue: she volunteered to do all his driving for him. I don't remember how she coped with the children, she must have had babysitting arrangements for the evening and night work. Anyway, we were greatly relieved.'

Michael Grieve may have been relieved – and grateful – that Primrose was doing the driving, but he did not like her, nor she him. Dr Grieve's gentle wife Heather was aware of Primrose's dislike for her husband. Primrose would gossip about Dr Grieve to the practice receptionists, and when word reached Heather she accosted the reception staff and told them if they had anything to say about her husband they should say it to his face, or hers, but not to Primrose Shipman.

'The impression we got was that Fred was quiet and hard-working, and that Primrose was the bossy one,' says Heather Grieve.

It was one of Primrose's 'friends', a receptionist at the practice called Marjorie Walker, who eventually precipitated the discovery of the truth behind his blackouts – and brought his career to a grinding, if temporary, halt in July 1975. Mrs Walker, who is now dead, was in the chemist's shop of Harold Lever, diagonally across the road from the practice. She was behind the counter in the dispensary, probably because she was friendly with the staff. The book detailing prescription of dangerous drugs had been left open, probably because the chemist was taking the opportunity to alert someone as to what was going on. It showed that Fred Shipman was prescribing substantial amounts of pethidine.

Pethidine is an opioid analgesic with similar properties to morphine. It was synthesised in the 1930s and was hailed initially as a wonder drug because it was believed to have no addictive properties. Even when it was discovered to be potentially addictive, it remained – and remains – very popular as a painkiller in childbirth. Occasionally midwives, who had access to it and, believing it to be free of addictive properties, took it for all their aches and pains, became dependent on it. For longer-term use (for instance for gallstones and renal colic) it can still be prescribed with care, because much larger dosages are required than for morphine, making it easier to fine-tune treatment and avoid addiction.

According to the controlled drugs book, Fred Shipman had been prescribing large amounts of pethidine on the practice account. The account existed (it was, and is, common for surgeries to have such an account) to enable the doctors to obtain a limited supply of drugs for carrying around or keeping in the consulting room for instant treatment of patients. He had also been prescribing large amounts in the names of various patients on his list.

Marjorie Walker went back to the Abraham Ormerod Medical Centre. The first doctor she met was John Dacre. She told him what she had seen, and he asked her to keep quiet about it. He checked with the pharmacist, and then spent a weekend (while Fred Shipman and Michael Grieve were on duty) investigating. He visited various patients whose names had appeared in the register as having had pethidine prescribed for them: they were able to tell him that they had never been given the drug.

The first that Fred Shipman knew about John Dacre's investigation – and the first the other doctors knew – was when Dacre called a meeting of all the medical staff in his consulting room after surgery hours on Monday afternoon.

'What's all this then, young Fred?' were the words he used, before telling the astonished others what he had found out.

Fred appeared outwardly calm, but did not deny what had happened. His initial reaction was that if he cured himself of his addiction to the drug, he would be able to carry on working. He said he had become hooked on pethidine at medical school when he was required to try it, as part of his training. 'Can't we just ride over this?' he said.

But the others, led by Michael Grieve, insisted that he must go into hospital for treatment, and that they would need to replace him. He initially agreed, and after a long discussion he left the building. The others stayed behind, going over the situation they were now in, all of them horrified by what they had learned about him.

'We had no clue, even after the episodes with the black-outs,' says Dr Grieve. 'We were shattered to discover he had epilepsy and doubly shattered to discover he didn't, but was an addict.'

Half an hour after Fred left the medical centre, he returned. He was angry, and announced that he was not leaving the practice, and nor was he going into hospital. The other partners were forced to ring the practice solic-itor, who told them that they had grounds to sack him for misbehaviour. The lawyer said that the onus would then be on Shipman to sue them for wrongful dismissal which, in the circumstances, he was highly unlikely to do. When they told him what they were planning Shipman stormed out, flinging his night bag (the bag provided by the prac-tice for home visits to patients) in through the back door of the premises in a fit of temper.

A Home Office drugs inspector, whose job was to rou-tinely monitor the prescription of controlled drugs, came to the practice and interviewed Shipman there. With the help of his partners, the GP was booked into a world-famous psychiatric centre in York, The Retreat. Although privately run, The Retreat had a philanthropic approach to members of the medical profession, and Fred Shipman may have been treated there free or for very reduced fees. (Times have changed, but even now doctors are sympa-thetic to the problems of members of their own pro-fession. The current literature about The Retreat says: 'The Retreat excels in providing anonymity to those people who are in the public eye or who have high profiles within their profession, including healthcare profession-als.') The doctors in Todmorden naturally thought very highly of The Retreat. Dr Grieve did his medical training at Guy's Hospital in London, where the psychiatric clinic was named the York Clinic as a tribute to the pioneering work in mental health done in that city.

In 1975, when Fred Shipman went there, there were 320 new admissions, among them 103 suffering from various kinds of depression, 58 from alcoholism and just 4 from drug addiction: recreational drug use was nowhere near as widespread in the 1970s as it is today. It was a benevolent regime – in 1975 The Retreat was one of only three medical institutions across the UK to win a five-star award in a *Sunday Times* survey of hospital food.

When Fred Shipman arrived, he would follow the same procedure as all new patients: he was by no means the only doctor to go to The Retreat for treatment for alcohol or drug abuse, and he was accorded no special privileges. Dr Michael Bearpark, a consultant psychiatrist at the hospital from 1961 to 1984, has no specific memories of Shipman, but describes the routine for new admissions: 'Relatives would take them into the dormitory where they would undress, put on pyjamas and go to bed. After a physical examination they would be prescribed medication for the night, usually a sedative, and a careful watch would be kept on them for twenty-four to forty-eight hours.

'A new admission was called a "parchment", because the parchment, or file, with all the patient's details would be handed over from one nurse to another when they went off shift. For the first few days everything would be taken very gently. The new patient would be prescribed librium and phenobarbitone, if there was thought to be any chance of convulsions. They would more or less go straight into detox. Withdrawal from drugs is rarely as bad as people think.'

Depending on the level of addiction, coming off pethidine would be similar to having a bout of flu – headaches, runny nose and eyes, and generally feeling under the weather, but lasting no longer than a week or two. Dr

Bearpark says that alcoholics could be free of their addiction in six to eight weeks, but that the treatment took longer for drug addicts. It was to The Retreat that detectives from West Yorkshire Police came, accompanied by the Home Office inspector, to interview him, in November 1975, about the forgery of the pethidine prescriptions, and when he came out of hospital it was with the prospect of a court case hanging over him.

After his arrest, his whole future – and that of his wife and two children – was in jeopardy. The General Medical Council, the body which polices the behaviour of doctors, was informed and had the option to suspend or strike his name off the register of doctors allowed to practise. But when his case came up at the relevant committee meeting, it was decided to take no action against him; unofficially, he had been advised to get treatment and rehabilitation for his addiction, which he was already doing, and to promise that in future he would avoid temptation by not carrying supplies of controlled drugs in his surgery. Today, the affair would have been handled very differently.

'Nowadays we would look at him on the grounds of health impairment,' says David Morris Johnson, spokesman for the GMC. 'In the case of a doctor with an addiction problem, he would be assessed by psychiatrists. Depending on the outcome of that, there would be a voluntary regime of restrictions placed on the doctor: he would have a supervisor (a psychiatrist) who would monitor him, deciding when he was fit to return to work, and he would be allowed to accept jobs only with the approval of this supervisor. Because there was no open hearing into his case, it appears it was not regarded as a desperately serious problem: it seems that the belief was that he could overcome it.'

It took his partners in Todmorden months to sort out the formalities – they had to buy him out of his share in the practice – and of course it was a time of great upheaval for the family: because he was unable to work they could not keep the house in Todmorden, and Primrose, with six-year-old Sarah and three-year-old Christopher, was forced to move back home to live with her parents in Wetherby. The buyers of the house were horrified by the state it was in: it was neglected and dirty, and the new owner rallied friends to help her clean it before moving in. It's difficult to know why Primrose's previously conscientious housekeeping had lapsed. Perhaps the strain of having to combine looking after two small children as well as driving her husband around to all his home visits was telling on her. Whatever the reason, it was a complete change for Primrose: she had been brought up in the stern Oxtoby household to believe that cleanliness was next to godliness. She had been taught to cook, clean and be proud of her environment; in the honeymoon years of their marriage, when they played house in their tiny flat in Leeds, both she and Fred had embraced cosy domesticity. All that, however, had changed.

The Shipman family vanished instantly and completely from Todmorden. Eric Crossley, their neighbour, only realised they had gone when he saw the house empty. There was, of course, a great deal of gossip – Todmorden is a small, enclosed community. As one resident says: 'If you kick someone in Cornholme someone in Walsden says ouch' – Cornholme and Walsden being tiny villages at either end of the town.

'It was common knowledge in the town that he left because of drugs. It was what everyone talked about, because he had been so well thought of. Because he was a doctor, everyone was horrified.'

Edna Oxtoby told one of her friends in later years that she took Primrose and the children in 'out of duty – after all, it is not the children's fault'. We can only speculate about the atmosphere in that dark, gloomy household, the air heavy with the Oxtobys' reproach and 'told-you-so' smugness. But whatever the reception she gave Primrose, Edna's Christian duty was clear to her, and for several months she and George provided a home for them. The relationship between them and their second daughter was seriously fractured, though, and from the minute Primrose and Fred re-established themselves, Primrose broke off all communication with her parents.

In order to work and support his family after his stay in The Retreat, Fred initially took a short-term contract with the National Coal Board, based at Doncaster. At the time, the NCB was carrying out an extensive programme of health reviews among miners, checking them for incipient emphysema and pneumoconiosis, lung diseases caused or aggravated by conditions in the pits.

He and Primrose were reunited, settling in a detached house set back from the main road that runs through the mining village of Rossington, near Doncaster, about a quarter of a mile from the pit medical centre.

The case against him came up at Halifax Magistrates' Court in February 1976. He pleaded guilty to eight offences, and asked for sixty-seven more to be taken into consideration. He was charged with three offences of obtaining a controlled drug by deception, three of unlawful possession of a controlled drug, and two of forging declarations of exemption from prescription charges. He was fined £75 on each of the charges and ordered to pay the NHS compensation of £57.78 for the drugs he obtained illegally, a total of £657.78. To put the fine in perspective, the 1999 equivalent would be £2,736.36. He was allowed to pay £50 a month, a hefty amount (£208 in today's money) which must have made the next year very difficult for the family (and perhaps exacerbated the problems between Primrose and her family, if they needed financial help).

In court it was revealed that when the police visited him, Shipman immediately admitted that he had been injecting himself with 600 to 700 milligrams of pethidine a day (which would mean as many as fourteen injections), and had started because he was depressed. As his depression worsened, he claimed, he had increased his dependence on the drug. His defence solicitor also claimed in court that Shipman had been frustrated after joining the Todmorden practice because his ideas for improving it were met with opposition (a suggestion that Michael Grieve emphatically refutes – but the doctors in the Todmorden practice knew nothing about the court case until they read it in the local papers).

Some of the pethidine he prescribed had been genuinely given to patients: in those cases he would prescribe a large amount, collect the prescription himself, and only give the patient a portion of the total amount. In other cases he had forged prescriptions without giving any to the patient. He had forged the signature of a matron at a local nursing home where he cared for some of the patients, and had also signed the backs of the prescription forms to obtain exemption from charges.

The court was told that the drug squad officers were satisfied that he had not sold drugs to any third party, nor had he deprived a patient of a drug they needed.

Two people, both neighbours from Sunnyside, appeared in court as character witnesses for Fred Shipman. One, a retired music teacher who is now dead, said he was a neighbour, friend and patient of Shipman's, and was very impressed with his ability. The other, Ken Fieldsend, also spoke of his confidence in Fred Shipman as a doctor.

'This is indeed a sad case,' the presiding magistrate, Dr Maurice Goldin, told Shipman as he stood in the dock. 'It is something which, it seems, has been going on for a long time, and no one could be more aware of the dangers involved than yourself.'

Shipman's reaction when he heard the sentence is not recorded, but despite the fine, he must have been relieved to have got away so lightly. He had managed to keep his profession, his wife had stood by him, and, at the age of thirty, he had a future ahead of him – although he was still living in Doncaster doing temporary work for the NCB at the time of the trial, he had already found himself a new job, far away from his troubles.

The arrest and trial of Fred Shipman in the mid-1970s may have been over a relatively trivial matter (at least, trivial when compared to fifteen murder charges), but there are interesting parallels with what would happen twenty-two years later, including his ability to inspire friends and neighbours to support him. (He and Primrose remained such good friends with Ken Fieldsend and his wife Marie that they returned to Todmorden in the early 1990s to attend Marie's fiftieth birthday party.)

There are questions to be asked about Fred Shipman's time in Todmorden. Was he really a drug addict? Or was he already using the pethidine to indulge his strange compulsion to kill? The blackouts would suggest genuine addiction, but they could have been a cover, because he realised that he would be found out. As he demonstrated with Mrs Grundy's will, he is a particularly bad forger – he makes little attempt to cover his traces. Perhaps the blackouts were another cry for attention, a bid to be stopped before his compulsion got out of hand.

His outraged reaction – throwing his bag through the door – when his partners announced they were sacking him suggests he genuinely was trying to get away with it: he did not crumple and plead for help. But Fred Shipman is a man of great contradictions, and back in 1975 these were no less apparent than they are today.

Since his arrest in 1998, detectives from Greater Manchester Police have been to Todmorden to go over the background to his previous conviction and ask questions about patients who died while he was caring for them. They have heard stories from ex-patients of his about how he was nicknamed 'Dr Phet' because of his rumoured willingness to prescribe amphetamines for anyone who asked for them. But it is all a very long time ago, and evidence is very hard to come by; many of the people who knew the Shipmans are now dead, including the doctor, Brenda Lewin, who was the closest of the partners to Fred and Primrose, and the receptionist Marjorie Walker.

We may never know exactly what was going on in Todmorden. Dr Grieve maintains he was not killing anyone – but then, so, many years later, would the doctors who were in practice with him in Hyde.

By the time he came up in court Fred Shipman had already secured a job in County Durham, more than a hundred miles away from the disgrace of Todmorden. He joined the South-West Durham Health Authority, working as a clinical medical officer. The post is now obsolete, but at that time it involved liaison between the health authority, the general practitioners in the area and local community groups. Fred Shipman's work involved looking at children's health care in the Bishop Auckland, Crook and Willington areas of the county.

One great attraction of the job was the cheap housing: the family were given a home in Newton Aycliffe, eight miles north of Darlington. With Fred's court fine to pay off, there was no question of embarking on another mortgage. They paid £7 10s a week (just under £30 in today's money) for a brand-new semi in Rylstone Close, a cul-de-sac and therefore a relatively safe area for the children to play in. Sarah and Christopher joined in with the other local kids, and went to the local primary school, Woodham Burn.

Mrs Ann Robson, who still lives in the Close, remembers Primrose as the mother who would always go out on to the street to quieten things down if the children were getting too rowdy. The Shipman children, she remembers, were well-behaved and polite.

'We knew they came from outside town, but they never said where. We didn't socialise, but Primrose was quite friendly. She always had a smile on her face. We scarcely saw her husband as he worked out of the town.'

The Shipmans spent only eighteen months in Newton Aycliffe. Fred Shipman had developed a taste for general practice, and his job with the health authority was, to him, a stepping stone to being rehabilitated in the eyes of his peers.

He wanted to be a GP again. And before too long, a job advertisement in the *British Medical Journal* caught his eye. It was for a practice in Hyde.

# 6
# Uneasy Partners

The young woman was nervous. It was her first day on the road as a drugs rep, travelling round visiting GPs in their surgeries to persuade them to prescribe the drugs her company manufactured. Drug companies can vastly increase their profits if they persuade doctors that theirs is the best preparation on the market.

This young rep, who was in her twenties, had an appointment at Donneybrook, one of the two very large practices in Hyde. She waited anxiously until morning surgery was over, and was then taken into an upstairs room to meet three or four of the doctors who were available to see her. Except one they were all friendly, although not exactly enthusiastic about listening to yet another pitch from yet another rep. The one who glared at her when she came in was small, bespectacled and bearded. He did not smile or chat with her, as the others did. She explained that it was her first day in the job since her training, and the others all wished her luck and paid attention as she went through her routine, promoting the wonders of the particular drug she had been taught to sell.

As she spoke, the small, angry-looking doctor got up

and started to prowl restlessly round the room. Suddenly, he turned on the drugs rep and started firing questions at her. He demanded to know more about the side-effect profile of the drug she was promoting, impatiently refused her time to reply to him, then badgered and browbeat her until, terrified and overwhelmed, she burst into tears. He walked out of the room, leaving the other doctors to console her, fetching her a cup of tea and reassuring her that life as a drugs rep was not always going to be like this.

Did she give up her new career after only one day? Or was the blooding she got at the hands of one acerbic GP enough to prepare her for all the vicissitudes of life as a sales rep? We don't know: certainly, she never came back to Donneybrook.

And Fred Shipman, the doctor with the caustic tongue, how did he feel after his victory over such a young, inexperienced and inadequate adversary? He was pleased with himself, secure in having proved his intellectual superiority, convinced that his colleagues had been left in awed admiration of his clinical knowledge.

If his drugs conviction had caused him any loss of confidence, if the years in Todmorden and Newton Aycliffe had sapped his self-esteem in any way, he had put it behind him. He was in Hyde now, and he was here to stay.

Hyde clings to the eastern edge of the Greater Manchester sprawl: just a mile or two beyond it is the majestic Peak District, an outstandingly beautiful area of dark peat and white limestone, wild and lonely despite its position wedged between industrial Yorkshire and industrial Lancashire. Within minutes' drive of Hyde it is possible to be in Derbyshire, Cheshire, Lancashire or Yorkshire, each with its own distinct appeal.

The town of Hyde itself is not beautiful. It isn't one of the pretty stone towns of the Peak District; architecturally and historically it turns towards Manchester, to the rapid industrial expansion of the eighteenth and nineteenth centuries, to the dark Satanic mills of the cotton industry (most of them now pulled down, or used as office and warehouse space).

The Town Hall in the centre of Hyde is a large, ornate, red-brick Victorian building, with the ugly grandeur of its vintage. Many much larger towns cannot boast such an imposing, solid focal point. The library, in matching brick and similar style, is also much bigger and more impressive than its counterparts in towns and cities across the country. Hyde, these self-important buildings proudly boast, was once successful and wealthy, a mill town made rich in the boom years of the Industrial Revolution.

Today Hyde is no longer prosperous but nor is it relentlessly poor. It is a town where money is tight, bargains are sought, conspicuous expenditure is avoided: but it is also a town which retains its old-fashioned dignity. Although it has been absorbed into the massive sprawl of Greater Manchester, it keeps its own identity. It is a close-knit community where the same families have lived for generations, knowing and supporting each other; where church and chapel are still full on Sunday mornings; where respectability and a good name are still highly prized; where there has been only a relatively small incursion of Bangladeshi immigrants to change the balance of the population. 'I've lived here thirty years, but I'm an outsider, not a local,' says one resident.

The Town Hall self-consciously fronts the market square, opposite the Clarendon Centre, a concrete and glass 1960s shopping centre, backed by a monstrous multi-storey car-park. The modern development has a feeling of impermanence about it – unlike the Victorians, its architects were not planning for posterity. Inside the shopping mall the sense of transience continues; most of the shops are small units selling cheap clothes, and changing hands on a regular basis. The town is not big enough or wealthy enough to support a Marks & Spencer or a BhS, and although there is a small branch of Tesco, the flourishing supermarkets are of the pile-it-high, sell-it-cheap variety.

Since the closure of the mills which, two centuries ago, changed a small agricultural community into a flourishing town, employment prospects for local youngsters have been limited, and work has to be found for many at the more prosperous centre of the Greater Manchester conurbation, or in the neighbouring towns of Stockport, Oldham and Ashton-under-Lyne. Until the last year or so, the three biggest local employers were a glue factory, the Senior Service cigarette factory, and a firm making protective gloves and industrial footwear. Now all three have closed or moved away, the cigarette factory laying off its final 3,000 workers just three months before Fred Shipman came to trial. The glue factory is missed by those who worked there, but not by residents in its vicinity: the air was frequently filled with the smell of boiling bones, a smell known locally as 'The Kingston Stink', and the subject of a twenty-year battle with the local council over environmental pollution, which culminated in the factory's closure.

Hyde has few claims to fame: Tameside is the birthplace of a few well-known names like Geoff Hurst, Barbara Castle and Mick Hucknall, but what it lacks in famous ex-residents it more than makes up for in infamous ones – it was in Hattersley, a huge council estate attached to Hyde, that Myra Hindley and Ian Brady were living when they carried out their final two murders. That case appalled the nation and resonates down the years: Hindley and Brady had been behind bars for nearly thirty-three years at the time of Fred Shipman's arrest, yet their crimes are still fresh in the collective memory of Britain. In Hyde, where they were arrested and where the

full gory details of their crimes were first heard at committal proceedings, nobody who was old enough to
remember the events of 1965 will ever forget them, and it
was with a sickening sense of *déjà vu* that the town prepared itself for the media onslaught of the Shipman trial.

What is it about this place? The question has been
asked endlessly in the months since Shipman's arrest.
Rumours have flown around the town of witches' covens,
seven separate ones, meeting in the hills above Hyde and
creating a concentration of evil which has spawned these
horrific crimes. Sheer coincidence can be the only possible, rational explanation: lightning does strike in the same
place. But that does not make it any easier for the people
of Hyde to endure.

There was no portent of what was to come when Dr Fred
Shipman arrived in Hyde in 1977, to join the
Donneybrook practice. One of the seven doctors at
Donneybrook, Dr John Bennett, was retiring, and the
remaining team advertised in the *British Medical Journal*
for a replacement. Fred was one of several applicants, all
of whom were interviewed.

'He freely admitted he had had a pethidine habit and a
conviction for it, but he said: "I am off it. I don't use it.
You will have to trust me." We all liked him and felt it was
fair to give him a chance, so we took him on on a six-
month trial basis,' says Dr Ian Napier, who joined one
year before Shipman.

Dr John Smith, who has now retired, also remembers
the interview, and being impressed by the way Shipman
owned up to the problem, explaining that it had been
brought on by stress. 'He was well qualified and he talked
well at the interview – Fred can certainly talk.'

Donneybrook was an unusual practice. It was founded
in December 1967 when seven doctors in the town, who
had been split between three different practices, decided

to team up in one purpose-built centre in the middle of the town. The seven had been covering for each other at weekends and evenings for many years, so were used to working loosely together. When they announced their plans, the other seven doctors in the town decided that they, too, wanted to have better premises, so eventually a large building was erected, split into two halves, with separate entrances for the Donneybrook practice and the others, who became known as the Clarendon practice.

It was the first time in Britain that all the family doctors in one town had been concentrated under the same roof. The official opening of the building was covered by local television news programmes, and a photograph of the original fourteen doctors made the front page of the magazine *World Medicine*.

Although the doctors at Donneybrook split the costs of the building (which they owned jointly) and ancillary staff like receptionists and cleaners between them, they each had their own list of patients (they were, in the jargon of the profession, single-handed practitioners – they did not become a proper group practice until seven years ago, after Fred Shipman had left). This meant that they reaped the rewards of their own work; if they used the facilities of the practice more, they paid more into the general expenses, but they also kept any extra money they earned by having bigger lists or offering extra services.

Fred soon proved to be industrious and popular with patients, and before long he had a patient list of 2,300, one of the largest in the practice.

'He was well liked by patients because he put himself out for them. He'd volunteer to visit them. Most doctors see a patient and say to them, "If it's not better in a day or two, give us a ring." Fred would say, "I'll drop by in a couple of days to see how you're doing." It made a very heavy workload, but he didn't seem to mind. He was everybody's idea of an old-fashioned doctor. Most of us work on a knee-jerk response to demand: it is all we have time to do. But he didn't seem to mind how hard he worked,' says Dr Ian Napier.

Dr John Smith, who was one of the founding members of the Donneybrook team, remembers that for most of the fifteen years that Shipman worked there he regarded him as a kindred spirit. 'We had similar attitudes. We used to chat about gardening, holidays, wine: he'd tell me about the wine he brought back from camping holidays in France. He had a sense of humour, you could enjoy a laugh with him. As a doctor he was kind; there's lots of folks who stood by him when he was charged, just wouldn't believe it.'

The practice manager at the surgery for twenty-five years was Vivien Langfield, known as Val to her colleagues. She was there from the day the Donneybrook practice opened until 1992, when she took early retirement to become minister at the Abney United Reform Church in Mossley, near Oldham, having been ordained in 1991.

Although their relationship deteriorated, she liked Fred Shipman when she first met him. 'He was dark, Jewish-looking, with a beard. I like men with beards.' In his early days at Donneybrook, while he was 'on trial' at the practice, Fred, Primrose, Sarah and Christopher lived in a rented house in Lord Derby Road, Gee Cross, for just over a year. It is, today, a neat modern semi with an immaculate garden, but when the Shipmans left the owner, who wanted to sell it, was distressed to find that it was dirty and neglected, just as the house at Todmorden had been.

The family soon moved to their own home, in Roe Cross Green, a cul-de-sac in Mottram in Longdendale, an attractive village about fifteen minutes' drive away from the centre of Hyde. The area is leafy, secluded, and the surrounding roads contain plenty of large, expensive detached houses. The Shipmans' home, where they moved in 1979, is not one of these: it is a four-bedroomed semi-detached, built in the 1960s, and allowed to deteriorate into shabbiness, with peeling paintwork and a terse notice telling people to 'Shut This Gate'. The road itself, a cramped mixture of houses of different ages and designs, is generally well-maintained and the gardens well-groomed. The Shipmans' home, with a garden that backs on to the busy A6018, lets the others down.

With the financial problems they brought with them, the hangover from the drugs charge fine and the time when Fred was unable to work, it was not a surprising house for them to buy; it would have cost about £25,000 at the time, well within the mortgage range of Fred's salary. As well as taking on the financing of the house, he was also paying back a loan to buy his share of the Donneybrook building (there is a fund from which GPs can borrow, interest-free, the capital to buy into a practice). With the purchase of his share in the property came, by the working arrangements of the practice, the list of patients from the doctor who was moving on.

What is surprising is that in over twenty years practising in Hyde, the Shipmans have never upgraded to a bigger or better home. There is nothing wrong with number 15 Roe Cross Green, but on the salary of a GP, in an area where house prices are not inflated, it has neither size nor exclusivity; it is not what most people would expect for a doctor and his family. By the time of Fred Shipman's arrest the house was worth £75,000 and the other residents all expressed (as well as the more obvious emotion of shock at finding themselves in the middle of a media maelstrom) puzzlement and a tarnished feeling of both pleasure and pride that a doctor lived in their road.

Having put down roots, and being determined to make the best of things (now there was no more help available from Primrose's parents) they had two more children: David was born on 20 March 1979, and three years later, on 5 April 1982, Sam followed. These two boys, now young men, have never seen their Oxtoby grandparents.

'When Fred joined Donneybrook we all went out for a meal to a restaurant in Disley,' says Maureen Smith, wife of Dr John Smith. 'It was a tradition when someone left or someone joined: on the whole we didn't socialise at other times.

'I asked Primrose, conversationally, if living in the Hyde area was handy for her in terms of seeing her family. She said, "I have nothing whatsoever to do with my family." I was really shocked, it sounded so extreme. She didn't just say she didn't get on very well with them: she said it very definitely. I bumped into her in the supermarket a year or so later and I asked her, "Have you made it up with your family yet?" To me, it seemed a terrible thing not to have contact with your family. But she said, "No, and I never will."'

Mrs Smith's instincts made her dislike Primrose: she would have been more forgiving if Primrose had seemed in any way upset by the split from her family, but her intractable stance shocked the older woman.

'It seemed so final, as though she had completely made up her mind, and there was no way she would ever be friendly with them. I thought that either they must have done something really terrible to her, or she was very stubborn and rather childlike.'

Similarly, she formed an instant adverse opinion of Fred, deciding he was 'sneaky and shifty'. At the time, her husband had no complaints about Fred, and neither did Dr Ian Napier. Gradually, though, Dr Shipman's colleagues began to notice that although he was pleasant towards them, and endlessly tolerant with his patients, he was very rude, snappy and demanding with the other staff at the surgery – and with people they had to deal with, like the hapless drugs company rep who was reduced to tears.

The Reverend Vivien Langfield, Val, had more opportunity than most to observe this side of his character. Prior to working at Donneybrook she was a day-nursery manager at a cotton mill: the closure of the mill cost her her job, but coincided fortuitously with the opening of Donneybrook. Throughout the twenty-five years she was there, she had more trouble from Fred Shipman than all the other doctors put together.

'He was known for his bad temper. It was a joke among the reception staff. We would tease each other: "If you do that again you'll have Fred blowing his top." We would say "Good morning" to the doctors as they arrived, but Fred would never reply. He would just go to his room, the last one at the end of the corridor, without saying a word. He never responded to our greetings. We all felt that he was ignorant.'

She remembers him occasionally falling out with the other doctors, but he reserved his real venom for members of the reception staff. He would take a dislike to certain of the 'civilian' staff for some small reason (or, often, for no obvious reason) and would, from then on, continually find fault with them. He resented anyone who stood up to him, preferring the young, junior staff who accorded him the respect he felt he deserved. As practice manager Vivien was responsible for the non-medical staff, and would defend them: inevitably, she became a target for Shipman's attacks. He repeatedly told her that if she could not run the practice properly, she should hand in her notice – the implication being that in his opinion she did not run the practice properly.

On two or three occasions he ordered her to sack receptionists who, she felt, were performing the job more than adequately.

'He took a dislike for no apparent reason, and that was

it. If I mentioned it to other doctors they would not go against him; their attitude was that if that was what Dr Shipman said I must do, then I must do it.'

In fact, although Vivien Langfield was not aware of it at the time, the other doctors did stand up to Shipman – over her. According to Dr Ian Napier, at the monthly meetings of the doctors he was constantly pushing for the practice manager to be sacked.

'He'd say, "She's got to go," and be constantly nagging away about her. But the rest of us liked her. She didn't do anything wrong – Fred's dislike of her was entirely personal. It is a measure of her character that she shrugged off his terrible rudeness.

'For the last year or eighteen months that he worked with us, he refused to speak to her. He told her: "Don't speak to me, write everything down and put it on my desk." Every time she tried to tell him something he'd repeat: "Write it down and put it on my desk."'

Dr Napier vividly remembers the visit from the drug company rep, on her first day in the job. 'He rubbished her in front of the rest of us. He just kept haranguing her. He'd trip her up and attack her: "You don't even know the side-effect profile of this drug you expect us to use on our patients," and so on. He reduced her to tears, just kept on and on until she cried. It seemed to make him feel smug and self-satisfied. He was trying to prove he was superior by humiliating her. It made the rest of us feel very uncomfortable, and sorry for the girl.

'He would never harangue us, his medical colleagues, like that. He was quite pushy in practice meetings, he liked to have his own way with his ideas. But it was polite.'

According to Vivien Langfield, Shipman was not always polite behind the other doctors' backs. He would mimic Dr Derek Carroll, who was fifteen years older than him and who has since retired. When Vivien told Dr Carroll, because she felt Shipman's mocking of him was unfair, he told her not to make a fuss: 'It's better to let Fred have his own way.'

She recalls an incident when Shipman was roasting one of the receptionists over some minor inefficiency, and his attack was so bilious that one of the other doctors interjected, 'Hey, Fred . . .' Shipman turned on his colleague and snapped, 'This has nothing to do with you. I would appreciate you keeping out of it.'

'I think some of the other doctors were frightened, or wary, of him. Although I didn't sit in on the monthly practice meetings – I would present my report and then leave – I did see the agenda, and many of the items were ideas put up by Fred. I must give credit where it is due, some of the ideas were very good. Some of the other doctors did not bother putting up ideas at all; they left it to Fred to make the running. But he got annoyed if they didn't like what he was proposing.

'He could have been more co-operative with the other doctors. This was supposed to be a professional partnership, but as far as he was concerned his views had to prevail. As far as the non-doctors were concerned, he treated them in a "below stairs" manner. They were not important, not allowed to hold views and in his eyes were only there to perform menial tasks.

'He was a bully who demanded that people look up to him and have regard to his position. If anyone queried anything to do with one of his patients he would say, "I am a good doctor. I have all the qualifications from Leeds Medical School. I have passed my exams," implying that you had better listen to him.

'He was very cruel when he made me fire people: he was lucky that nobody took him to an industrial tribunal, because they would have had a good case. When I suggested consulting the other doctors he would say, "Never mind the other doctors, I have told you what to do. Just do it." On one occasion he ordered me to get rid of a big woman receptionist by Friday. He didn't like people who were forceful, who stood up to him. He kept asking me if I had fired her. He didn't do the dirty work himself. He was a coward,' says Vivien.

When Shipman was being particularly rude and sarcastic to one of the reception staff, the woman turned on him and said, 'My own husband doesn't speak to me as you do.' Answering back marked her down as a target for more mean-spirited attacks. His weapon of choice was always sarcasm: he never raised his voice, and even his most blistering attacks would be delivered in a quiet and controlled way. If it suited him, he would be nice to the staff, although as far as Vivien is concerned, it was always for a reason, never from a genuine impulse to be pleasant.

It was not only the reception staff who were in the firing-line for his bullying, although they were his easiest prey. He would also be very critical of the cleaners. On one occasion he left instructions for them to remove his desk from his office in order to clean under and around it. The cleaners could not get the desk through the door into the corridor, so they left it stuck in the doorway and told him to move it himself if he wanted his office cleaning.

'He just pushed the desk back to its original position,' says Vivien. 'He didn't really want the area cleaned: it was just a demonstration of his power, another example of his control-freak mentality.'

He was acknowledged by all the staff, however, both medical and ancillary, as hard-working (one of the other doctors described him disparagingly as 'a workaholic'). Work certainly seemed to dominate his life: he would let other doctors go home while he saw the last of their patients for them.

'He could be arrogant and supercilious in his manner, but I was never aware of him falling down diagnostically,' says Dr Napier. 'I think he was a sound doctor. His main failing was that he always had to prove he knew more and was better than anyone else.'

He was also inclined to have strong enthusiasms which ended abruptly – from 1980 to 1988 he was heavily involved with the local St John Ambulance, holding the posts of Divisional Surgeon, Area Surgeon and Area Commissioner, but appeared to lose interest almost overnight, and withdrew entirely. Similarly, for a while he was on the Parent–Teacher Association of Longdendale High School, the comprehensive that all his children attended. He is remembered for the inquisition he once ordered into the tea and biscuit fund, demanding receipts for provisions supplied.

For a time in the 1980s he was heavily involved in GP politics, as a member of the local Family Practitioner Committee (now known as the Area Health Authority) and secretary of the Local Medical Committee (LMC), which represents doctors in their dealings with the health authority and other bodies. Again, he became involved with great zeal but then pulled out rapidly, causing some problems for his successors.

As part of his duties for the LMC he would assess other GPs, checking that their surgeries had adequate facilities, heating and cleanliness. (With an irony that becomes apparent in retrospect, he rebuked one very popular GP because his surgery was 'untidy'.) He also had to deal with problems brought to his notice by other GPs. In one case he was approached by two doctors who were very concerned that their partner was abusing drugs. He was very sympathetic towards the doctor who was using the drugs, telling the partners who brought the matter to his attention that they should try to help the addict.

'The point is, we were trying to help him. But we also had a duty to our patients,' says one of the other doctors. 'Not knowing anything about Fred's own background, I said to him, "A drug addict is always a drug addict – they don't change." He said, "Imagine, if you help him and it works, the satisfaction you will feel."

'We were in touch with Fred several times over this problem, and we naïvely assumed he had set the ball rolling for something to be done – we assumed he had passed it on to the GMC. Eventually, we discovered that Fred had told nobody and done nothing, so we got in touch with the GMC ourselves, and an inquiry was held.

'Perhaps it was not his job to pass it on, but we felt he left patients at risk by increasing the delay and by not telling us that he was doing nothing.'

Subsequently Fred Shipman gave interviews to journalists from two medical journals, *Medeconomics* and *General Practitioner*, about the problems of dealing with alcoholic and drug-addicted doctors: in both cases he made no mention of his own conviction, and talked only about this case, complaining about the time it took to get anything done and advocating a much faster system of dealing with addiction and alcohol problems.

He was happy to pontificate to journalists about any aspect of his work as a GP, and was regularly quoted on a variety of issues. While he was on the LMC he appeared to thrive on his position. Chairman to his secretary was Dr Wally Ashworth (later to become the Shipman family's GP), who became a personal friend.

'I met him at a meeting, years ago,' Dr Ashworth recalls. 'He struck me from square one as able and dedicated – or, as I see it, addicted to the job. He was always talking about the job, and he seemed to have all the latest info at his fingertips. He could talk well at meetings – he was probably the most politically active GP around here. At that time there were twelve of us on the Tameside LMC [it is now a much bigger West Pennines committee]. When he opened his mouth, he knew what he was talking about. He had a good personality for committee work: when we got some admin person in front of us, he would wipe the floor with them.

'He may not have had the fullest insight into the depth of the issues he tackled, but he knew the letter of the law. He isn't a great brain, but he read up about things. In debate he could be aggressive, fiery, forthright. I had a lot of respect for him, but to misquote Shakespeare, sufferance would not have been the badge of his tribe.'

Dr Ashworth remembers another embarrassing incident when Shipman attacked a drugs company rep who was addressing the LMC (a separate, but disturbingly similar, episode to the one where he reduced the rep at Donneybrook to tears). 'She was giving a talk and she got something clinically wrong. He tore her apart, viciously – he almost had to be hauled off. It's as though he had to prove himself superior, and she was an easy target.'

Fred Shipman did not socialise regularly with his colleagues. Some of the others played occasional games of golf, or had a drink or meal together, but he rarely joined in. The tradition of having a farewell party for doctors leaving the practice, especially if they were retiring, continued, and Fred would usually bring Primrose to these occasions – to the surprise of other guests at one party she brought a baby with her, not one of her own children. It transpired that she was working as a childminder, and the baby, whose mother was a teacher, was in her care. She bottle-fed the baby in the midst of the gathering. During school holidays she would have several children, whose parents were working, to look after.

Although Primrose occasionally called in at the surgery (as all the wives did) she was never openly chatty with the reception staff or the other doctors' wives. Vivien Langford is not sure whether this was Primrose's own choice, or whether she was under instructions from Fred not to fraternise. After the problems over her gossiping to the reception staff at Todmorden, it is possible that he had warned her not to get too close.

The Shipmans certainly did not go in for entertaining at their own home. They did not give dinner parties or even informal suppers for friends. Despite Primrose's undoubted skill as a cook, the impulse to socialise from his student days had gone. But there was one occasion when his colleagues from Donneybrook and their partners were invited to number 15 Roe Cross Green: the eighteenth birthday party of his daughter Sarah, in February 1985. It is remembered as a pleasant and unexceptional event – perhaps the most telling thing about it, which would be wholly unremarkable in the context of any other family, was that the house was clean and tidy.

There was an even bigger splash of Shipman hospitality the following year, in 1986, when Fred celebrated his fortieth birthday with a party at the York House Hotel in Ashton-under-Lyne. It was a sit-down meal, attended by colleagues and their partners, the Shipman children, and family friends.

There were other events that he snubbed. At the end of 1989 the practices of Donneybrook and Clarendon, which functioned entirely separately from each other, joined forces to hold a twenty-first birthday party, commemorating the historic establishment of the building they shared. It was held at Dukinfield Golf Club, and staff past and present were invited with their partners, a total of more than 150 people. But Fred and Primrose Shipman were conspicuous by their absence. The Mayor of Hyde, a Labour councillor, had been invited, and this prompted Fred to accuse the organisers of being 'politically motivated'.

When his old adversary Vivien Langfield took early retirement to become a full-time minister, he would not come to the party the surgery threw for her. There was a presentation and speeches in the reception area, and although Fred did not attend, it would have been impossible for him to be in the building and not realise what was going on. Once the presentation was over he went up to Vivien and asked when she was retiring. She was taken aback by the question, and replied, 'Today.'

'Oh, you won't be here on Monday, then,' he said, walking away.

'It was a strange experience, I didn't know what to make of it. He didn't say goodbye or wish me luck. He didn't like anyone else to be in the limelight. I suspect in many ways he was shy, and his bombastic arrogance was a cover for his insecurity,' she says. 'He hated anyone else being fêted, given attention. Perhaps he lacked love and affection in childhood. He never talked about his roots, or where he came from. We all assumed it was Yorkshire.'

When his father died in January 1985, Fred appeared to be completely unmoved. When Vivien said, 'I am sorry about your father,' he replied, 'Are you? I'm not' and walked away. He did not take time off work for the funeral, but he may have been more deeply affected than he appeared. Kate McGraw, who had worked as a nurse attached to Donneybrook but was not there at the time, bumped into another nurse who said he was in a bad way.

'She told me he was hanging on in, just this side of a nervous breakdown. She said he was just about keeping himself together, but appeared devastated. He'd never really talked to me about his father, but I knew the death of his mother upset him a great deal, which I always assumed was why he was so good with women patients, particularly older women.'

One reason he may have been upset after his father's death was because he realised that the house in Nottingham, where he grew up, had been left to his sister Pauline, who was still living there at the time of their father's death. When Pauline decided soon after the death to sell the ex-council house in Longmead Drive, she sunk all the capital from it into a house she shares today with her brother Clive, his wife and daughter. She has a self-contained 'granny flat' in the modern semi-detached house in Long Eaton, five miles south of the city centre of Nottingham. Not only had Fred failed to inherit a third share of the Longmead Drive property (worth, at the time, about £30,000), but he also realised that on Pauline's death her stake in the new house would pass to Clive and his family. He had, effectively, been cut out of his share of his father's home, and it caused a rift between him and his brother and sister.

His father died suddenly, of a heart attack, at the age of seventy – Pauline found him on the floor in the kitchen when she arrived home from work. He had bought the house after his wife died, for £5,500, because he realised that on his death Pauline might be forced to move out into much smaller council accommodation. He wanted to guarantee her future. Ursula Oldknow, who still lives in the house next door, remembers him discussing it with her mother, who had similarly just bought her house in order to leave it to Ursula.

'My mother told him to do it – she said they had to make sure "the girls", that's me and Pauline, would be all right after their deaths. I remember him saying that it would be good because, being roughly the same age, Pauline and I would be good neighbours for each other.'

But soon after her father's death Pauline decided she did not want to continue to live on the Edwards Lane estate, and she sold up.

The rift between Pauline and Clive and their brother Fred, and Fred's assertion that he did not mourn the passing of his father, adds to the picture of the Shipmans as an isolated family, cut off from normal family ties. They had no contact with the Oxtobys and no close contact with Fred's family: they were living increasingly in a world of their own making, a world in which Fred's view of himself as superior to everyone else was allowed to flourish and prevail.

His need to be right, and to prove to everyone that he was right, showed in small, silly ways, as well as in matters of practice policy. He was always sarcastic about Vivien Langfield's involvement with the United Reform Church, and her training for the ministry, making comments like 'You'd better ask Miss Langfield, she's the Christ follower.' Yet, despite these disparaging remarks about Christianity, she remembers him having an argument with one of the other doctors about the number of loaves and fishes Jesus produced in the miracle on the shores of Lake Galilee: as ever, he was determined to be right (even though he later told the police, when asked about his religion, that he was agnostic).

'His whole personality radiated an "I know best" manner, even on things like that,' says Vivien. 'He thought he was cleverer than anyone else, and he needed to be looked up to.'

When in 1990 the government insisted as part of the Patient Charter proposals that all practices should be computerised, Shipman did not like the idea – he always resented anything being imposed upon him. He claimed he was going to raise the matter with his MP. But when he saw, fairly quickly, that computers were rapidly becoming standard, he changed his tune and began to push for them. He liked to give the impression that he was computer literate; technophobes like Wally Ashworth could be easily blinded by his little knowledge, and gained the impression that his friend Fred was a whizz on computers. Others, who themselves knew something about the new technology, were not so easily dazzled, and whenever he had dealings with anyone who really understood computers, it was apparent that his knowledge was superficial (as he would find to his cost one day).

★

There were deaths during his time at Donneybrook, old ladies who died before their time. Shipman's partners noticed nothing – they couldn't be expected to, as he worked on his own, with his own patient list. Not only that, he was careful: scared, perhaps, after the Todmorden experience. But there were unexplained, suspicious deaths, classic Shipman deaths: elderly victims, living alone, whose deaths came as a shock only to those immediately around them. Their ages meant that the deaths would not make any statistician raise an eyebrow: seventy, seventy-four, sixty-nine, eighty-three. All within the range that death comes, but all untimely, undeserved, unforgiveable.

Winifred Arrowsmith died in April 1984, six and a half years after Shipman arrived in Hyde. She was living in a flat at Chartist House, a fifteen-storey tower block in the centre of Hyde. The block has a warden to check on its elderly inhabitants, and a social club, where lunches are laid on, on the ground floor. Winifred, who was seventy when she died, moved to the block on a temporary basis, while her old home was being renovated, then decided she would like to stay.

But unlike many of the residents, she did not need much help with running her life. She was fit, active and fiercely independent. She had arthritis, which limited her mobility, but she was able to take care of herself, cooking all her own meals (she didn't bother with the lunches at the social club). Her flat was immaculate and she was very content, her main companion being a budgie she doted on, which was allowed to fly free about the living room. She loved reading, always wore floral dresses, and never seemed to feel the cold.

Like so many of the old ladies who were on Shipman's register, Winifred had lived through hard times: an unhappy marriage had left her bringing up three children on her own, and she had always had to work for a living, in the hat trade. But she was resilient and cheerful and was enjoying a contented retirement, and that's how the warden at Chartist House, Jenny Unsworth, can still picture her. Although Winifred was not involved with the social club, she was chatty and friendly with the other residents, and Mrs Unsworth remembers her for her proud demonstration that, although she was arthritic and a little bit plump, she could bend down and touch her toes like a teenager.

It was to Mrs Unsworth that Fred Shipman went on the day of Winifred's death. He asked her if Mrs Arrowsmith was in, saying that he had knocked at the flat and there was no reply. With Mrs Unsworth to let him in with a master key, he went back to the flat. Inside, Winifred Arrowsmith was dead, sitting in an armchair as if she had fallen asleep.

Winifred's daughter-in-law, Maureen, had been to see Winifred the day before her death. 'She didn't say Dr Shipman was coming to see her. I'm sure she would have told me if she was expecting him. He did always go to see her at home, because she had trouble getting about with her arthritis, but the only time he came out to her was to give her a repeat prescription for her arthritis tablets.

'When they found her dead she had just had her dinner. The potato peelings were still on the worktop, and she'd had a Fray Bentos steak pie, one of her favourites. I remember thinking that she couldn't have been gone long because she always used to tidy up straight after her meal. It was all so sudden, and we were all very distressed. She thought very highly of Dr Shipman.'

Dr Fred Shipman's Donneybrook years are defined not by the way he conducted himself while there, but by the manner of his leaving. His departure from Donneybrook says as much – and more – about him than all the rudeness and arrogance he displayed to the staff he considered beneath him, all his ingratiating kindness towards his patients, all his attempts to impress his peers with his superior medical knowledge.

The Donneybrook practice functioned efficiently and well, according to an agreement drawn up by the original seven doctors, with the help of their accountants. Doctors came and went, retiring or moving on to other jobs in other parts of the country. There were never any problems – until Shipman left.

He betrayed the trust and confidence of his colleagues. Although what he did was technically, legally right, his colleagues viewed it as unethical and immoral, and it cost all the other six doctors a substantial amount of money – over £70,000 in the first year, and at least £20,000 a year from then on. Dr John Smith has never spoken a polite word to him since; Dr Ian Napier remained on civil terms, not knowing until after Fred had gone the full extent of the damage he had done to his colleagues; others in the practice describe what he did as 'despicable'.

The Donneybrook agreement, which, as one of the founding members, John Smith was in part the architect of, assumed that all doctors who leave would pass on their list of patients to the incoming GP taking their place. It was in this way that Shipman acquired the list of Dr John Bennett. He built it up, but to start with, he had a viable patient list to earn a living as a member of the practice. He bought a one-seventh share of the building from Dr Bennett.

When he left, he said he was planning to move to Yorkshire, but could not find a suitable practice there. He claimed that he did not want to stay at Donneybrook because he did not agree with GP fundholding, and that, because of a loophole he had found in the contract, he was taking his list of patients.

This hit the other six doctors hard, in four different

ways. First, and most significant, because they had no
list to offer an incoming GP, they could not advertise his
post and replace him. This meant they lost his contribution to the running costs of the building and ancillary
staff, about £20,000 a year. As these costs remained the
same for six doctors as for seven, the others had to shoulder his share.

Second, they had to buy out his share of the building
for £23,000. They did this with a bank loan, which iron-
ically they finished paying about three months after his
arrest.

Third, they had to pay Shipman's tax bill of almost
£30,000. In those days (1992) tax was paid on the previous year's profits, and as Donneybrook was run as a
company, Shipman's tax was computed in with everybody else's. The company accountants approached him
after he had left to pay his share of the joint bill, but he
refused. The tax bill was raised against the company, not
the individuals, so there was nothing the other six could
do to force him to pay. They discussed suing him, but
eventually decided against. It was by no means certain
they would win: although once again their position was
morally right, he had found another legal loophole to
exploit. Litigation is time-consuming and expensive, and
in the end they decided it was better to accept their loss.

The fourth way in which he hit the Donneybrook practice was by taking two of the staff. Although he was
capable of verbally abusing and humiliating some of the
staff, others were loyal to him. He promised his colleagues
that he would not poach staff, but eventually he did.

'The first we knew was when he came to us and told us
that he had been to a solicitor and had found a technical
flaw in our agreement, which meant he could take his
patient list with him and just pull out of our practice,' says
Dr Smith.

'It came as a bolt from the blue. The agreement had

always worked because everybody else was honourable. But this was immoral. As one of the originals I was particularly angry. I had been very proud of how we had it running. It was beneath contempt to exploit a loophole in a contract that he had been perfectly happy with when it was his turn to join the practice. Nobody had ever taken their list before.

'He planned his exit very carefully. He was devious, making plans for some time without letting any of us know that he was even thinking of leaving. He had never struck me as untrustworthy before, but I now think he is totally devious. From the point that I heard he was leaving I never spoke to him. We were all very angry about what he had done, forcing us to become a six GP practice. It was all so underhand and selfish.

'He claimed he didn't want to stay with us because he was opposed to fundholding, but he was the one who pushed for fundholding, and after he set up on his own he very soon went into another fundholding arrangement with other single-handed practitioners – which shows what a mockery it was. Morally, he defrauded us. He stole patients from us.'

For the first few months after severing his agreement with his partners, Fred Shipman continued to work from the Donneybrook building, of which he continued to be a part-owner until the others bought him out. When he had found his new premises, about three hundred yards away from the Donneybrook building, he left without any fanfare. His relationship with his former partners was hardly warm.

'I told him that we were parting on good terms, but that he would find, by virtue of choosing to work on his own, that he would become an outcast,' says Dr Napier. 'And that's what happened. When you are a one-man dictatorship, you can effectively do what you want. It is easy with hindsight to judge why he chose to move into practice on his own: whatever problems we had with him, there is not one of us who wasn't absolutely shocked by the news of his arrest.'

Dr John Smith agrees. 'He was shifty, arrogant, treacherous, but that does not make you suspect someone of being a mass murderer.'

Although the doctors who were present at his original interview always knew about his conviction for drug-taking, there was a strange corollary to his leaving for the reception and administrative staff. A budget manager who was employed to take over from Vivien Langfield was demonstrating her computer skills to the rest of the staff, and pulled Shipman's CV up on the screen. It was the first time that any of the non-medical staff knew of his conviction, and it means that when the practice data was computerised in the early 1990s, somebody inputted his criminal conviction along with his other details.

It would not be the only time that information stored on a computer worked against Fred Shipman.

# 7
# Going it Alone

**D**r Fred Shipman moved into The Surgery in July 1992. Compared to Donneybrook it is an unprepossessing building: a shop among a row of shops, lifted out of ordinariness by an attractive green-painted wrought-iron architrave running the length of the block. The situation is good, just 100 yards away from the market square and the Town Hall, on the main road through the centre of Hyde. (Although it is called Market Street, to the older residents who made up a large proportion of Shipman's patients, the road is known as 'Hyde Lane', a name that passed out of official use decades ago.) Number 21 is the second to the end of the terrace of shops, with a well-stocked chemist's shop on one side, two Indian restaurants within a few yards, a used car lot and a pet-grooming parlour opposite, and the much bigger, prosperous-looking purpose-built Brooke Surgery just along the road (from where the doctors who left the Clarendon practice now operate).

The property on the other side of The Surgery used to be a branch of the Halifax building society, and when it closed down Shipman had designs on these larger premises. He began negotiating with a young woman doctor in the town, Dr Lisa Gutteridge, to become his partner if he could expand into this extra floor space. She met him once to talk about it. 'I suppose you could say I had a lucky escape,' she says, adding that he seemed a very nice chap.

Since his arrest, the building next door has become a bathroom fittings centre. This property, like his, is owned by a company called Placehold Ltd, and managed for them by a commercial property consultancy. Shipman took out a twenty-year lease when he moved in, paying rent of about £300 a week. (Since his arrest, the rent has been paid by the West Pennine Health Authority, who have kept the practice running with locum services.)

Poignantly ironic is the name above the charity shop directly opposite number 21: Age Concern. Shipman must have seen it every time he left his premises. He had his own concerns for the aged on his list, concerns that were given free reign once he started to practise in his own premises. His house calls gave him the greatest opportunities to commit murder, but The Surgery itself proved a haven for him, saving him the trouble of knocking on a door with a syringeful of morphine in his medical bag.

Edith Brady drove at her usual slow speed through Hyde, a tailback of impatient motorists behind her. She was on her way for her regular three-monthly vitamin B12 injection for her pernicious anaemia – or 'pernickety' anaemia, as she called it. She was a familiar sight at 'Shippy's' surgery, enjoying her visits to the doctor's: her daughter Pamela would joke, 'Are you going to the staff dance, then?' and Edith would reply, 'Just wait until you're bloody old.'

The family nicknamed Edith 'the incredible shrinking woman', because as she grew older and her bones thinned, her height went down to less than five feet.

Pamela has a clear picture in her mind of her mother's last moments, sitting on the examining table in the room behind Shipman's consulting room, waiting for him to come in to give her the injection.

'I can just imagine her sitting there, her little legs dangling because they weren't long enough to reach the floor, twiddling the handles on her handbag, which she always did, waiting for the doctor,' says Pamela, whose policeman husband Roger Turner was the first to be told of Edith's death.

'Shipman rang him and told him it was about my mum. My husband asked, "How bad is it?" and Shipman said, "How bad do you want it? There is no way she is walking out of here." Yet, despite the anaemia and diabetes, and an operation on her knee, she was active and in good health.'

Edith, who was twice-widowed, was seventy-two when she died; a woman whose life, while very much her own, is also an emblem of the times she lived through. There are many thousands of women like her, hard-working, loving, humorous, tough; women who have struggled hard all their lives and who deserve a quiet old age surrounded by the families they have cherished. Her death was untimely, unfair and unforgiveable. She died on 13 May 1996, on the table where Shipman injected her.

He told her family that he had gone through to the examination room and found her dead. He said there was no need for a post-mortem, and at the time Pamela and the rest of the family were relieved. 'I thanked Dr Shipman for looking after Mum. I said to him, "I'm glad she died here, instead of in her car when driving, or on her own." We even laughed about it in the family, saying that at least she died where she was happy, at the doctor's.'

The day before she died Edith looked after two of her great-grandchildren all day at their home, and while there she cut the lawn and trimmed the privet hedge. She drove herself to her final appointment with the doctor in her little green Proton car; both Edith and the car were well-known in Hyde.

Edith was born in the town in 1924, one of a family of six. Her father was one of the first-ever tank drivers in the First World War. Edith left Leigh Street School and started work as a machinist, but within a year the Second World War broke out, and she joined the Wrens. Based in Scotland, she had a tender love affair with Cliff Walker, an electrician on the aircraft-carrier HMS *Argos*: he, too, was born and bred in Hyde. They married when Edith was nineteen, and when she died fifty-three years later, his love letters to her were found, carefully preserved in a biscuit tin.

Cliff served on the Malta convoy, dodging German planes and U-boats on the most dangerous run in naval history. Their oldest child, Geoff, was three before Cliff saw him. Then came two other children, Pamela and Ken. After the war times were hard, and Cliff tramped the streets looking for work until he found a job with the chemical giant ICI. At first the family lived in a run-down terrace with no running hot water and a tin bath, but eventually they got an ICI house, then a council house in Newton. They moved to another council house, in Bearwood Close on the other side of Hyde, after a tragedy next door: the neighbour's little daughter died when her nightie caught fire, and although Edith tried to rescue her by wrapping her in a quilt, it was too late. After that, she could not bear looking at the house where it had happened.

Sadly, just as their children were grown up, Cliff died of a heart attack. Edith was devastated: she had run to get help when he had severe chest pains, and by the time she returned he was dead. He had served the community all his life, as a retained firefighter and as a driver for the St

John Ambulance, as well as his full-time job. Because he was an electrician, he was always being asked to help out neighbours with electrical problems, and never said no.

Six years later, Edith married Eric Brady, a butcher, whom she had known for many years. They were happy, both working hard, Edith in an office job with Castrol, the oil company, and Eric at Wall's, the sausage-making company. They loved family parties, and on quiet weekends would drive out into the local countryside for picnics.

Then, in 1988, a double tragedy struck the family. First, Eric died while in hospital for a heart by-pass operation. Six months later, Edith's youngest child Ken, her 'baby', and his girlfriend were killed in a fire which gutted their home in Godley. It was a blow from which she never really recovered. When the house was rebuilt she moved into it, to be near his memory. For eight years, until her own death in 1996, she mourned him.

Pamela felt she could do nothing to console her mother and was relieved when her mum's acute distress at Ken's death began to ease.

'I wanted her to sell the house, to let go of him, and eventually, shortly before she died, she agreed to move,' says Pamela, whose affectionate memories of her mother are etched with humour. 'Mum was always pottering about the town – she seemed to know everyone, and she was always nattering. She knitted and made rag dolls for her great-grandchildren. She loved parties, and she did all her own decorating. She'd had a hard life, a lot of grief, but she enjoyed a laugh and a joke. She was a trusting person, careful with money because she'd never had much, but she put on a good table and everyone was welcome. She reminded me of the famous old comedienne Hylda Baker – independent, strong, and funny. Her mind was completely sharp, she remembered all the birthdays in the family. She kept everything important in a biscuit tin – old women always have biscuit tins. It was hard to get her to throw anything away. I would say, "Mum, sling it out – you even keep bus tickets." But she would say, "If you keep it long enough it'll be worth something one day."

'We only started to wonder about her death after Shipman had been on the news. My husband mentioned her death at work, and the police investigated. We're in the same position as lots of other families: we want answers.'

Edith Brady was not the only patient to die at Shipman's practice. On the death certificates of four other women the place of death is given as '21 Market Street, Hyde'. It sounds like a very ordinary address, but what the death certificates do not make clear is that 21 Market Street is also known as The Surgery. In just over three years, five women died there. Although statistics for deaths in doctors' surgeries are not kept, a straw poll of several GPs reveals just how unprecedented this is: most, throughout long careers, have never experienced more than one tragic death on their premises, even though they are in group practices with combined lists of patients which far outnumber Fred Shipman's. Many have never known a death at the practice, although some talk of calling ambulances for patients suddenly taken very ill, only to have them die later in hospital.

Calling ambulances was not something that Dr Shipman was very good at, although he often told relatives and friends that he had summoned them, and that he had then cancelled them when it was obvious the patient was dead. He had no idea, when he told these lies, that one day detectives would plough meticulously through ambulance control records and telephone company audits to prove that the calls were never made.

Joan Harding, who was the first of the five to die on his premises, may have been eighty-two, but she was fit and

active. She had never married, but had led a fulfilling life
as a social worker (or welfare worker, as they were called
in the days when Joan did the job) and enjoyed her retirement. She'd just spent a happy Christmas with the family
of her 'adoptive daughter', Brenda McKinney, whose
mother had been a close friend of Joan's.

When she woke up with a pain in her shoulders, on 5
January 1994, she decided to go to the doctor's. Her GP
was Fred Shipman. She'd followed him from the
Donneybrook practice to his new surgery when he moved
nineteen months earlier. She liked him. He never made
you feel you were wasting his time, he always remembered everything about you and had plenty of time for a
chat. Joan rang her usual taxi driver, but he wasn't free to
take her down to the centre of Hyde from her home in
Joel Lane, Gee Cross. But if she could get to the surgery
herself, he'd be able to pick her up and take her home, he
said. She said she'd ring if she needed him.

Next she rang Brenda, who lived just a few hundred
yards away, but Brenda had another appointment fixed
for that morning. So she rang a friend, Marion Bolton,
who lives in Stockport. Marion picked her up and they
drove together to The Surgery. Marion parked outside
and went in with Joan. As usual, the waiting room was
packed and every patient was being given the Shipman
treatment: consultations rarely lasted less than twenty
minutes. Eventually Marion, worried about the time running out on her parking slot, told Joan she would sit
outside in the car to wait for her.

Within minutes one of the staff from The Surgery
came out and told Marion that Joan had died while
having her blood pressure taken. Her death came as a
complete shock to everyone who knew her – she had not
appeared seriously ill to anyone who spoke to her that
day.

For Brenda, it was a terrible blow. 'I was like a daughter

to her, and she was like a mother to me after my mum died. She worried about her health a bit, but she had nothing more than the usual aches and pains at that age,' she says.

Joan was cremated and her ashes went back to her original home, the Isle of Man. At the time, although friends wondered why it had happened so suddenly and why, being in a surgery, she hadn't been resuscitated and saved, they accepted it. After all, she was old and, as the doctor said, she had simply had a massive heart attack.

Eighteen months after Joan Harding's death, Bertha Moss also died at The Surgery, on 30 June 1995. The 68-year-old widow, who was known to all her friends and family as Betty, had lived an eventful life, and her huge family (seven children, twenty-one grandchildren and ten great-grandchildren, plus stepchildren and stepgrandchildren) were expecting her to enjoy it for a lot longer. Although she was under the weather when she went to see the doctor, she went shopping on Hyde Market only a couple of hours before her death.

Betty was married three times, finally finding happiness with her third husband, Brian Moss, after her children were grown up. Brian, who had also been married before, spotted her in The Cotton Tree pub in Dukinfield, and before he had even spoken to her he told one of her six daughters that he intended marrying her. He had made up his mind that she was the one for him. His judgement was good, because for the three years from their marriage to his death they were very happy, making what those around them describe as 'a great comedy double act'.

They moved to Blackpool, living in a caravan. Betty, who had always worked in chip shops, took a job in a café. One night, after a silly row, she threw Brian out into the rain – he turned up on the doorstep half an hour later saying, 'Good evening, madam. I hear you're looking for a gardener.' Betty burst out laughing and the row was forgotten.

When Brian was diagnosed with cancer of the liver, the doctors told Betty but told her not to tell him. Brian's sister-in-law, Jackie Moss, who became a close friend of Betty's, recalls what happened: 'One day Brian kept on about buying a car. He'd received some money in compensation for an accident at work. He was making plans and eventually Betty burst into tears, saying, "Don't keep on about the car, Brian." Then he said: "How long have I got?" She told him, and they spent the rest of the day locked in the house, crying with each other. Then Brian eventually said, "Right, no more crying, we will have to sort a stall out," meaning his funeral arrangements. Then he said, "I've not met the rest of your children – we are going on holiday to visit them."'

Five of Betty's seven children had emigrated to Australia, and she and Brian enjoyed a happy stay with them. After he died, she went back, planning to spend the rest of her life there. But she missed England, and moved to Hyde to live with her daughter, eventually getting her own place.

Although it took her a while to get over Brian's death, she was always good fun. Her sister-in-law Jacqueline went on holiday to Greece with her, and remembers her for her jokes and the laughter they shared. For the last few years of her life she had a close friend, a widower who lived in Stockport, who would share meals with her and holidays in Eastbourne.

Jackie Moss saw her on the day she died. 'We were both shopping on the market. She looked a bit off colour, and she said she was going to the doctor's to have her heart checked. She said she would ring me and let me know how she got on.'

When Jackie got no reply from Betty's phone that

evening, she rang Betty's daughter Jane, and heard the shocking news that Betty had died at Shipman's surgery, apparently (according to what he told Jane) after he had monitored her heart and she was getting dressed. He said he was putting his equipment away and she had a massive heart attack.

In the death notice in the local paper the family included the line: 'Special thanks to the family doctor for his care and attention.'

'No one was suspicious,' says Jackie. 'But we were shocked, we did not expect her to die. She was such a great personality, the sort of person you took to straight away. A grand woman and great company, the best company anyone could wish for.'

Less than three months later, another old lady went to see the doctor she trusted and liked so much and never made the return journey home from 21 Market Street. Dora Ashton was eighty-seven, the widow of a farm labourer. She lived in a neat terraced house in Mona Street, in the centre of Hyde, and thought nothing of walking the half-mile from there to the doctor's surgery for her regular three-monthly check-ups.

Being active was part of her life. She had worked for the electrical engineering company Ferranti before the war, and then during the war for the Chief Inspector of Armaments at Dukinfield, testing shell cases, which was an unusual job for a woman. Her last job, before retirement at the age of sixty-five, was as a laundry worker at the local hospital – she took great pride in starching the nurses' uniforms and hats.

Dora, who had three grandchildren, lived with her son James in Mona Street for ten years, moving in with him after her husband died and her home in Stalybridge was burgled. She'd had an active social life in Stalybridge, playing bingo and going to Mothers' Union meetings at the local church, and when she moved to Hyde she simply switched her allegiance to a different bingo hall and a different church. She also joined the ladies' darts team at The Bush pub, remaining a regular player until she was eighty-three.

It was when she came to Hyde that she registered with Dr Shipman because her son James, a widower, was one of his patients, and thought highly of him. 'I recommended that Mum go to him, and she loved him to bits,' says James. 'She thought he was marvellous. She would turn in her grave if she knew what had happened, she had such faith in him.

'I only saw him a couple of times because my health is good, but he came to the house on quite a few home visits. When he came he would chat to us while he checked Mum over, though I never really saw what he was checking. He always seemed very nice.'

About a year before she died Dora was mugged in the street, an incident which took away a lot of her confidence: her health seemed to be less good from then onwards, although she was still fit and active.

On the day of her death James spoke to her on the phone from work. She told him she had prepared him an egg sandwich and left it for him, because she was going to The Surgery for her check-up. James told her to get a taxi because it was raining. 'What's an umbrella for?' was her characteristic reply.

Soon after James arrived home there was a phone call from the doctor's surgery. He was told that his mother was ill and they were getting an ambulance to send her to hospital.

'I rushed down to the surgery and she wasn't there. I thought they'd got her off to hospital very quickly. But then Dr Shipman told me what had happened. He said she'd been waiting for her appointment, and when he called her she stood up and collapsed. He told me she'd had a stroke. He said he took her into his room and she keeled over again, and this time it was another stroke and it killed her.'

Mrs Ashton was taking tablets for a heart condition. Because of her age, her family accepted the doctor's explanation of what had happened.

It was eight months later, on 13 May 1996, that Edith Brady became the next person to die in The Surgery. Then, for a whole year, nobody else died there, until 29 May 1997, when Ivy Lomas, the 63-year-old widow of an engineer, walked in for a routine check on a pain in her arm and never walked out again.

She was a regular attender at The Surgery; over the years she'd had a number of ailments, but none of them serious. The main problem in her life was coping with the demands of her son, Jack, who had psychiatric problems. On the morning of her death she went with a neighbour to Brindle House, a support centre, to sort out various things for her son. She also went by taxi to collect some of his clothes from a residential home where he had, until a few days earlier, been living. When she told her neighbour her arm was troubling her, the neighbour put it down to carrying the bags of clothing.

Her friend walked with her to the bus stop to catch a 3.30pm bus into Hyde to see the doctor. She had the first appointment of the afternoon session, at 4pm, but was so early the waiting area was closed. Recognising her, however, the receptionist let her in. The receptionist noticed that she was quieter than usual, and seemed a little unwell.

Dr Shipman arrived back at 3.55pm. He asked her into his consulting room and then called out to his receptionist that he was going to the treatment room next door. He emerged twenty-five minutes later to tell the receptionist that he had a problem with the ECG machine. He looked tired and flushed. He then dealt with three other patients before calling the receptionist to tell her that Mrs Lomas had died in the treatment room. He said he had tried to resuscitate her, and asked the receptionist, Carol Chapman, to contact her relatives. When this proved to be difficult, the receptionist called the police.

Sergeant Phillip Reade arrived, was shown the body, and was told by Shipman that she had come to the surgery with bronchial problems, and that he had put her in the treatment room to rest. He had then found her dead. He made a macabre joke to the police sergeant: he said that Mrs Lomas had been such a nuisance he had considered having part of the seating area permanently reserved for her, with a plaque above it to this effect: 'Seat belonging to Ivy Lomas.'

When the police sergeant asked the doctor what he had done when he found his patient had died, Shipman replied, 'Nothing.' Seeing the look of puzzlement on the policeman's face, he added: 'This lady was beyond resuscitation, she was quite clearly dead.'

Despite his feelings of disquiet, Sergeant Reade, like so many others in this case, accepted that Shipman was a doctor and therefore knew best. It was only when he heard about the investigation into the GP fifteen months later, that he contacted his colleagues on the case to share his worries about Mrs Lomas's death.

On her death certificate Shipman said she had died from a heart attack and from obstructed airways caused by smoking. Sixteen months after she was buried in Hyde Cemetery, the body of Ivy Lomas was exhumed, and Shipman was charged with murdering her.

Inside, The Surgery is bigger than it seems from the street. It covers three floors, with the reception area, a consulting room and an examination room on the ground floor, two offices on the first floor, and a larger room at the top, used for administration. One of the first-floor offices was used by nurses, and by a psychotherapist, Colton Reid, to whom Shipman referred some of his patients (GPs are allowed funding for these extra services).

Practising alone meant that he could choose to decorate the building how he liked, and what Fred Shipman likes are pigs. His home in Roe Cross Green is full of pig ornaments, and The Surgery had posters of pigs on the walls in the waiting area and in his consulting room, as well as a large pink money-box in the shape of a pig on the reception desk, in which he collected loose change for his 'Patients' Fund'. Along the corridor were prints of steam trains, and pride of place on the wall of his office went to a large caricature of Shipman himself, without his beard but with a large moustache and a big grin on his face, done by one of his patients. On his desk there was a maxim: 'Every Day's a Bonus'.

But practising alone meant more than just being able to choose his own decor. At Donneybrook, although he ran his own patient list, there was always a risk that someone on the staff would notice that he had more deaths than the other doctors, that rumours would start and that, because of his previous track record with pethidine, the other GPs would be keeping an eye on his prescriptions of controlled drugs (although, in fairness, this would have been extremely difficult, if not impossible, for them to do).

If there were murders while at Donneybrook they were secret, occasional, private pleasures: opportunities which, when presented to him, he perhaps could not resist. He controlled himself, did not go looking for them, did not see them as a source of financial gain. If he killed, it enabled him to perfect his killing, but the deaths were sporadic, unconnected, and there was never the slightest reason for any of the staff to raise an eyebrow. Was he aware of holding himself in check? Was his desire to set up a practice on his own underwritten by a conscious need to let the death toll rise? Probably not, but like an embryonic alcoholic who finds work in a pub, or an inchoate paedophile who gravitates towards jobs and hobbies involving children, underneath all his rationales for leaving Donneybrook there could have been a subtext. To be on his own meant freedom from the fear of being found out – the perfect crimes could be committed perfectly safely.

At Donneybrook, too, there was a clear memory of Todmorden: of the humiliation of being caught out; of how he had had to persuade the police and everyone else that the massive amounts of pethidine he prescribed were for his own use; of the narrow escape he had. Donneybrook was his second chance, and he was keen not to blow it. But as the years rolled on, and he became more and more secure both in his reputation as a doctor and his skills as a killer, the shame of Todmorden receded. He was arrogant enough to give interviews to medical journalists about the abuse of drugs by doctors, without ever once referring to himself.

The other doctors who were in practice with him at Donneybrook feel sure that he did not murder while he was there – they believe the staff would have noticed. But police now believe he did kill while there, but not with the abandon that The Surgery gave him.

Now, on his own, his superiority complex took over, his arrogance grew, his self-belief became total. At Donneybrook he had been able to harangue, browbeat and bully his subordinates, the ancillary staff and the drugs reps, but he had rarely crossed swords with his equals, the other doctors. Yet when he reached the haven of The Surgery he became even more convinced of his own infallibility, and was even prepared to tackle his fellow professionals. Dr Ian Napier, his colleague from Donneybrook, encountered him a few times at Thursday lunchtime lectures held at the postgraduate centre at Tameside Hospital. GPs are expected to attend a certain amount of in-service lectures every year, to prevent their medical knowledge stagnating and keep them up to date with new thinking in the profession.

'If I saw Fred there I avoided him, because he was embarrassing,' says Dr Napier. 'As time went on he became more and more bristly, like a hedgehog. He'd interrupt the speaker – usually some eminent professor – and harangue him. Everyone would be embarrassed, thinking, "Oh, God, Fred, sit down and shut up." He got up everyone's nose – we'd all think "Oh, no" if we saw he was there. He was irascible, bad-tempered, yappy, like a Jack Russell snapping at everyone's heels. He'd be trying to prove himself, and I imagine he thought we were all impressed by his knowledge. He was certainly very smug about it. He didn't realise that he was making a fool of himself.'

Dr Wally Ashworth, who served on the local medical committee with Shipman, remembers him getting on to a similar hectoring roll with a senior administration officer of the health authority.

'Fred got a bee in his bonnet about some new diktat, something or nothing really, an irritation rather than something to go mad about. But Fred really went for this man. Fred had done his homework, as he always did when he was going to challenge someone, and the argument was so heated that they nearly came to blows. Fred always needed to prove he was right.'

For several years before his retirement Dr Ashworth, a larger-than-life character with a down-to-earth turn of phrase, also operated a single-handed practice, and he can see how easy it was for Fred Shipman, who already had an inflated sense of his own importance, to slip into a 'God complex'.

'There's nobody to challenge you. You can convince

yourself you know it all. Your patients look up to you as if you are God. Lots of GPs are puffed up with their own image: it's a job that takes you up a peg or two, not down a peg or two. There is a hell of a lot of pressure on single-handed practitioners – the bureaucracy, the paperwork – it's all out of control nowadays. When you're working on your own there is nobody to even talk to about it. And you can't share any diagnostic worries you might have, so you get used to believing all your decisions are right.'

Like his Donneybrook colleagues, Wally Ashworth believes that Shipman was a sound doctor. When he was not killing his patients, he treated them very well, always insisting on prescribing the appropriate drug regardless of its cost. 'He had a bit of an obsession, quite rightly, about all the cost-cutting that has come in. He felt very strongly that if a drug was the right one, he shouldn't have to look at the price tag,' says Wally.

Patients appreciated this attitude, too: he certainly made sure they knew when he was prescribing expensive drugs for them. He would tell them, 'This is going to cost me a hundred pounds – but it's what you need, so you shall have it.'

When he left Donneybrook, one of the reasons he gave was that he did not like the new (optional) system of GP fundholding. To the astonishment of his colleagues at Donneybrook, no sooner had he set up at The Surgery than he joined the Tameside Fund-Holders Consortium, a group of single-handed practitioners who worked together as fundholders in order to be able to buy drugs and equipment at discounted prices. The other six GPs in the group were taken aback to discover that Shipman's drugs bill was twice as big as anyone else's: he had an obsession with anti-cholesterol drugs and was prescribing them to large numbers of his patients. But when he was taken to task by the other fundholders in the consortium he simply laughed.

His relationship with his patients was almost always good. One or two people in Hyde today talk about not getting on well with him, about his being brusque and off-hand if you asked too many questions, or of days when he was, to use the local word, 'nowty'. But there was a long waiting list to be taken on by The Surgery, and this was because for the vast majority of patients he was that rare thing: an old-fashioned doctor who had endless time for his patients, did not fob them off on locums and partners, made house-calls without demur and treated everyone personally and warmly, at the same time making it clear to them that he was a well-qualified and very professional doctor. He would repeat the litany about being well qualified ('I have passed all my exams, I am a good doctor') either as a haughty put-down, or with a twinkle in his eye as he wrote out yet another prescription for one of the elderly ladies who doted on him.

'He always made a fuss of the old dears. He'd enjoy putting a smile on their faces by joking with them, being a little bit flirty,' says the nurse, Kate McGraw. 'It was his way of cheering them up. They went to him for a tonic.'

She was not one of his patients, 'although I often wished that I was. If it hadn't been for the two-year waiting list to get taken on, I'd have joined his surgery.' As a health-care professional, she knew that he was held in high regard by his patients.

'He'd go far beyond the normal call of duty for a GP. One of his patients lost a thumb and finger in an accident. When he arrived home from hospital he was in great pain, and Fred spent hours at his home, constructing a makeshift sling, and just talking to him for half the night. He'd call in on patients on the way home from work and on his way in to work in the morning. If he was worried about someone, he'd call.'

Like everyone else, Kate had no reason to see anything other than exceptional altruism and dedication in Fred

Shipman's willingness to make home visits. Other doctors marvelled at his ability to do it – they all feel under so much pressure that seeing sick patients in their own homes is something they discourage.

'I have no idea how he found the time,' says Dr Ian Napier. 'But that's what attracted patients to him – he was everyone's idea of an old-fashioned family doctor.'

June Evans, councillor for Werneth Ward on Tameside Borough Council, became one of his patients in 1984 when she, her husband and her three daughters moved into Hyde. A dark-haired, energetic woman, she sums up the feelings of so many dedicated supporters of Shipman – people who, initially at least, could not believe any of the charges laid against him. The idea that he would deliberately hurt or kill patients was a heresy to them, and even now they find it difficult to accept his guilt.

'When I moved here I was told I would be lucky to get on his list – and I still regard it as lucky, because he was such a good doctor. I was expecting my third baby, and having had problems before with the first two, I was worried. He was very sympathetic and supportive,' says June.

'I worked as a driver for the ambulance service, and I never heard a bad word said about him. After his arrest, I just could not believe it. I wrote a letter of support to his wife and family, then sent a card to his staff. I went into The Surgery to read all the cards; every one told a personal story of how good and kind he was.

'He never judged you, never criticised you. When you were in his surgery he treated you like the only patient he had. Whether you needed five minutes or twenty-five minutes, he never let you see that time was a precious commodity to him. I was in awe of him, and I adored him. When I was down, he was always there for me. He'd hold my hand and talk me through my problems. He kept me afloat when I thought I was drowning. I felt he knew me better than I knew myself. I was besotted with him.'

In his consulting room, Shipman would always pull his chair round to the patient's side of the desk, so that he could talk more intimately, with nothing between them. Whether he refreshed his memory beforehand with a glance at their notes, or whether he really did have a phenomenal recall of the medical and personal histories of more than 3,000 patients, he always gave the impression to each one that he valued and knew them.

'He would talk to me about the future of Hyde, about the problems of his profession. He would get angry when he talked about the pressure to prescribe cheaper drugs: he worried about how he would keep up the standards expected of him,' says Councillor Evans. 'He never hesitated to refer me to a specialist, and he would give me the necessary medicines even though he would tell me that it was costing a lot. I always felt my conversations with him were on three levels: as a friend, as a doctor and as a caring member of the local community.

'Perhaps we asked too much of him. I've seen him working when his own health has been bad, but he would never talk about it, always made light of it. A lot of people in this town worshipped him, and although a great many kept quiet or changed their tunes after his arrest, there were others, like me, who found it so hard to believe. When I met someone else who felt highly of him, we'd latch on to each other, as if we shared some shameful secret.'

Although Shipman's patient list was made up predominantly of older women, he was popular with young families and with teenagers, too. Rebecca Evans, one of June Evans's daughters, was eighteen when he was arrested, and was as shocked as her mother by the news.

'I had to go to him a couple of times for emergency contraception, the morning-after pill, and he prescribed it without question. He was never judgemental. Young people could go to him with any problems: you could talk

to him about drugs, pregnancy, anything that was bothering you. I'm only five feet one inch tall, and when I was
about eleven I was very worried that I wasn't growing.
When I went to see him I said, "I know it sounds a really
stupid thing to be worrying about . . ." He said, "If it
bothers you enough to come and see me, it's not stupid."
That was always his attitude.'

There are many people in Hyde who want to tell stories about the kind Dr Shipman, of the lengths he went to
to help people in mental distress as well as those with
physical problems, of the way he came out over bank-
holiday weekends or in the middle of the night without
ever complaining. His popularity spoke for itself: he had
3,000 patients, a large number (the average for a GP in
Britain is 2,700, and the top limit is set at 3,500).

It is easy to lose sight, in this welter of adoration, of the
true nature of Fred Shipman. While playing the devoted
doctor, dealing with the ingrowing toenails, indigestion,
vaccinations and other minutiae of a GP's life, he had his
own agenda. His thoughts were frequently elsewhere. As
he scribbled prescriptions and made smiling inquiries
about his patients' lives, he was planning his next murder,
his appetite for it growing as the years went by, until in the
last few months of freedom he was killing regularly and
frequently. Yet, unlike most serial killers, there was no
clue in his outward demeanour: he did not appear to be
disturbed, excited or out of control. His façade was so
good that even today there are those in Hyde *whose own
relatives have died at his hand* who say they would go back
to him tomorrow for treatment if he were freed.

There appears to have been only one prerequisite for
his exceptional service: he basked in the regard he
inspired, which June Evans sums up in her choice of
words – 'besotted', 'adored', 'worshipped' and 'in awe
of' are all descriptions she uses of her feelings towards
him. More articulate and more perceptive than most

people, she is able to express sentiments that many other patients struggled to convey, and were even ashamed to admit, yet the strength of her attachment to him is typical. The average GP does not inspire such passion. Importantly, her descriptions have a strongly religious overtone. If Fred Shipman saw himself as God, he was able to share this vision of himself with his faithful congregation, his patients.

Even those who died at his hand were faithful to him to the last – they rolled up their sleeves to receive his final ministration, the injection that would send them peacefully from this world. These were not savage, brutal murders; they were the handiwork of a man who believed he was all-powerful, and the ultimate power is that of life and death. But although many of the killings were motiveless, apart from his own compulsion to exercise his power, there were some from which he definitely wanted a payoff.

The polished dark-wood settle in Mabel Shawcross's home in Stockport Road, Hyde, was a fine piece of old oak furniture, the sort of thing that antique-dealers would fight over. It had always been promised to Mabel's great nephew: as a spinster, she had no children of her own but was particularly close to her niece Joan Sellars and Joan's family.

So it came as a great shock when, the day after her aunt's death, Joan and her husband Bernard went to Dr Shipman's surgery to collect the death certificate, and were accosted by the GP who told them that Mabel had promised him the settle. Joan was taken aback, but dismissed it by telling Shipman that it was going to her son.

'Afterwards Bernard and I talked about it. It seemed so indelicate, asking for it like that, the day after she died. I felt it absolutely wasn't his, that my aunt had never promised it. It seemed a very cheeky thing to do – but at least he said it pleasantly, which is different from the way he spoke to my daughter-in-law immediately after Aunt Mabel's death.'

Mabel, who was seventy-nine, died on 22 January 1998, and her body was found by a neighbour, who called the police. The police rang Joan's daughter-in-law; they had found a letter from her in the old lady's living room.

'Then she got a call from Dr Shipman, who was very off-hand and rude with her, asking what relationship she had to the deceased. My daughter-in-law tried to explain – after all, it's complicated, because she is the wife of Mabel's great nephew. He was very short with her.'

When Joan heard the news of her aunt's death, she was shocked. 'She was fit and well, with a very youthful outlook on life. She had no major health problems. We were very close. I regarded her as a second mother, and she treated my children as her grandchildren.

'When we went to collect the death certificate Shipman said, "She probably had a stroke." We thought it sounded very vague, but it never occurred to us to ask for a post-mortem. You trust doctors, don't you?'

The next shock for Joan and her husband was when the police called to tell her they suspected that her aunt was one of Shipman's victims. She was cremated, and he was not charged with her murder.

'The police are hoping that one day he will tell the whole story, so that the relatives can get some peace. But from my brief encounter with him I don't think he will ever talk,' says Joan. 'I'm so glad we did not let him have the settle – if we hadn't been as close as we were to my aunt we might have believed him and let him have it.'

Shipman was never shy about asking for money or gifts from his patients. One widow remembers telling him that her son was getting married and leaving home. He spent the next ten minutes trying to persuade her to sell the big house she was living in and buy herself a small flat. He could even tell her exactly what her house was worth.

'I didn't think a great deal of it at the time, but now I think he may have been sizing up my wealth. He could obviously get his hands on my money better than he could get his hands on my house, which may be why he wanted me to sell it.'

Most of the approaches he made to patients for money were for his Patients' Fund. It is not unknown for doctors' practices to have a special fund into which bequests can be paid, to help fund medical provisions at the surgery. Most practices only need such an account when they find themselves the unexpected recipients of a patient's generosity: many wealthy people, especially older ones, litter their wills with grateful rewards to their doctors, dentists, and others who have helped them.

What is unknown is for GPs to openly tout for money from patients. Shipman had a notice behind his reception desk telling patients that they could leave money to The Surgery in their wills. He also had the large pink piggy-bank for the Patients' Fund. He held raffles and organised potato-pie suppers in a local pub or hall all in aid of the fund. Patients assumed it was normal, and gave generously: every so often, notes would be posted on the bulletin board in the reception area saying how much had been raised, and what it had been spent on.

A myth grew that because of the fund, The Surgery was awash with state-of-the-art medical equipment. In fact, most of the equipment there was second-hand and outdated, or was the sort of kit that drugs companies will supply free to practices. A locum who worked at The Surgery described it as adequately, but certainly not well, appointed.

The brazenness with which Shipman courted donations for the fund has shocked other doctors. 'I found that whole fund very unusual,' says Dr John Smith. 'We had a fund at Donneybrook, set up after someone left us some money, but we certainly didn't advertise it or hold fund-raising events. We regarded it as part of our job to provide the necessary equipment. With our fund we bought extras, like ripple beds for bed-ridden patients.'

Dr Wally Ashworth describes it as 'very abnormal' for a doctor to ask for money, or to suggest that wills should be made in his favour. 'Fred told me a story once about a patient, an elderly woman, who was always at his surgery, always sitting in the same chair. One day he said to her, "Mrs So-and-so, we'd like you to sponsor that chair." And she wrote him a cheque for £50.

'He was very hot on money, he was always screwing it out of the NHS, legitimately. He knew every little thing we could claim for. Every injection you stick in a kid's bum has to be recorded and claimed for, and Fred was on top of all that.'

The information about how GPs are paid is contained in a loose-leaf, three-inch thick book, *The National Health Service General Medical Services*, colloquially known by doctors as 'the red book'.

'Fred was an expert on the red book – I think he read it every night before going to sleep, he knew it so well,' says Wally Ashworth.

The Patients' Fund was administered for him by two trustees, and there is no suggestion that the money from the fund was misappropriated. It was set up by retired policeman Len Fallows, a loyal patient of Shipman's, three months after the doctor moved to his new premises. Mr Fallows talked to him about the cost of equipping the new surgery, and asked if there was anything he needed. Shipman told him that other people had also made offers, and asked Mr Fallows to run a fund he was going to set up. In eighteen months the fund raised £2,700, used to buy nebulisers for asthmatic patients, a diabetes testing machine, a foetal heart detector, and an electro-cardio-graph machine.

'It is a case of patients helping patients and showing their appreciation of Dr Shipman,' Mr Fallows told the local paper in 1994.

But Shipman was also prepared to solicit personal bequests, to himself rather than to the fund, from patients – and, astonishingly, to help himself to cash and jewellery from the houses of the many women he killed over his years at The Surgery.

Valerie Cuthbert, a 54-year-old retired publican, left him £250 in her will. Others whose relatives found valu-ables missing after their deaths included Mrs Ada Warburton, whose purse was empty and who had jew-ellery missing; Mrs Pamela Hillier, whose ring had vanished; Mrs Alice Black, whose jewellery had gone; Mrs Elizabeth Battersby, whose money had disappeared; and Mrs Mary Walls, who lost rings and other property.

After his arrest the police looked into Shipman's bank accounts in great depth. There was nothing unusual, no substantial deposits or withdrawals. But as most of the thefts from his victims were in the form of petty cash – most of them had no more than the contents of their purse to steal – there would be no reason for it to pass through his accounts. The valuable jewellery he stole was probably sold across the Pennines in Sheffield – there are plenty of jewellers and pawnbrokers who would take it without asking any questions. What was found in the Shipmans' house was not valuable, although there was lots of it.

In the six years that he practised at The Surgery, Shipman killed a great many people; most of them, but not all, elderly; most of them, but not all, living on their own. He got away with it, year after year, because of the way he selected his victims, and because he was in a posi-tion to cover up their deaths in ways that were never challenged: after all, he was the doctor, and as countless people have said during the research for this book, 'You trust the doctor, don't you?'

But Fred Shipman's need to kill was growing. The brakes were off and he was, by the time of his arrest, careering out of control, killing at an ever-increasing rate. He was suspected of averaging three or four deaths a month, and in February 1998 he is believed to have killed an astonishing seven people in four weeks, with another six the following month. Despite this – and it must have preoccupied him – he was always able to maintain the fiction of being a caring, committed doctor, and a happy family man.

But what was life in the Shipman family really like?

Fred and Primrose had been married for thirty-two years by the time he was arrested in September 1998: a long marriage by any standards, and an apparently successful one. They have four children – Sarah, whose conception precipitated their marriage and who was thirty-one when her father was arrested; Christopher, who was twenty-seven at the time; David, who was nineteen, and Sam, who was sixteen.

It would be wrong here to dwell in any detail on the children – they are, by all accounts, decent kids who must now find themselves facing a bleak future, their lives blighted by their father's crimes. Sam, the youngest, who lived at home during the time his father was on remand, knows at first hand what it means to be closely related to a notorious murderer. During the long wait for the trial, as tension grew among the townspeople of Hyde, he was attacked in the street on one occasion. In the early hours of New Year's Day, 1999, Primrose Shipman's car, a red Ford Sierra, was stolen from outside the family home in Roe Cross Green, and, after a police chase, crashed into the gateway of Dukinfield cemetery – the cemetery where, just three weeks earlier, the body of Sally Ashworth had been exhumed. Officially, the police put it down to joyriding: two youths who were caught running away were charged with taking the car, dangerous driving, and driving without insurance or licence. Perhaps they genuinely did not know whose car it was, or the irony of its final resting place, crumpled against the gates of a cemetery, but local rumours class it as a tiny act of retribution against the Shipmans.

There was constant media interest in the family. One reporter even tracked Sam down at college, where other students rallied round to protect him. (He was doing an agricultural course, and there were volunteers offering to consign the journalist to a slurry pit.) In a letter to his friend Wally Ashworth, Fred Shipman himself describes Primrose stonefacedly shutting the door on an ITN reporter, a woman who subsequently knocked on the window and shouted through the glass to try to persuade Primrose to put her side of the story on camera. Primrose ignored her, and she left as disappointed as all the other reporters who walked down the path in the hope of getting an exclusive talk with Shipman's wife.

The children's relationship with their father cannot ever have been easy, particularly for the younger two, who were at home as his appetite for murder grew. They were not exempt from his need to control. Vivien Langfield, who worked at Donneybrook, remembers one revealing incident, when David was nine and Sam was six. Primrose rang her husband to ask when he would be home, because the two boys were at the table, waiting to eat. He told her to keep them there: they were not to eat until he sat down with them. When he did eventually arrive home they had both fallen asleep, hungry, at the table.

David would go to the Donneybrook surgery every Saturday morning for a lift home from his father at lunchtime. He was about ten years old at the time. On one occasion Shipman ordered him to fetch his overcoat for him, but David went into the wrong consulting room and could not find it.

'He went berserk at the boy,' says Vivien. 'I told him he shouldn't talk to a child like that. He turned and told me very firmly that it was nothing to do with me. Which it wasn't.'

Sarah was the most open of the Shipman children, and used to help out at Donneybrook during her school holidays. She told staff she was not happy at home and was desperate to get away, because her father was so selfish and strict. When she left school she moved to Brighton, to do a catering and hotel management course. She now lives and works in the centre of Manchester, having bought her first home (about a mile away from Strangeways Prison, where her father was held for most of the time he was on remand). She is the only member of family who keeps in touch with her grandmother, old Mrs Oxtoby, visiting her in Wetherby occasionally.

All the Shipman children have been brought up to be well-behaved and disciplined. When Sarah and Christopher were small, Jenny Unsworth, the warden at the Chartist House flats, was asked to babysit for the Shipmans on New Year's Eve, 1978.

'I had met Dr Shipman through my job, and he rang and asked if I knew of a babysitter – he said their babysitter had let them down. My husband and I were staying in with our children, so I went up to the house in Lord Derby Road that the Shipmans were renting at the time, leaving my husband to look after ours.

'Sarah and Christopher were beautiful children, then aged eleven and seven. Before he left for the party, Dr Shipman said, "Christopher will go to bed at 9pm, Sarah at 10pm." I couldn't believe it when they just went up at the time he said. They were as good as gold.'

The children went to Mottram Church of England junior school (with the exception of Sarah, who was already senior-school age when the Shipmans arrived in Mottram). When the school needed funds for a new roof, Primrose Shipman served on the committee, alongside senior detective Ian Fairlie (who retired recently as a Detective Chief Superintendent with Norfolk Police). Fairlie, who was part of the original Moors Murders inquiry, remembers Primrose as noisy, strong-willed and single-minded. Fred, on the other hand, was quiet and extremely hard-working.

'We organised numerous social events, fêtes and so on, to raise the money, and Fred was always there first and last to put up stalls and take them down again. He seemed reserved, introverted, and the last person I would have marked down as a murderer. I've dealt with scores of murderers, but as a policeman I had no indication that there was anything wrong.

'I knew them for twelve years. They would attend all the dances and social evenings, although I never saw them up on the dance floor. Primrose was rather large. Fred was very reserved – he would sit at a table and people would go up to him to speak, but he didn't circulate.'

Ian Fairlie went to the Shipman home a couple of times, on school committee business. He was never invited inside, which struck him as odd. 'But I didn't think too much of it. There was certainly no outward sign of affluence, but you simply got the impression they were the kind of people who did not care about material things.'

Sarah and her brother Christopher both then went to Longdendale High School, the local comprehensive. Christopher was very bright, but always on the edge of any social event, as Fred had been in his schooldays. But Christopher enjoyed performing: he was good at drama, and liked, as Fred does, to be the centre of attention.

After A-levels he went to university and now works for a major national building firm.

While they were at Longdendale, Fred served from 1981 to 1983 as chairman of the PTA. Alan Garlick, who was deputy head and head of modern languages, remembers him for an unusually expansive Shipman gesture: after an exchange visit with French students, which Sarah was part of, the PTA hosted a dinner for the organisers of the exchange, and Fred paid for half the cost.

'It was a very generous gesture,' says Mr Garlick, who is now retired, and who remembers Fred Shipman as a hard-working member of the association, very involved with school activities.

But the Shipmans went off Longdendale High and sent their two younger children, David and Sam, to West Hill High School in Stalybridge, a boys' school with a good reputation locally. David, a quiet boy, was at university in Newcastle at the time of his father's trial. He set a precedent for his younger brother by becoming head boy at West Hill during his final year there; Sam, described by school friends as very smart and hard-working, was able to emulate him three years later, and both boys are remembered for taking their responsibilities seriously. Although Dave was quiet, Sam was happy to bark out orders to the prefects.

Sam was diagnosed as dyslexic early in his school career, and was allowed extra time when taking the compulsory SATS exams. After school he started his agricultural course. He has inherited Fred Shipman's talent and passion for rugby; he plays for Ashton Rugby Club and has also turned out for the county team. He is described by Steve Hett, who was steward at the club, as 'an excellent rugby player'. Fred Shipman involved himself in the organisation of the Under-15s team at the club, and presented the club with a trophy. He organised rugby tours for the younger players to Ireland and Wales, described by another parent as 'roaring successes' because of the meticulous detail of the organisation. But he was never part of the inevitable social scene which exists around any rugby club. 'He'd have the odd pint, but he kept himself to himself,' says Steve Hett. 'He certainly wasn't one of the regulars propping up the bar.'

Primrose would occasionally help out at the club, roped in with other mothers to butter sandwiches and serve teas. But it was not a milieu in which she felt confident or happy: another mother describes her as 'not really fitting in – everyone else knew each other and socialised, but she seemed uncomfortable'.

Wally Ashworth, whose wife is involved with the club, remembers seeing Primrose once parked near the club in the Renault Espace that was the family car. She was sitting there, staring into space. 'She looked very miserable, but I didn't stop to speak to her. She looked as if she wanted to be left alone,' he says.

Although there is plenty of evidence that Primrose was in thrall to her husband (who would never cease to remind her, implicitly if not explicitly, that he was her intellectual superior), it would be simplistic to assume that she was totally dominated by him. All those years under Edna's iron thumb had made Primrose strong, and she was tough enough to stand up to Fred when she needed to. The incident when the two boys were not allowed to eat until their father returned home sparked a major row, and there are some who lived close to the family who assumed that it was Fred who was henpecked, and Prim who was the dominant partner.

In the road where they lived, Roe Cross Green, they kept themselves to themselves, but this was not unusual, as there is no real community spirit in a road where most residents disappear by car to Manchester or Stockport to work. Apart from the odd conversation about the mending of a fence or the cutting of a hedge, there is little contact between neighbours. A petition to stop a footpath being closed about eight years ago is the nearest the road has ever come to having a sense of identity. The nearest pub, The Roe Cross, is part of the Toby Inn chain, but is not used as a 'local' by the residents in the road. The Shipman family probably patronised it more than most, having Sunday lunch in the carvery on a regular basis, and with the Shipman boys working there as kitchen porters and waiters at different times to supplement their pocket money. The family are remembered at the pub only for being unremarkable.

That is also the verdict of most of the neighbours, although there have been murmurings of disquiet about the state of the house, which, even from the outside, is visibly neglected and dirty. Wally Ashworth, the family GP, is puzzled by the state of it. 'That's a real baffler, that is. Why would anyone live like that? It was ultra, ultra messy.' His surprise would be echoed by members of the police investigating team, when they eventually went inside number 15.

The long hours that Fred Shipman worked – visiting so many of his elderly patients at home – meant that he was not seen much in the street. He once told the nurse, Kate McGraw, that he regretted not seeing more of his children growing up: this was probably just a conventional conversational gambit because he clearly could have spent more time at home had he organised his working life differently. When he was at home, he worked in the garden; Fred's social contact with neighbours was limited to a chat about gardening. For several years he collected newspapers on behalf of the Scouts, which brought him into more contact with the other residents than anything else, but it was only a doorstep conversation over a bundle of papers, and he stopped the collection more than ten years ago.

Sandra Walker, who lives with her husband and grown-up children a few doors away from the Shipmans, was unimpressed by them. 'The whole family are loners, you never see them with other people. We have always found them a bit odd. He seemed to be a hen-pecked husband – quite small, always quiet, and she was a big woman. When the kids were younger she always seemed to be watching, and would knock on doors to complain. Dr Shipman would say, "Just leave it Primrose, calm down," but she ran right over him. It was as if he didn't have a mind of his own. She was an abrasive woman, and her house was a mess. None of the kids in the street liked her.'

But even though they did not get close to their neighbours, Fred and Primrose did have some staunch friends who stood by them after Fred's arrest, including Primrose's friend, Jayne Stokes, and her husband Robert. For a time the two women ran a sandwich shop in the village of Hadfield, two or three miles from Mottram. It was called 'Jayne and Prim', and was open to sell sandwiches to the workers on a small industrial estate, the shop hours dovetailing with the changing shifts. It was not a success, and Primrose and Jayne were delighted to be able to sell the lease. One of their customers described them as looking 'like Pinky and Perky, two little fat women'. After abandoning the sandwich enterprise, Primrose went back to childminding, the job she had done when the family first moved to Hyde. She may have been motivated in part by an affection for children, but there was also a strong financial motive, and at one point she stunned her customers by upping her rates without notice.

Primrose's unprepossessing looks and size are constantly remarked upon. The most charitable assertion about her is that she seems a jolly person (and somewhere, buried beneath all the burdens that life with Fred Shipman has imposed on her, there must still be the carefree, jolly Prim of the 1st Wetherby Guides and the Number 38 doubledecker).

Kate McGraw, however, to whom Shipman confessed that he married Primrose because she was pregnant, considers that the doctor 'felt he'd married beneath himself, really. But he stuck by her.'

Yet there was no reason for Primrose, the stocky, pleasant-looking young woman of the Wetherby bus, to be an embarrassment to him: she may not have had his education, but she was bright enough, and physically attractive enough, to have kept pace with her aspirational husband.

At some point, though, it seems she gave up. She gave up cooking, cleaning and keeping her weight in check. It is possible that she resorted to eating because it was the one area of her life that Fred could not control. Or perhaps, true to the girl who seemed not to care about her looks or her clothes, she really is oblivious to the constant assessment by appearance that goes on in modern society. She has not asked for medical help with her weight problem, nor does she seem in any way bothered by it: if it hurts, she keeps the hurt hidden.

# 8
# Early Misgivings

**F**or many months and years, the tide ran with Fred Shipman. These were perfect crimes: apparently motiveless, with victims whose deaths, although a shock to those around them, were not questioned, committed by a murderer who had access to the means of killing and who was, because of his position and because of his own reputation as a particularly caring doctor, above suspicion.

But there were in Hyde a few people who began to notice that there was a scourge at the heart of their close-knit community, that a terrible sequence of events was in train. These people are the heroes of this story, because without them it is possible that Dr Fred Shipman could still be at large, still be administering his unique brand of care in the community. It is partly thanks to them, and their watchfulness, that Fred Shipman is now behind bars: they may not, as individuals, have been able to stop his killing spree, but they made vital contributions to the build-up of evidence against him.

John Shaw is a giant of a man, big in stature and big of heart. He retired at the age of sixty-four in the summer of

1999, but for more than eleven years he was a taxi driver in Hyde. Not just any crackly-radioed on-call cab ferrying holidaymakers to the airport and drinkers home after nights out, however; John Shaw saw himself as a specialist, and the vast majority of passengers who climbed into the comfortable back seat of his thirteen-year-old blue Volvo were old ladies, regulars who used him every week to chauffeur them to the post office to collect their pensions, to the supermarket for their bulky groceries, to the bingo evenings and coffee mornings that punctuated their quiet days. They booked John directly by phoning his wife Kath, or simply asked him to turn up at their front doors at the same time each week.

To the old ladies of Hyde, his bulky frame was reassuring. He carried their shopping, changed lightbulbs, fixed gates and even on one occasion had to help one of his regulars out of a surgical corset he had taken her to the hospital to have fitted. In short, he was a lot more than a normal taxi driver: he was a friend. His charges were very modest, and he was used to the oddest of tips – he's been given pies, cakes, magazines, tins of cat food. He never minded: after an eventful and at times sad life, John had settled in middle age with his third wife Kath into a contented routine, ferrying his old ladies around and earning just enough to be comfortable.

He enjoyed his work. He never had any hassle from his elderly customers, they never threw up all over the cab or refused to pay (although sometimes they clean forgot to pay, and John could never bring himself to ask for money. Kath would get a call an hour or so later from the elderly passenger, apologising and promising to give John double the next week). He was amused by them, fond of them, they were part of his life as much as he was part of theirs. In the card index system that Kath kept on the windowsill next to the phone in their cosy flat, there were a couple of hundred names, and he knew them all personally.

From time to time, one of his old ladies would die. It was always a sad event, and sometimes John would have the time to go to the funeral. When Renee Sparks died in October 1992 it was particularly poignant: because she was arthritic, John always carried her bags into the kitchen for her after her regular Wednesday trip to the shops, and knew her well.

'She was more than a customer, she was a friend,' he says. 'I'd taken her out on the Wednesday and she was fine, lively and normal, only her arthritis bothering her. The next Monday I got a call from her niece cancelling her bookings because she had passed away. Apparently she had not felt well, she called the doctor, he came and shortly afterwards she had a heart attack and died. I was very surprised. Although she was seventy-three years old, I felt she had a lot more years left in her.'

At the time, John had no suspicions that there was anything amiss. But as the months and years wore on, he started to become uneasy.

'If you work with old people, you expect deaths, but not the sort of numbers I was getting. My list of regulars was being cut back all the time. It was not that I needed the business, because there were always more waiting to get on my list. But it began to feel wrong, and about three or four years ago I noticed that all those who were dying went to the same doctor, Dr Shipman.

'I didn't know him, I've never met him or even seen him. But his name kept cropping up. In the end, I was coming home and saying to Kath, "You'll never guess what . . ." and she'd say, "Another Shipman patient?"

'At first we'd say it with a smile, because neither of us could believe it was anything more than coincidence, based on him having a practice with lots of old women on his books. But after a bit I began to get really worried, and when it got to be one death every three or four weeks, some time in 1996, about two years before his arrest,

Kath started to write the names down on a loose piece of card at the front of my card index system.

'I was getting upset about it, and I wanted to go to the police or to somebody in authority, I didn't know who. Kath didn't want me to do anything: she said nobody would believe my suspicions against a doctor, especially a highly regarded and popular doctor. We thought that if I had it all wrong – and it was very hard to believe that he could be killing them – then I could be done in court for defamation of character.

'I thought about going to his surgery, confronting him. Perhaps that would have stopped him – but it would not have got justice for all those who had already died.'

Kath, too, was beginning to be upset because she could see the effect on John. Not only was he losing valued friends and customers, but he was at a loss to know how to help, and was feeling guilty that he was doing nothing to stop the mounting death toll. Many times they came close to going to the police; many times they held back because of the sheer enormity of what they knew they would be saying.

Eventually, John heard about the death of Kathleen Grundy, who was not one of his regulars but, as an ex-Mayoress, was well known in the town. The woman who told him had been speaking to Mrs Grundy the evening before she died, and knew that all she was suffering from was indigestion.

'I asked my usual question: "Who was her doctor?"' says John. 'When I heard the name I was expecting to hear I made my mind up to speak to the police.'

For the past year or so John had been calling at the Hyde Club every Monday evening for a soft drink (he does not drink alcohol). Hyde Club is a sturdy red-brick building in Bowling Green Street, the street named after the immaculate bowling green laid out behind the club. It is a tiny oasis of northern, masculine traditions: there are snooker tables, dart boards, cheap beer and the bowling green. Founded more than a hundred years ago by the mill owners and businessmen of the town, it is dark, wood-panelled, with red banquettes and a large portrait of the Queen dominating the main function room. Women are tolerated, but it is a male preserve.

Hyde Club has a unique role in the story of Dr Fred Shipman's downfall. It was within the portals of the club that some of the main players – those who (to use an analogy that Shipman the rugby player would appreciate) picked up the ball and ran with it – were able to share their misgivings with each other. Crucially, a stalwart of the club, president since 1997, is Stan Egerton, the detective inspector who initially led the inquiry and who formally arrested the doctor.

But when John Shaw went into the club after Kathleen Grundy's death, he knew nothing of any police inquiry, nor had he heard any rumours of a forged will. All he knew was that this was one death too far. He sought out Stan Egerton and told the detective that he needed to talk to him, privately. Stan gave him his business card and told him to call the next day.

But by the following morning John had had second thoughts, all the old doubts crowding in again. It was not until he heard that Mrs Grundy's death was being investigated as a possible murder that he again sought out DI Egerton at Hyde Club. He told him about all the customers he had lost.

'How many?' asked Stan Egerton.

'How many do you want? I've got a list of about twenty.'

'Bloody hell! How far back do they go?'

'About six years.'

'Bloody hell – we're only investigating the last eighteen months.'

John Shaw's list of twenty names, all of them customers

of his who had also been his friends, was added to those the police already knew about, and the inquiry, which was already rolling, grew.

John Shaw and his wife Kath are left nursing a guilt, a feeling that they should have acted earlier, and perhaps some lives would have been saved. But DI Egerton has reassured John: his word alone would not have brought down a respected GP.

'Stan has told me that if I'd gone to the police when I first had suspicions nobody would have believed me. They'd have assumed I had a grudge against Shipman. How could I, a taxi driver, question the work of such a popular and highly regarded doctor?'

As he talks, he strokes Dinky, the elderly cat which once belonged to Renee Sparks and which John volunteered to adopt after Renee's death – a death which may have been caused by Dr Shipman.

'This cat, if she could talk, could have been called to give evidence. She was in the room when Mrs Sparks died. This cat is a witness to murder,' says John.

John Shaw and his wife were not the only people in Hyde who were beginning to notice something sinister was happening. At Frank Massey & Son, Undertakers, they would have recognised the interchange between John and Kath:

'You'll never guess what.'

'Not another of Dr Shipman's patients?'

For Alan Massey, his daughter Debbie and her husband David Bambroffe, it started in much the same way as it did for John Shaw. They began to notice Fred Shipman's name coming up with more frequency than usual; they began commenting to each other; for a long time they could not accept the awful reality.

The Massey family firm has been in business since 1903, founded by Alan's grandfather. Alan learned the business from his father and uncle, working alongside them in the undertaking side but also apprenticed to them as a cabinet-maker: the two trades went hand in hand in the days when undertakers made their own coffins. When Alan took over the firm, he moved to premises in the centre of Hyde. Business grew, as the population of Hyde expanded, and as other undertaking firms were taken over by large groups. The Masseys remain a family firm, rooted in the community, well known to the townspeople, and offering the sort of service and continuity that their customers value. Bereaved relatives often tell them that they want 'Mum to have a funeral exactly the same as Dad', and as long as they can give Alan the year of Dad's death, he can dig out the file with all the details.

With three daughters and no sons, Alan was unsure that he would be able to hand the company on within the immediate family. To his great delight, however, his daughter Debbie, after trying her hand at other jobs, asked to join him, and now she and his son-in-law David have taken over a great deal of the work. Alan, three years older than Fred Shipman, has served as a magistrate on the Tameside bench since 1987, a role he enjoys and which puts him even closer to the heart of the local community.

The Masseys are a cheerful bunch, open and friendly. They treat their customers with the greatest respect, and Alan has passed on to the two younger members of the firm the message that was drilled into him by his father: whoever you are burying, never forget that they were somebody's mum or dad, and must be buried with the care that you would give your own mum or dad. But their manner is not gloomy or reverential: Debbie is a bubbly, attractive, friendly young woman, in her late twenties at the time of the trial, who inspires the confidence of the families she deals with.

It was in late 1996 or early 1997 that the Masseys first

became aware of the number of patients of Dr Shipman's they were being called to, and for a few months, although they commented on it occasionally between themselves, they made the same rationalisation that others who were suspicious did: he is a GP with a lot of elderly patients on his list, so he is bound to have more deaths than a GP with a younger patient base. They knew his reputation – Debbie and David were patients of his, so was Alan's wife and his other two daughters, one of whom suffers from epilepsy.

'He took her on to his list knowing that her drugs would cost a lot of money over the years. Not all GPs will do that,' says Alan. 'My wife thought he was wonderful, as did most of the patients we ever spoke to about him.'

'We were very happy going to him,' says Debbie. 'He always had plenty of time for you. The old people we dealt with were all made up with him; they thought he was marvellous, and they'd ask for funeral donations to be made to his surgery fund. You never heard a bad word about him, and that's why it was so hard to accept what was happening.'

It was not just the number of deaths that began to alarm the Masseys. There were other factors which were unusual, notably the circumstances in which they found the bodies of his victims when they were called out by the families. They were all sitting in easy chairs, fully dressed, often with a sleeve rolled up as if for an injection. A lifetime dealing with death has made Alan Massey well aware that it rarely arrives in such an orderly manner: people who die of sudden, unexpected heart attacks or strokes are usually found on the floor, often in a kitchen or bathroom. If they have been ill for some time, they usually die in bed wearing their nightclothes.

'Of course, there are people who die peacefully in their armchairs, so finding one or two bodies like that would not cause any surprise. It was the fact that they were *all* in that position,' says Debbie.

'I can only remember one of Shipman's deaths in recent years when the person was in her nightie, and that was one who died at 10pm. The others all passed away during the day, and they were all in the same position, almost as if they had been arranged to be found like that.'

Another factor which raised the eyebrows of the under-takers was the very high preponderance of women among the Shipman patients they dealt with. 'You do get more old ladies than men, because men die younger, and we knew he had a reputation for being good with old ladies. So again, for quite a while you accept it.'

As the comments between the members of the business became more open, and they realised they were all notic-ing the same things, they began to discuss it properly, and serious worries started to creep in. It was, nonethe-less, a huge leap from their disquiet to actually voicing suspicions that the GP was killing his patients. Right up until the death of Mrs Grundy, none of them had used the word 'murder': it was just too big a thought, too unlikely, flying too much in the face of public perception of Dr Shipman, their own trusted and respected family doctor.

But they knew something was going on, and they did not know how to deal with it. They did not, in Debbie's words, want to 'kickstart something'.

'If I'd said something to a family, and the coroner had become involved, a post-mortem, and then it turned out there was nothing wrong, how would I have felt? Relatives don't like post-mortems. They were always so grateful when there wasn't a need for a post-mortem. On several occasions I've heard them say how grateful they were to Dr Shipman for arranging everything without a PM. Our reputation could have been badly damaged – and apart from that, it would have been terrible to have cast suspi-cion on Dr Shipman if he was innocent.'

But suspicions were growing. Debbie, a naturally

chatty young woman, would say to the bereaved relatives when she was arranging a funeral: 'Had your mum been ill long?'

Invariably, families of the Shipman victims would reply that the deceased only had a cold, or some other trifling ailment. She found herself increasingly dealing with deeply baffled families. Although all deaths are a shock, when the deceased is elderly the family are usually prepared for it, aware that their relative is in failing health. Yet with the Shipman deaths she was constantly hearing how well the dead person had been, how active, how much they were looking forward and planning ahead for holidays and family celebrations. Nor were they all old – there was a growing number of them in their fifties and sixties.

She and David and Alan were also surprised that so many of Shipman's patients had died alone: when an old person is ill, they usually have someone with them as they die. Even more odd, in their long experience in the business, was the fact that the doctor himself was there on a number of occasions when they were called out, and they heard stories of him being in the house at the time of the death.

Eventually, Alan decided he would go to see Shipman himself. By this time, the Masseys had begun to collect names in their heads of deaths they were unhappy about. Alan had been talking to a home help who worked in the town, and she'd mentioned that the home helps, a band of hard-working women employed by the council to help with housework for the elderly and handicapped, had also begun to notice that their clients were dying off at an unusual rate, and they'd registered the Shipman connection, too.

Although he was not a patient at The Surgery, Alan booked an appointment at the end of the afternoon session, not long before the end of 1997. He had to wait;

Shipman's famous chatty, caring style meant that patients always had a long wait. Most of them did not begrudge it – they appreciated the fact that the doctor always took his time with them, and knew he would do the same for others.

Eventually, Fred Shipman came out of the surgery, handed a file to his receptionist and turned and beckoned Alan to come through. He was calm and seemed in no way surprised to see the undertaker, whom he had met many times professionally. For Alan Massey, the first sentence was difficult, and he was embarrassed. But he'd come with a purpose, so he got on with it: he told the doctor that, as an experienced undertaker, he had concerns about the number of funerals he was arranging for patients of The Surgery.

Shipman was unabashed. He was not indignant, angry or outwardly surprised. In retrospect, Alan Massey is himself surprised at the doctor's calmness, but at the time he was relieved to find a potentially awkward situation defused by the benign and friendly manner of the GP.

'He told me, "There's no need to be concerned. It's all in the book, and anyone can look at the book." He gave me the deaths book which all doctors fill in, entering each death and the cause of death. It proved nothing: there was a medical term for the cause of death in each case, but it meant nothing to me, a layman.

'But I was reassured, mainly because he was so calm and matter-of-fact about it. He certainly didn't act like someone with something to hide, or someone who was nervous. I came away, after about fifteen minutes, feeling that perhaps we had been putting two and two together and making five. He seemed exactly what people said he was – a caring, conscientious doctor who put himself out for his patients.'

Alan's fears were allayed, but Debbie was unconvinced. Soon after her father's visit to The Surgery, on Christmas

Eve 1997, Dr Shipman called in at the funeral parlour to countersign a cremation certificate for another doctor. The rules for burying or cremating bodies are different: a body can be buried on the signature of one doctor, but to release a body for cremation requires a three-part form, an Authority to Cremate (issued by the crematorium on the authority of the Home Office), which has to be signed by two doctors as well as the medical representative of the crematorium. The first doctor, either the GP or the hospital doctor dealing with the patient who has died, fills in the first section of the form, giving details of the deceased's previous treatment and the cause of death (and including a statement that the doctor has no financial interest in the death). A second doctor, who must not be a partner of the first, then has to examine the body and confirm the cause of death.

For carrying out the second procedure doctors are paid a fee of £41 (which is handed over by the undertaker and then appears on the funeral bill). It is known among cynical GPs as 'ash-can money', and for most involves a trip to the undertaker where the body is stored, a peremptory examination of it, and a signature. For some GPs it is seen as a perk of the job: 'The more you burn, the more you earn,' they say.

As one GP explains: 'You cannot very easily ascertain the cause of death just by looking at a body, but you take it on trust that your colleague, who has been dealing with the patient, has got it right.'

Signing 'second part' cremation forms is therefore generally nothing more than a rubber stamp of the first doctor's diagnosis. It is through the signing of second parts that undertakers get to know local doctors, and Fred Shipman was certainly known to the funeral directors in Hyde. It was not just at the Masseys' firm, but at others in the town as well, that his behaviour was remarked upon: he would insist on giving the body a very thorough examination, turning it over and checking it in much more detail than his colleagues would, always wearing surgical gloves.

He made the same remark, flippantly, every time: 'Got to check the back, you never know whether there's a knife wound or a bullet hole.'

He was always pleasant and friendly, and when he arrived at Massey's a couple of weeks after Alan's visit to him at his surgery, to countersign the cremation form for another doctor, he made his familiar joke to Debbie: 'Got a knifing or a shooting for me, have you?'

'No,' said Debbie, 'you won't find one here – you'll have to go elsewhere for that.'

After he examined the body he filled out the form, and then asked Debbie if she had any spare blank cremation forms that he could have.

'I said to him, "Hey, it's Christmas, you've got to be good. We want a bit of a holiday, too, you know." He just laughed and said, "There's some pending." I took that to mean that he had some patients who were very ill and might die over the Christmas period. True enough, we were called out to one that evening – but it wasn't someone who had been ill at all, prior to Dr Shipman calling. It was another typical Shipman case.

'He wasn't open about what he was doing, but again he didn't seem at all bothered by my jokey allusion to the number of deaths among his patients.'

By the New Year of 1998 Debbie and her husband David had become ever more convinced that things were not right, although Alan still felt they were in danger of making a terrible mistake if they tried to do anything about it.

As more and more people died (two in January of that year, but a record seven in February), Debbie became more and more determined that the doctor had to be stopped. She remembers the occasion when she and her mother were out shopping in Stockport and she phoned the office to be told that another woman had died. Hearing that it was another Dr Shipman case, Debbie made up her mind.

The countersignatures for Shipman's cremation forms were almost always given by doctors from the Brooke Surgery, the new surgery set up across the road from his (a breakaway group from the large Clarendon practice) where seven doctors were in partnership. They were the nearest to him, and after his uncomfortable departure from Donneybrook he was not about to ask any of his old colleagues to countersign.

Debbie Massey had already exchanged a few jokey remarks with the Brooke doctors as they popped in and out of the Masseys' office to sign the forms. 'Another of Fred Shipman's,' she'd say, or one of the doctors would say, 'What – not another of Freddy's?'

Eventually, she decided that she would speak properly about her fears to one of the Brooke team. She chose Dr Susan Booth, a married woman in her forties with an open and friendly manner, because she felt she was approachable. The next time Dr Booth came in to the funeral parlour, Debbie took her to one side and shared her concerns with her.

'She told me she would go away and discuss it with her partners,' says Debbie.

A few days later, the telephone at Debbie and David's bedside rang on a Sunday morning, before 9am. Their immediate thought was that it was a call to another death, but instead it was Dr Linda Reynolds, another member of the Brooke team. She wanted to contact Alan, Debbie's father, who was away on holiday in Spain. She would not tell Debbie what the call was about, but she was insistent that she needed to speak to him urgently.

Debbie knew that Dr Reynolds was not her father's own GP, and her next thought was that it might be about her grandfather. She then realised the call was probably about Dr Shipman, so the next day she rang Dr Reynolds.

Linda Reynolds already had suspicions about Shipman. She had been working at the Brooke Surgery for eighteen months, and shortly after arriving had met Shipman, and found him pleasant and polite – although subsequently he barely acknowledged her. Towards the end of 1997 she had commented to her partners that Shipman often seemed to be present at the death of his patients.

'In my years of practice I had found presence at death to be a most irregular occurrence (two or three times in ten years),' said Dr Reynolds. But she was assured that it was 'the product of the caring nature of Dr Shipman, a doctor who would visit unannounced when he was concerned about his patients' condition. He was well known for this trait and it had been accepted by the community.'

After Debbie Massey voiced her own worries to Dr Booth, the Brooke partners had discussed the matter at one of their regular practice meetings. Dr Reynolds was on holiday at the time, and it was only when she herself told Dr Booth that she was signing rather a lot of cremation forms for Shipman that she heard about the undertakers' concern. At the time, Dr Reynolds estimates that she was signing a cremation form on average once every ten days – and as the other partners were also signing them, in rotation, she realised that a surprising number of Shipman patients were dying. So she made contact with Debbie, and she and Susan Booth went together to meet Debbie and her husband David at their office.

'Dr Booth and I visited Miss Massey in February 1998. Miss Massey had noticed that all the patients she was concerned about were female, living alone and were found dead by Dr Shipman. She found it difficult to understand how Dr Shipman had gained access to the

*Dr Harold Frederick Shipman, shortly before his arrest.*

*Fred Shipman's birthplace in Nottingham.*

*Shipman aged five (third from right, back row).*

*Shipman at Burford Infants School (centre, wearing bow-tie).*

*Shipman aged fifteen, at High Pavement Grammar School.*

*Shipman, aged seventeen, relaxing on a rugby tour in the north-east (note the natty waistcoat).*

*The Donneybrook Medical Centre, where he first practised in Hyde.*

*The surgery at 21 Market Street, Hyde,*
*where five patients of Dr Shipman died.*

*The Shipman family home at 15 Roe Cross Green,*
*Mottram-in-Longdendale.*

Number 79 Joel Lane, the £200,000 home of Kathleen Grundy, former mayoress of Hyde. Shipman was accused of her murder and of forging her will.

Paul Spencer, witness to the forged will of Kathleen Grundy, with a friend.

*The death certificate of Mrs Grundy declared she died of 'old age'. In court Dr Shipman maintained she had a drug habit.*

CERTIFIED COPY
Pursuant to the Births and

OF AN ENTRY
Deaths Registration Act 1953

DEATH

Entry Number 148

Registration District
Sub-district    Tameside
                Tameside

Administrative area
Metropolitan District of
Tameside

1. Date and place of death

Twenty-fourth June 1998
Loughrigg Cottage, 79, Joel Lane, Gee Cross, Hyde.

2. Name and surname

Kathleen  GRUNDY

3. Sex
   Female
4. Maiden surname
   of woman who
   has married      PLATT

5. Date and place of birth

2nd July 1916   Hyde  Cheshire

6. Occupation and usual address

Widow of John GRUNDY University Lecturer
Loughrigg Cottage, 79, Joel Lane, Gee Cross, Hyde, Cheshire.

7. (a) Name and surname of informant

Angela WOODRUFF

(b) Qualification

Daughter

(c) Usual address

Wagstaffe School House, Crown Street, Harbury, Leamington Spa, Warwickshire.

8. Cause of death

I(a) Old Age

Certified by H.F.Shipman  M.B.

9. I certify that the particulars given by me above are true to the best of my knowledge and belief.

A.Woodruff

Signature
of informant

10. Date of registration

Twenty-fifth June 1998

11. Signature of registrar

C. L. McCann Registrar

Certified to be a true copy of an entry in a register in my custody.

*Superintendent Registrar
*Registrar                19.8.98.  Date
*delete as appropriate

IAP 003656

*The exhumation of the body of Irene Turner.*

*Angela Woodruff, Mrs Grundy's daughter, who turned detective to expose her mother's will forgery.*

*Murder victim Kathleen Grundy.*

*Murder victim Joan Melia.*

*Murder victim Bianka Pomfret.*

*Murder victim
Winifred Mellor.*

*Murder victim
Marie Quinn.*

*Murder victim Marie West.*

*Murder victim Norah Nuttall.*

*Murder victim Maureen Ward.*

*Murder victim Ivy Lomas.*

*Murder victim Kathleen Wagstaff.*

*Murder victim Lizzie Adams.*

*Murder victim Irene Turner.*

*Murder victim Jean Lilley.*

*Murder victim Pamela Hillier.*

*Murder victim Muriel Grimshaw.*

*Undertaker Debbie Massey, who buried many of Shipman's victims.*

*Taxi driver John Shaw, who 'lost' twenty of his customers to Shipman and also told the police about his misgivings.*

*Dr Shipman poses for cameras after the news broke of the police
investigation into Kathleen Grundy's death.*

*A dejected Fred Shipman in handcuffs after appearing on remand at Tameside Magistrates' Court.*

*Detective Superintendent Bernard Postles, who headed the investigation into the Shipman murders.*

*Detective Inspector Stan Egerton.*

*Smiling Primrose Shipman (right), with her friend Jayne Stokes, with whom she ran a sandwich shop.*

patient, and she knew that on several occasions there had been no contributory illness. She also stated that a local taxi driver had expressed similar concerns to her. At no time, in any of these patients, had she found any obvious external sign of malpractice,' said Dr Reynolds, in a statement issued during the trial, by which time she herself was terminally ill.

Debbie and David were relieved to find that Dr Reynolds had her own misgivings.

'It made us realise we weren't imagining it. Dr Reynolds said she would monitor things, and would find out who to approach. It was a load off our shoulders – we knew we'd done the right thing in sharing our worries, and we felt sure that Dr Reynolds was taking it seriously. The ball was no longer in our court.'

The Brooke partners again discussed the matter, and compared death rates between their surgery and Shipman's. They agreed there was, in Dr Reynolds' words, 'considerable cause for concern'. After consulting the Medical Defence Union, who urged caution, Dr Reynolds eventually decided that she had no moral alternative but to take action.

It was on 24 March 1998 that the South Manchester Coroner John Pollard took a call from Dr Reynolds. John Pollard liaises all the time with GPs and hospital doctors, and he is used to handling queries over individual causes of deaths, and post-mortem results. In a normal day, about twenty such phone calls come into his office, which is housed in an uninspiring 1960s office block in Stockport. But this was something he had never encountered before.

John Pollard is a down-to-earth criminal lawyer, working in an area where he deals regularly with gangland killings, deaths through drunken brawls and a range of premeditated murders, and he never dismisses any potential evidence. His initial instinct was that Shipman was just dealing with a heavy caseload of the elderly and infirm, but he could see that it merited a closer look.

'I quite often get phone calls from doctors who are not happy with the cause of death put on a cremation certificate by the GP who has been treating the patient, and suggesting that it might be better if there is a post-mortem examination of the body. But in all those cases I have been asked to look at, the cause of death may be slightly different after the PM, but nothing untoward or unlawful has ever been revealed,' he says. 'This GP expected me to order an investigation, to be carried out very subtly, to find out whether Doctor Shipman was signing certificates wrongly.'

Agreeing that it merited looking into, the coroner contacted Greater Manchester Police at Tameside, the borough which includes Hyde, and DI Dave Smith was assigned to carry out an investigation. Stan Egerton, the DI who knows Hyde and the people of Hyde well, was away on holiday: he insists, even with local knowledge, that he would not have come to any different conclusions from DI Smith, allowing for the tight restraints placed on the investigation. These included not giving to Fred Shipman any clue that an investigation was being carried out and, importantly, not revealing the name of the doctor who had prompted it. (Dr Reynolds had told Pollard that she wanted to protect her professional relationship with Shipman, and did not want him to know that she had expressed doubt about him).

'I wanted an inquiry made, but made in a very careful way,' says John Pollard. 'The position of the other GP would have been totally untenable if he turned out to be a conscientious GP and then learned that she had reported him.

'I was quite satisfied with the inquiry the police made, but it came to nothing. They didn't see anything that was wrong at that time. It was, in my view, a full investigation within the limits imposed, without blowing the gaff to Shipman.'

Among those interviewed by the police were the Masseys and Dr Reynolds. After the interview the Masseys heard nothing more about the police investigation. DI Smith revisited Linda Reynolds and told her that Dr Shipman was well loved, and there was no apparent motive for him to be harming his patients. Dr Reynolds was unhappy about the thoroughness of the investigation, but felt she could do no more. The inquiry was wound up, with the DI and his superiors satisfied that there was no evidence.

'The investigating team looked at medical records, but what we did not know at the time was that Dr Shipman had amended those records,' says Detective Superintendent Bernard Postles, who headed the massive Shipman inquiry. 'There was tittle-tattle, gossip if you like, around the town about Dr Shipman, but no evidence of wrongdoing. There are no statistics kept for death rates of patients to doctors. They just don't exist. We did not have the evidence to apply for an exhumation, or to arrest him.'

But it was not an entirely fruitless exercise. It may not have saved the lives of Winnie Mellor, Joan Melia and Kathleen Grundy, three elderly ladies who were murdered between that phone call from Dr Reynolds to the coroner and the arrest of Fred Shipman. But it laid down a marker. So that when the next unexpected phone call came to John Pollard about a suspicious death involving Dr Shipman, he was ready to take it very seriously.

# 9

# Where There's a Will

At his computer keyboard on 10 December 1997, Dr Fred Shipman accessed a patient's records by using her surname, Pomfret, as a password, and then began to type, two-fingered, details of visits she had made to him over the previous weeks, complaining of chest pains. As he wrote, 49-year-old Bianka Pomfret was propped in a chair, dead, at her home in Fountain Street. Nobody knew she was dead except the man who had killed her, Fred Shipman. He was covering his tracks, creating a false medical history.

There was only one major problem – and one that Shipman, no more computer literate than most of his generation, did not predict. The hard drive of his computer was making a permanent, ineradicable, time-dated copy of the words he was typing. In the seventy minutes before Bianka Pomfret's body was discovered, he made ten false entries, dated back over the previous ten months.

He had no idea that, just a few months later, a computer expert at Greater Manchester Police would read the evidence, as damning as the swirl of a fingerprint, on the hidden hard drive of the practice computer. He should have known: the software company that provided the package used in thousands of GP practices, including his, had an advisory panel to help them design it. Fred Shipman served on that panel.

German by birth, Bianka Pomfret, who was the second youngest of Shipman's victims, met her ex-husband Adrian when he was serving in Germany with the British Army. She had one son, William, who is married with two children. Although she and Adrian were divorced three years before her death and he had remarried, the couple remained close, with Adrian calling to see her a couple of times every month. In the late 1970s Bianka had been diagnosed as manic depressive, a serious psychotic illness that makes life very tough for the sufferer but also for all those around them. Despite the divorce, Adrian still felt a degree of responsibility for her, and she always discussed her plans and financial arrangements with him. He knew that she had planned to leave the bulk of her estate, worth about £60,000, to Dr Shipman in her will, with a small bequest to her psychiatrist. Adrian persuaded her to change the will, pointing out that it would be better for her son and his wife and her grandchildren to inherit it. She changed it, leaving everything to her family, just two weeks before she was murdered: when he injected her with morphine Fred Shipman probably did not know that the will had been changed, and his legacy excluded.

Bianka was devoted to Dr Shipman. During the latter years of the marriage, when Adrian had suggested moving house, she had refused because it would have meant changing GPs.

'She thought the world of him, in a nutshell,' says Adrian, a demolition expert. 'She said he was excellent, very caring. She needed to see her GP on a regular basis, once a week or even more. She was also being treated at Tameside Hospital, but she regarded Shipman as her main support in life. Your average GP wouldn't give a great deal of time on a weekly basis to someone who had mental problems and was already under the care of the hospital. With most GPs it's in and out, here's the prescription, off to the chemist. But he wasn't like that; he had an old-fashioned bedside manner, nothing was too much trouble for him.'

Adrian visited her on the Sunday, three days before her death, and she complained of having chest pains. She said she had had flu, and that Dr Shipman was also treating her for angina. He was going to call in and see her on the Monday or Tuesday, she said. She also had an appointment with her parish priest, Father Denis Maher – she waited for him in the church after Mass, to ask when he was going to pop round and see her at home. He promised he would make it on Wednesday or Thursday evening. 'Is that a promise? I'll be expecting you,' she said.

The following day, she had a regular consultation with her psychiatrist, Dr Allen Tate, who said she was lonely and depressed about the prospect of Christmas. But although she voiced suicidal thoughts, she told him she did not really want to die. The next day, one of her mental-health support workers visited, and spent some time with her; she talked about having flu, but seemed otherwise to be well. On the morning of her death one of her neighbours, Paul Graham, a mechanic, was outside working on his house. He saw Bianka moving around inside her house and watching television, and she waved to him.

'I didn't know her well but she was a very nice lady. She had a puppy – her Yorkshire terrier died – and I would walk the dog if she was going out for the day. She kept herself to herself, but we'd chat over the wall. I went to work at 2pm. Her death came as a complete shock.'

During the morning, at 11.30, Bianka rang The Surgery, and then called again at 1.10. Shipman called round to see her that afternoon. At 5pm another psychiatric support worker called, and when there was no reply looked through a window. She could see Mrs Pomfret fully dressed, on the settee, as if asleep. The support worker contacted William, Bianka's son, who, with his wife Gaynor, runs a local shop. William had a key, and he and the support worker went in. They found Bianka looking quite relaxed, with half a cup of coffee next to her, the TV on, and a cigarette burned halfway through in an ashtray next to her.

'I went over to my mum to feel her hands. They were cold. I felt her chest; it was warm. I opened her eyes and they were cold, like looking at the eyes of a fish. She was gone,' says William.

They called for an ambulance, and William rang Adrian, who had just arrived home from work. The ambulance crew asked their control to contact Dr Shipman; he is logged on their message system as saying that he had called on Mrs Pomfret earlier that afternoon, and that he had made arrangements to return. He went back to the house, certifying Mrs Pomfret (who had been moved upstairs by the ambulance crew) as dead, with coronary thrombosis and ischaemic heart disease as the cause. He told William and Gaynor, to their great surprise, that she had had angina for ten months: they were sure she would have told them, as she was not a secretive person and was preoccupied with her health.

Adrian Pomfret arrived just after Shipman left, and took on the unhappy task of ringing Bianka's parents and brother and sister in Münster. It was two weeks before Christmas, and the whole family was very upset. Adrian was surprised that a post-mortem was not being held, and mentioned it to William. William raised it with Dr Shipman, who explained that it was not necessary, as he had seen her recently and knew about her heart condition – the heart condition he had invented at a computer keyboard.

\*

Six months after the death of Bianka Pomfret came the death of Kathleen Grundy, the final murder, and the one which triggered the police inquiry.

The word was out in Hyde about the exhumation of Mrs Grundy's body and the search of The Surgery. People were beginning to ask questions, and rumours had reached the ears of journalist Brian Whittle. Realising that an exhumation was an unusual and very serious step for the police to have taken, he dispatched a reporter and photographer to see the doctor at the centre of all the gossip. Fred Shipman was no more outwardly abashed to find the press outside his surgery than he was to be accosted by Alan Massey about the number of deaths among his patients, or to find the police searching his home and business premises. He climbed out of his battered E-reg Espace, smiled affably, and told the journalists: 'You can have five seconds of my time for a photograph, but you must direct any questions to my lawyers.'

It was 19 August 1998, more than a fortnight since Mrs Grundy's body had been dug up. Shipman was still practising: The Surgery was as full as ever of patients wanting his attention. He appeared, certainly on the surface, to be calm, confident and unruffled by his problems. By the next day, when the story was broadcast across the national press and on radio and television, with speculation that nineteen other deaths apart from Mrs Grundy's were being investigated, he appeared unperturbed when he arrived at work – but the first patient to see him says he broke down in tears, telling her that he knew nothing about Mrs Grundy's will, and waving his hand in the direction of the Brooke Surgery across the street, saying, 'There are doctors over there who will see you if you like.'

A few days later, another patient found him calm, and he said: 'Primrose and I have talked about it, and I may get twelve years and be out in eight,' he told her, one of the few times he came close to admitting his guilt. Marion Gilchrist, a district nurse attached to The Surgery, had two conversations with him. On the first occasion, he closed the door of his consulting room and went through the circumstances of Kathleen Grundy's death, telling the nurse that he had seen the old lady the day before to syringe her ears, and had decided to take some blood because she looked awful. He told Mrs Gilchrist that he had suspected for some time that she had taken medication not prescribed by him.

In a later chat with Nurse Gilchrist he was very upset, and even cried. He told the nurse that he read thrillers 'and on the evidence they have, I would have me guilty'. Recovering himself, he joked that the only thing he had done wrong was not being able to arrange for Mrs Grundy's body to be cremated.

The other person he opened up to was Mrs Lesley Pulford, a patient visiting his surgery. He talked to her for about half an hour, telling her that he believed he was going to be accused of forging Mrs Grundy's will. He said the police investigation was destroying him.

'He was very emotional, his eyes welling up with tears. I remember thinking I should have been sat in his chair and he should have sat in mine, because our roles were reversed. He said that if he could bring her back "I would sit her in that chair and say look at all the trouble you've caused me. I didn't want her money, but after all the trouble, I would have it now," he said.

'He also said the staff had had a meeting, and planned to each have a week off on the proceeds of the will, and on the anniversary of her death they would give so much to old folks' homes and give some money to any patient who had a baby on that day, for a charity of their choice.'

When Mrs Pulford asked why he had not yet been arrested he told her that toxicology reports took a long time, because cases were prioritised. The patient felt very sorry for the doctor. 'I felt he just wanted to get it off his chest,' she said.

Like all doctors, he had legal cover from the Medical Defence Union, an organisation which provides doctors with insurance against legal actions (they are vulnerable to medical negligence claims, some of which can result in massive damages being paid to patients). His solicitor, Anne Ball, a slim, attractive woman in her early thirties, of the Manchester branch of the legal firm Hempson's, has done other medical defence work, but it is unlikely she had any idea what she was getting into on the day she took the first call about Dr Shipman. Hempson's, which was established more than a hundred years ago, has offices in London and Harrogate as well as Manchester, and describes itself as 'pre-eminent in the medico-legal field'.

But by this time, the police had at least some idea of the scale of the operation ahead of them. On 21 August, Detective Superintendent Bernard Postles set up an incident room at Ashton-under-Lyne police station, in a large room used for major inquiries. There could be no doubt in anybody's mind by now that this was a major inquiry. Bernard Postles had been involved from the beginning, as Stan Egerton's boss, and knew from the early days of the investigation that the case would go on developing. A preliminary look at the number of deaths among patients of The Surgery over the past twelve months had come up with more than thirty names. Who knew how far back it went?

Postles, a smart, dapper and intelligent man, forty-six years old at the time of the trial, is a career cop who has risen rapidly through the promotion system, passing not just the police exams but studying in his own time for a degree. Unlike some of the senior officers who hit the promotion trail from their first day in the force, Bernard Postles is well-respected and well-liked: his ambition is to be good at the job, not just a self-serving quest for bigger titles and bigger salaries. At the time of the trial he had twenty-seven years' service with Greater Manchester Police behind him, twenty-two of them with CID. He has worked in the Serious Crime Squad, the Major Incident Support Unit and the Drugs Squad. The Shipman case was close to his home ground: he and his wife live in the Tameside area.

Over the months they all worked together, the fifty-nine-man team increased their regard for him. They found him approachable and open. He occasionally threw the odd tantrum when he felt things were not being done as fast as he wanted, and his subordinates would warn each other if he was in a tricky mood. But there were few real criticisms of him and much that was admired. He never pulled rank over small things; if he was making himself a cup of tea and a police constable walked in, he'd make one for him, too.

Throughout the first few months of the inquiry, when the pressure was on, Postles would be in the incident room by 7.30am every day. He and DI Egerton would invariably be the first in. They would also both still be there twelve hours later, until eventually a rota system for late duty developed between Postles, Egerton and Detective Chief Inspector Mike Williams, who joined the inquiry as Bernard Postles' second-in-command after it had been going for a few weeks.

DCI Williams was a great asset to the team, a very experienced policeman with a laid-back approach to life which belies his intelligence and efficiency. Quietly spoken, with a great sense of humour and an ability to never get rattled, he provided, on the rare occasions it was needed, a good buffer between Postles and his team. Williams, a married man with grown-up children, was fifty at the time of the trial. He and Bernard Postles work well together, having first encountered each other in the

Serious Crime Squad, and he was confident enough to stand up for the team if he felt his superior was being hard on them. He was a very popular boss.

Under these two came two detective inspectors. Stan Egerton became head of outside inquiries; in other words, he co-ordinated the teams of detectives who were set to take on one of the biggest and most sensitive inquiries in British criminal history. His local knowledge, and his hands-on, hard-working approach to the job, made him invaluable, but he was also a popular man to whom junior officers could relate. He had been nicknamed Stan 'The Hammer' by Chief Superintendent David Sykes, the Tameside Divisional Commander, because of his no-nonsense approach to criminal investigations, and the name stuck.

DI Steve Fullalove was seconded from the Serious Crime Squad as office manager, a job for which this quiet, competent and very organised man was ideally suited. It was his job to delegate work to the civilian staff, to provide cars, computers and liaise with the Divisional Support Unit when extra detectives were needed. Fullalove was in charge of the paperwork: it was all funnelled through him and he brought up any problems at the management team meetings which were held every day, at 8.30am.

These four senior policemen were joined at some of the management meetings by John Ashley, a stocky, round-faced detective sergeant who is the acknowledged computer expert in Greater Manchester Police. His technical wizardry allowed GMP to bring the first British prosecution involving pornography on the Internet. Initially a self-taught computer enthusiast, he has been on several courses to expand his knowledge, and his expertise gives GMP an edge over many other forces where computer experts are civilians brought in from outside. John Ashley's role in the Shipman investigation makes him another of the heroes of this book: it was his computer evidence that came closest to breaking Shipman in interrogation; it was he who found, on the hard drive of Shipman's computer, the evidence that medical records had been tampered with.

The morning management team meeting would also be attended by two detective constables, one a statement-reader, whose job was to read all the statements, other incoming paperwork and sort out the important details; and one an action-allocator, who kept tabs on the workloads of the various teams of detectives and was, effectively, Egerton's right-hand man. After that meeting would be another one at 10am, for the remainder of the team. At least once a week Det. Supt. Postles would address everyone, but the rest of the time it was Stan Egerton's job to tell them what was going on and what they would be doing that day.

The nucleus of the team were Stan Egerton's men from Stalybridge sub-division (which covers Hyde, Hattersley, Hollingsworth and Dukinfield). He chose detectives he knew were good. Detective Sergeant Mark Waring, described by DI Egerton as the best DS he has ever met, had recently been commended by a judge for the prosecution file he put together on a serious murder case, and oversaw the compilation of the files on the Shipman case. Detective Constables Dave O'Brien, Perry Sinacola and Mark Denham were also hand-picked by DI Egerton from Stalybridge, and supplemented by DC Sally Reid, WPC Jackie Kings and DC Gary Schofield, from Ashton-under-Lyne (again, all personally chosen by Egerton). Detective Sergeant John Walker came in from Stockport and there were detective constables from Oldham, Rochdale, Bury and Stockport as well as two officers from the Drugs Squad, a team from the Fraud Squad and a plethora of civilian typists, computer analysts and researchers. There was a steady core of twenty-four detectives, but from time to time, when searches were being carried out, the numbers were supplemented by more from other divisions.

One of the Drugs Squad officers was a chemists' inspector, whose normal duty was to check on pharmacies and drugs held in doctors' surgeries. There were also two bereavement officers, trained to counsel families of victims in murder inquiries and road traffic accidents. A great deal of time had to be spent helping the relatives of the bereaved come to terms with what was happening. Unlike in a normal murder case, where it is obvious that a crime has been committed, these were families who had believed their relative had died peacefully and naturally. For many of them, especially where the death had occurred some time ago, the whole grieving process had to start again, even more painfully than before.

All of the officers were given as much information as possible at the morning meeting – gone are the days when lower ranks were expected to obey orders without knowing why. DCS Postles believes that he can get more out of well-informed and well-motivated officers than out of those who regard each day as simply another shift: his open policy certainly paid off, with everyone working long hours voluntarily, and a continual buzz of interest and excitement around the case. It was also vital to keep everyone informed so that seemingly trivial bits of information would not be overlooked.

Nobody, not even the most senior ranks, had ever worked on anything as big as this case, and there was instant hush and attention the moment the briefing meeting began each day. As evidence came in – and it came in very fast over the first few months – looks of amazement and pride in their collective achievements registered on the faces of all those involved.

Unlike some inquiries, where officers dragged away from their own divisions are resentful, knowing that work is piling up on their desks, there was a very high level of commitment. For the senior officers, and especially for Stan Egerton, who was briefing the team of detectives who were knocking on doors all over Hyde, it was necessary to keep stressing the need for an open mind. 'He may be an innocent man, and we have to investigate that way,' the detectives were constantly reminded. Despite the welter of evidence they were collecting, and their own inescapable feelings about the man they were investigating, Postles knew that it was vital to keep the investigation clean and fair, so that there were no legal technicalities which the defence lawyers could exploit.

Apart from the formal meetings of the team, The Greyhound pub, a couple of streets behind the police station in Ashton, and known to all the cops as 'The Fast Dog', became the unofficial winding-down venue, where Postles, Williams and Egerton would chat over a pint at the end of some very long days. DI Fullalove would rarely join them: he lived at the other side of the GMP area and faced a long drive home to his young family, and he was immersed in studying for promotion exams. Once a month, there would be a curry supper for the whole team, with £60 behind the bar from the pockets of the senior officers for them all to have a drink.

Morale was high, but there were, over the course of a long and difficult inquiry, some specific problems. On the morning of the first meeting, on 21 August, not all of the team were in place. Those who were already on the case assembled in the incident room, a large room used not just for major incidents in the Tameside area, but for any big GMP cases (the windows were covered with a plastic film which allowed the policemen and women to look out, but no persistent journalists to look in). The first task that Postles outlined to his staff was to get copies of the death certificates of all Shipman patients who had died since September 1997, and then to examine their medical records and start talking to their friends and relatives. At the same time, the investigations already initiated by Stan Egerton into Mrs Grundy's death would continue.

Over the next weeks detectives, working in teams of two, were given lists of five or six deaths to check out. If they found themselves dealing with one that was a potential murder case, then they would concentrate on it and hand the others on their list back to Stan Egerton, to be re-allocated.

Every death that was looked into was scored, in order to assess which ones should be given priority. A system, giving a maximum of five points, was devised:

1. Was the body buried or cremated? *Score one for buried.* (The police did not initially expect to get enough evidence on cremation cases.)
2. Were the family concerned about the circumstances of the death? *Score one for yes.*
3. Were there any causes for police concern (e.g. a cause of death not consistent with medical records, property missing, etc.). *Score one for yes.*
4. Had the medical records been altered? *Score one for yes.*
5. Give an extra point to any case which has scored four, making it a top priority.

In the end, as evidence mounted even in cases where the body had been cremated, the team were investigating scores of three, but they started out looking hardest at the fives. As 70 per cent of all bodies are cremated nowadays, and as they only concerned themselves with deaths outside hospital, they were able to keep the initial investigation to a manageable total of fourteen cases.

It was a difficult and sensitive job: some families did not want to be part of the inquiry, preferring to leave their dead relatives in peace. Others were upset that more was not being done in terms of investigating their particular case. Perhaps most difficult of all, some families were divided as to how much they wanted the police involvement.

For the police officers, it often meant long hours sitting with distressed and elderly relatives. The bereavement officers and the local Victim Support group were kept at full stretch, and were able to some extent to free up the detectives for investigative work. But at every stage, all of the officers on the case knew that they were dealing with very sensitive situations. To help them, Postles arranged for counselling to be available. They could approach a senior officer and ask for counselling or they could ring, in total confidence, a number to speak directly to a counsellor. By the very nature of the arrangement, it is not known whether any of them used the service.

Occasionally, when it was obvious that the stress was getting to an officer, he or she would be moved discreetly to a different area of the case. Some of the families were more difficult to deal with than others, and on one or two occasions the senior team were concerned that an officer was getting too close to an individual family.

There was another problem when one of the detectives, DC John Townsend, was involved in a car crash when he was off-duty. He had been working closely with the staff at The Surgery. Initially the staff had been very loyal to Shipman, but they co-operated with the police. As the inquiry continued, however, and DC Townsend won their trust, they became more open. His injuries meant that he could not work for two or three weeks.

The staff at The Surgery, receptionists and nurses, continued to work as normal, and so did Fred Shipman, defiantly turning up for work each day with a smile on his face. One of the first priorities outlined by DCS Postles at the first management team meeting was to find out how to stop him practising: it seemed ludicrous to hard-headed policeman, accustomed to instant response, that he was not suspended from duty as soon as the first suspicions surfaced. The police put pressure on West Pennine Health Authority to stop him holding surgeries, but it was not until 29 September (three weeks after his arrest) that Bernard Postles, Mike Williams and a police solicitor went to London to give evidence to an NHS tribunal. (One of the many areas in which the police would like to see procedural improvements is in the way doctors are suspended.)

Although Shipman did not obstruct the police investigation, he treated them with disdain. When DS John Ashley arrived to download the computer records, Shipman disparagingly reminded him not to damage any data: he spoke to Ashley as if he were ignorant, with only a cursory understanding of high-tech equipment. DS Ashley politely let him know that he was well up to the job, and Shipman backed off. No doubt he realised that he was in the hands of someone who knew more about computers than he did, but it is highly unlikely he realised just how much John Ashley would be able to track from the permanent records in the machine.

The media posed another problem for the police. Until the arrest and charge of Shipman, on 7 September, the press were free to carry on writing about the case. Under English law, after a person is charged the case becomes '*sub judice*', and the media are restricted in what they can report. They can give details of court appearances, including the charges, but nothing more. The aim is to prevent a future jury being influenced by background information acquired from newspaper or TV reports. For the last week of August and the first week of September, before he was charged, the case was making daily headlines, and speculation about the number of deaths was rife (although even the wildest shores of tabloid hyperbole only brought the figure near to half the probable total).

The *sub judice* law does not apply in other countries, and throughout the inquiry the team were inundated with requests for information from foreign news organisations: the enormity of the Shipman case was recognised abroad very quickly, with an Internet website dedicated to it. Television crews from all over Europe, Japan and America invaded Hyde. There were apocryphal stories of coachloads of Japanese tourists being driven down Market Street, their Nikons all focused on The Surgery. The town's inhabitants risked having microphones thrust in front of them every time they visited the market.

Postles was particularly concerned that the media interest did not cause problems for the trial. The most recent trial on this scale was that of Rosemary West, who was convicted of ten murders committed with her husband Fred (who hanged himself in prison before the trial). The West trial was almost jeopardised by the involvement of witnesses with newspapers – a main plank of the defence case was that the payment of money to witnesses rendered their evidence at least tainted, if not invalid. To avoid any repetition of such problems, all potential witnesses were advised not to speak to the media.

The people of Hyde were another problem for the police, not because they were deliberately obstructive but because, especially for those who knew Shipman personally, it was impossible to believe the enormity of what was happening. Many residents felt the police were unfairly targetting a good and caring GP who, at worst, was responsible for helping some terminally ill old people to a peaceful end. They believed, because the facts were not available and the town was stoked up with rumours, that Fred Shipman was either totally innocent, or a crusader for euthanasia. Many of them felt the police presence in the town was unnecessary and intrusive, and that the dead should be left in peace.

For local policemen, like Stan Egerton, it was an incredibly difficult situation. He lives in Hyde and is well known. He found himself ostracised by half the town: people he had known for thirty years avoided his company, or found it difficult to look him in the eye when they met. One woman accosted him in the street, spat in the gutter, and told him to leave Dr Shipman alone. At Hyde Club, where he is the president, he was aware of old mates shuffling along the bar to avoid talking to him.

It was an added stress on top of what was proving to be a very demanding inquiry. Unlike the other members of the senior team, he was never able to go off-duty: his neighbours, friends and all his social contacts were affected by the case. There is probably nobody in Hyde (apart, perhaps, from the Bengali population) who does not know somebody who is related to a victim or a suspected victim: in a small town, with a stable 22,000 population, the network of connections is complex and all-embracing. Kathleen Grundy alone must have been personally known to a substantial portion of the residents. Talk to anyone in Hyde and you hear stories of aunties, cousins, friends' relatives, in-laws and neighbours, all of whom are involved in some way with the police investigation.

In the weeks leading up to, and immediately after, Fred Shipman's arrest, The Surgery was inundated with cards, letters of support and flowers. The staff pinned the messages on the walls. There were moving tributes from those who had been treated by him, or who had had relatives treated by him; some, in fact, whose relatives would later turn out to be suspected victims.

The media, especially television crews, came in for as much criticism as the police. When a Belgian crew were filming at the back door of The Surgery one old man, a loyal patient of Shipman's, mistook them for Germans.

When they asked him what he thought about the number of deaths linked to Shipman he shook his stick at them and shouted, 'What about you lot? You murdered millions in the war!'

But alongside the deep sense of shock and unease that ran through the town there was, inevitably, a black humour developing, a humour born not of disrespect for the victims, but a mark of the resilience and stoicism of the people in the town. Quite soon after the news about Mrs Grundy's will became known, some wag slipped a notice into the window of The Surgery, which said: 'Where There's a Will, There's a Way'. There were jokes about Disney and Spielberg moving into the town to make films about the case: *101 Cremations* and *Shipman's List*. And when Stan Egerton began the grisly business of exhuming more bodies, the expression 'Life's a bitch, and then you die' was expanded to 'Life's a bitch and then you die – and then Stan Egerton digs you up.'

The information, which came on 2 September from forensic toxicologist Julie Evans, that there were large quantities of morphine in Kathleen Grundy's body kicked off the murder inquiry. It meant that the police had the evidence they needed to arrest Dr Fred Shipman. They did not rush: the confirmation of the morphine came on a Wednesday, and they arranged to arrest Dr Shipman by appointment the following Monday morning. They were satisfied by then that he was not a risk to the community (however arrogant he was, they felt he was not stupid enough to carry out any more murders while he was under such close police scrutiny). The police were well aware of the impact the case was having on the local community, and they wanted to minimise disruption. In arresting him by appointment they gave him time to organise a locum doctor to take over the running of The Surgery, so that patients would not be left stranded.

There was also more work to be done. They had to discover from the experts the properties of morphine – how
much do you need to kill someone? Was there any other
possible explanation for it being present in Mrs Grundy's
body? One very significant fact came to light as soon as
they talked to a forensic toxicologist: morphine never
degrades. As long as there is body tissue to test, it can be
found. Morphine has been found in thirteenth-century
mummies found in South America. So, if it was present in
Mrs Grundy's body, it would also be there in the bodies of
any other victims who had been buried. It was, by any
standards, a very stupid drug for a GP, with access to
other drugs (like insulin or potassium, both of which are
much harder to detect) to choose as a murder weapon.

The arrest was made by Stan Egerton at Ashton-
under-Lyne police station, at 9.18am on 7 September.
Shipman arrived at the police station with his solicitor,
Ann Ball. He appeared calm, controlled and to be expecting what was coming – it was his solicitor who looked
shocked when she heard the charges. He was charged
with the murder of Mrs Grundy, with attempted theft by
deception, and with three counts of forgery. He was held
in custody that night, and appeared in front of Tameside
Magistrates' Court the next morning.

Stan Egerton, the man who had started the whole
investigation and who was closer to the people of Hyde
than anyone else on the case, asked DCS Postles if he
could charge the doctor: he wanted to look Shipman in
the eye when he was accused of murder. He knew, as did
all the police team, that they were dealing with a rare and
exceptional criminal. Egerton was professional enough
not to let his pleasure at the arrest show. Postles agreed; it
seemed only fair that Stan 'The Hammer' should be the
first one to call Dr Harold Frederick Shipman a killer, to
his face.

# 10
# Digging Up Bodies

**D**rive south from the centre of Hyde for five minutes, through small crowded streets of terraced houses, and you come to another monument to Hyde's former status: the cemetery, as grand as the Victorian municipal buildings in the centre of the town. Hyde Cemetery has now achieved a notoriety all of its own – it was from here that the bodies of seven of the victims were exhumed, and it was from beyond the iron railings bordering the cemetery at the end of Knight Street that television cameras from around the world filmed the sad activities of the police and the exhumation specialists bringing the coffins up from their resting places.

To give as much dignity and privacy as possible to the victims, the exhumations took place in the middle of the night, and – with the exception of the first, Mrs Grundy – the bodies were returned to the earth, with, in most cases, a priest on hand to carry out a simple service, by the afternoon of the following day.

Walking around Hyde Cemetery on a sunny afternoon it is, to quote Emily Brontë, impossible to imagine unquiet slumbers for the sleepers in that quiet earth. The cemetery is orderly and well maintained, with phalanxes of black marble headstones in regimented rows stretching up the hill from the gate. Council workmen are busy working among the neat flowerbeds and gravelled paths. On the level ground at the bottom of the cemetery are the Muslim graves and the Roman Catholic graves, with other Christian denominations covering the slope, which is bordered by a road called Richmond Hill.

Only the occasional slash of newly dug earth showed where the bodies of Shipman's victims had been exhumed: without knowing their history, they looked for a few weeks simply like new graves. As the grass grew back over them, they have been absorbed again into the gentle order of their surroundings, and from their simple headstones generations to come will know nothing of their untimely ends.

Yet the cemetery can also be a frightening, unearthly place. When the first of the exhumations took place there, on 28 September 1998, there was a dank mist shrouding the graves, keeping the place dark long after the normal dawn. Police secrecy had worked: for this exhumation there was only one reporter and one photographer present to see the arc lights go on around the grave. The thin fog clinging to the ground deepened the unease of the police officers working on something so alien to their normal activities.

For some of them it was a completely new experience; for others, like Stan Egerton, it was already becoming a familiar procedure, although never one with which he felt comfortable. This exhumation, of Bianka Pomfret, was the fourth of the twelve that he would supervise. Apart from the detectives working on each case, he had five or six uniformed policemen on hand to keep the press at bay.

At some of the later exhumations, when TV crews and photographers turned up in large numbers, Egerton would tell his men to turn their arc lights on to the cameramen at the moment when the coffin was removed from the ground, dazzling them and preventing them getting pictures. His thoughts were with the families of the victims: he reckoned their grief was enough to cope with without seeing photographs of their loved ones being removed from their graves. (He showed little sympathy to the TV cameraman who accused him of damaging the camera by turning the arc lights towards it.) Dealing with intrusive press interest was an added, but anticipated, problem. At one re-internment a camera crew swept into the cemetery in a black limousine with black tinted windows, looking for all the world like a funeral car attending another funeral. The car braked, the crew jumped out, set up a tripod and started filming. Egerton told them to back off. They claimed, as a defence, that they were more than thirty yards away from the grave; the edited highlights of his reply were that he didn't care if they were three hundred yards away, they were not intruding on what, even in these unusual circumstances, should be a private family occasion.

Stan Egerton has always had a good, open relationship with the press. He has always been known to journalists as a cop who would give a good quote: he never pussyfooted around making diplomatic statements – if he felt a criminal was evil, he would say so, in colourful language. He described a rapist whose victim was a young mother who had a toddler and a baby with her when she was attacked as 'lower than a snake's belly'. Another time he condemned drug dealers as 'parasites living on the back of humanity'. All good headline copy, which may have made some of his bosses wince but successfully kept the crimes in the public eye.

He was not disillusioned by the behaviour of the media in Hyde because he expected it. Just as exhumations were new to the police, so they were new to the public and the press who service and nurture public interest. But he was saddened that there wasn't more respect for the families, some of them distraught, and that the re-burials, which should have been intensely private, dignified occasions, turned into media circuses. For himself, he could deal with any amount of press questioning – he speaks the same robust language as most reporters. But for the vulnerable, often elderly, relatives who stood by the gravesides of people they loved, and watched a coffin lowered into the ground for a second time, he felt a strong sense of responsibility.

After Kathleen Grundy, the second exhumation was that of Joan Melia, who died on 12 June 1998, twelve days before Mrs Grundy. She was the first of Stan Egerton's 'fives', the cases which scored five points and were therefore priorities. The exhumation of Mrs Grundy was the quantum leap: once morphine had been found in her body tissue, it was apparent to all the senior officers on the case that more bodies would have to come up.

It was 21 September, the early hours of a Monday morning, when Mrs Melia's coffin was raised from the earth of St Mary's graveyard in Newton. It is a traditional churchyard, attractive in its slight unkemptness and the higgledy-piggledy arrangement of the simple graves. Even with the industrial estate abutting it, and the maisonettes with balconies overlooking it, it is possible to see it as the inspiration for Gray's elegy, with millhands' and factory workers' lives and deaths substituting perfectly for the herdsmen and the ploughmen of the original.

In darkness the police and the exhumation experts assembled, trundling the small mechanical digger through an opening in a stone wall at the back of the churchyard into a high, windy field where the newer graves are. A policeman stood sentry on the balcony of the flats, in case any residents woke to the noise and arc lights and wondered what was going on. It was, in the manner of these things, an easy one: the ground was dry and sandy, there was room for the digger to get in. The re-burial, the same afternoon, was quick and simple, and there was no religious service.

The next night it was a different story in Highfield Cemetery, Bredbury, when the body of Winifred Mellor was unearthed. Another council-run cemetery, it is greener, more spacious, less crowded than Hyde Cemetery, bordered by fields and bushes. Yet the sense of openness is deceptive: when it came to exhuming Mrs Mellor, it was impossible to get the mechanical digger into the grave, and the digging all had to be done by hand.

A week later, the first exhumation in Hyde Cemetery, of Bianka Pomfret, took place. Her grave, in the Roman Catholic section of the cemetery, is three plots away from that of Marie Quinn, who would be removed from her final resting place two weeks later, and only six yards away from Alice Kitchen, whose turn would come four weeks after that, on 11 November. Their graves, in the lower part of the cemetery, were in damp earth: a spring flows through the ground of Hyde Cemetery and the lower areas quickly become waterlogged. Ivy Lomas, Irene Turner and Jean Lilley would all be disinterred from this cemetery on different dates in October and November: Ivy Lomas on 12 October, Marie Quinn on 13 October, Irene Turner on 10 November, Alice Kitchen on 11 November and Jean Lilley on 12 November.

In December, three more exhumations would take place. Sarah, known as Sally, Ashworth was the only body removed from Dukinfield Cemetery. Mrs Ashworth's grave, next to a thick privet hedge, caused problems: tree branches had to be cut back to get the digger in. But because she was buried in a family plot, with another coffin below her, the excavation did not need to be so deep as some of the others. This was the oldest of the graves opened, as Mrs Ashworth died in April 1993. Modern coffins are not made to withstand years in the earth – there was little left of this one, and the remains had to be carefully handled.

The following night, in the early hours of 8 December, the team were back at Highfield Cemetery to remove the coffin of Muriel Grimshaw, this time without any problems of access. And then, on 9 December, another raw, wintry night, the body of Elizabeth Mellor was exhumed from Hyde Cemetery, making the twelfth and final exhumation: by far the biggest total of modern graves opened for one inquiry. John Pollard, who issued warrants to Stan Egerton for each one, holds the record as the coroner who has ordered the most exhumations in recent history. It is not, he says, a record he ever aspired to.

'The most difficult thing was to view each application individually, not just think, "Oh, another one . . ." In each case, a senior police officer would explain the circumstances to me. There were various indicators, the prime one being that the people who died were not apparently ill. They did not have terminal illnesses, nor did they appear to relatives to be so unwell that they were imminently going to die,' says Pollard, who gave up his private law practice to become Coroner for Manchester South in July 1995.

'The only word to sum up my feelings would be amazement. It was like Topsy, it just seemed to grow and grow. My main concern throughout was to see that justice was done, but to balance that against the cares and considerations of the family and friends. Exhumation is a disturbing experience for everyone involved, including the police and, to some extent, myself as coroner, because I don't want to cause distress. But there is a need to prove if something has gone wrong.'

In every one of the twelve cases, the family of the deceased agreed to the exhumation. Had they not, the police could have requested it and the coroner issued a warrant for it anyway, but both Det. Supt. Postles and John Pollard were happier that it was being done with the support and approval of the families. They knew how sensitive the issue was and a great deal of soul-searching and care went into it. They checked that they were avoiding birthdays and anniversaries when they picked the dates for the exhumations. There were some possible victims where the relatives objected strongly to the idea of exhumation – John Pollard had at least one letter from a family stating their unequivocal wish not to see the body disinterred. The two men, Pollard and Postles, liaised regularly about the case, with, after the charges were brought against Shipman, the Crown Prosecution Service (the legal team handling the case) attending the meetings.

The main question was where to stop. They both knew that they could go on digging up more and more bodies, all of them cases which scored five on the points system. The tally of potential victims was growing daily: when a helpline for worried patients of Dr Shipman's was opened at the beginning of October by West Pennine Health Authority it was swamped with more than 100 calls in the first seven days, not all of them relevant, but many adding new names to the list. By the time of the final exhumation, the police total had increased to 131: even allowing that some would be genuine deaths from natural causes, it was a mind-boggling number and one which, as the senior officers were becoming increasingly aware, could put Shipman at the head of the list of British serial killers. (By the time Shipman came to trial, the total was over 140.)

'We reached a point where Detective Superintendent Postles had to say, "Yes, there is enough evidence on which to found a case and yes, we do not need to go any further because the balance of the evidential benefit from further exhumations and the distress caused to society in general has tilted in favour of distress and against evidential benefit,"' says Pollard, who made a point of being present at some of the exhumations. He was not required by law to be there, but felt it was part of his duty to make sure everything was done properly and as tastefully as possible.

'My main role as far as any dead body within my jurisdiction is concerned is that I am the custodian of the body, and I have to make sure that nothing happens that shouldn't. I have been extremely impressed with the way the police have carried out the exhumations, with dignity but also professionalism.

'I don't think anybody gets used to it. Forensic officers get used to attending post-mortems, but an exhumation is far more distressing. We are all aware that here you have somebody who has been laid to rest, we all know the phrase "rest in peace", and we were acutely aware that we were disturbing that peace. It wasn't someone who had just died: this was someone who had had a funeral, been laid to rest – all of us were disturbed and distressed by what was happening. Even some of the very experienced police officers, men who have seen it all, were visibly distressed at times. The coffins and the bodies were sometimes in a poor state.'

It was not only the effect on relatives and families that Postles and Pollard discussed; they were also concerned about the whole community, aware that not just the act of exhuming bodies, but the worldwide media attention it was drawing to Hyde, were problems for the townspeople. There was a sense of shock pervading all areas of life.

'The feeling of sorrow and sympathy for the families and friends of the deceased broadened out into sympathy for the whole community. It is a small, close-knit community, and they have suffered greatly as a result of what's gone on,' says Pollard. 'The town of Hyde will cope well, because these are good, solid northern people who are resilient. They will see that though this is a horrific thing to have happened, there is an awful lot in Hyde that is good – far more good than bad.'

Alan Massey was on holiday with his wife in the upmarket resort of La Manga, Spain, when a neighbour rang and told them to switch on Sky News. The image they saw as the television screen lit up shocked them: the footage was of one of the exhumations at Hyde Cemetery, filmed in the early hours of the morning. There, in the foreground, was his daughter Debbie and son-in-law David.

'You don't expect to see your daughter on telly when you're in Spain – and certainly not walking out of a cemetery in the dark,' he says.

Debbie and David were required to be at the exhumations where Masseys had carried out the funeral, to confirm that the right coffin was being removed. Their firm had been responsible for nine of the twelve graves that were opened: it was a tiring time for them, as they had to be at the cemetery at 2am and then carry on with the family business all day as usual. With the police team doing the exhumations in batches, there were stretches of three days at a time when they got no more than three or four hours' sleep a night.

For Debbie and David, it was the first time they had ever been present at an exhumation, and for them the most noticeable feature was the smell: an unpleasant smell, stronger in the more recent graves. The older ones had a peculiar woody, damp smell.

For the funeral directors, it was a difficult time. Living and working in the town all his life, Alan Massey knew personally five of the women whose bodies were exhumed. Supervising the burial of friends and acquaintances is difficult enough, but watching the process happen in reverse feels unnatural, even to an undertaker. When, years earlier, Alan Massey had been asked to tender a quote for exhuming graves inside Strangeways Prison, he turned it down because he felt strongly that his job was to bury people, not to disinter them. He could not have predicted the role his firm would subsequently play in the biggest number of exhumations of the recent dead outside a war zone.

Debbie and David were not, of course, the only people working very long hours during the hectic weeks in which bodies were being exhumed. Removing the bodies from the ground was just the first step; the next was to carry out a post-mortem. In the case of Mrs Grundy, a second post-mortem had to be conducted on 14 September, by the pathologist appointed to work for Shipman's defence, Richard Shepherd. But for the other eleven, the defence pathologist was asked to be present at the post-mortem carried out at Tameside General Hospital, in Ashton-under-Lyne, by Dr John Rutherford. In most cases Shepherd was able to be present, but once or twice a different pathologist was used. (The defence wanted to hold separate post-mortems each time, but the police felt it was proper, for the sake of the families, to re-bury the bodies of all except Mrs Grundy the same day as the exhumation, and the coroner agreed with them.)

A normal post-mortem, carried out routinely to establish a cause of death, takes about an hour and a half. A forensic post-mortem, when the search is on for criminal evidence, lasts about five hours. It starts with a detailed examination of the body, lasting about an hour and a half to two hours, noting any bruising or needle-marks, and taking samples from hair, nail clippings and scrapings from under the nails (although nail scrapings were not relevant in the Shipman case). Sometimes an injection causes external bruising; it always causes some internal bruising. With the Shipman victims, because the bodies had started to decompose, the pathologist never found evidence of injections.

After photographs are taken of the body, the chest is dissected, starting at the chin. The throat is examined for signs of strangulation, in which case the little bones in the neck are broken, or for the internal bruising caused by choking. The lungs, heart, kidneys, spleen and other organs are removed and closely examined: the heart, in particular, was relevant to the Shipman case, because the pathologist could tell from it whether the victims had died from heart disease or a heart attack. The lungs are examined for signs of pneumonia, and the whole body is investigated for evidence of cancer. The contents of the stomach are inspected, and samples are taken from the liver and kidneys.

When it became apparent that the exhumed bodies had not died from the causes of death put on their death certificates by Shipman, and there was no other obvious cause of death, the organs and muscle tissue samples, taken from the thigh, where the muscle is thick and therefore better preserved, were sent away for toxicology reports to the North-West Forensic Science labs at Chorley. It took about two weeks for the laboratory to report back to the police. Mrs Grundy took longer, as the forensic scientists at the lab did not know what they were looking for. After morphine was found in her body, they knew to test for it in all the others.

Morphine is a narcotic analgesic, a painkiller extracted from the head of the opium poppy. It works by acting directly on the area of the brain where pain is perceived, and blocks the flow of pain signals. Medically, it is the most valuable of all painkillers for severe pain, used in short-term courses for severe pain after surgery or accidents, and in long-term, managed doses for the terminally ill. It causes euphoria, a feeling of well-being and mental detachment: the benefits which heroin users become addicted to (heroin is the popular name for diamorphine, a double strength morphine). There are also adverse side effects including vomiting, drowsiness and constipation – and addiction. Given in large enough quantities it depresses breathing and reduces blood pressure to a dangerous level, and ultimately causes death. The only small consolation available to the families of Fred Shipman's victims is the knowledge that they died peacefully: morphine derives its name from Morpheus, the Greek god of sleep, and their deaths would have been a relaxing, pain-free journey into sleep.

DI Stan Egerton attended all the post-mortems. Over his long career he has been present at many: it used to be routine procedure for young policemen to be thrown in at the deep end with a post-mortem, but nowadays the situation is handled more sensitively, and only officers who feel happy with the procedure are required to attend. For the mortuary staff, too, these were strange occasions – the vast majority of post-mortems are carried out on the newly dead. Although everything was handled with the greatest possible respect, there were moments of levity. After Stan Egerton once famously put his Wellington boots on the wrong feet in the dark at 4am before an exhumation, the next time he arrived at the mortuary he found his overshoes painted with a large L and R.

The re-burials of most of the bodies took place at 2pm on the day of the exhumation. The police paid for the new coffins and the re-burial costs. The first, apart from Mrs Grundy, was Joan Melia.

After her death, Joan Melia's neighbours were astonished to discover that the attractive, energetic widow was seventy-three. She looked like, and acted like, a woman at least ten years younger. She had just returned from a holiday in Menorca, with the man who had loved her and been loved by her for twenty years, ever since her marriage broke up. They were already talking about their next holiday: there was a great deal to look forward to.

On the day of her death, 12 June 1998, Joan went to see Dr Shipman at 11am. She suffered from occasional bouts of asthma, and she was beginning to feel off colour, as though she might be going down with a heavy cold or flu. She wanted to get some antibiotics to knock out the bug as fast as possible: the last thing Joan wanted was to be laid up during the summer. There was so much to do, so many places to go . . .

Derek Steele, the man she called her 'boyfriend', drove her to The Surgery. The couple did not live together. They had met while Joan was still married, and when, eventually, she left her husband they had become even closer. But having gained her independence, Joan liked to keep her own home. She saw Derek most days, and they holidayed together; their lives were completely intertwined, but because she neither lived with him nor was related to him, Dr Shipman did not know of the existence of Derek Steele in her life.

No doubt the doctor thought she was a lonely old lady, whose distant nieces and nephews would find nothing strange about her sudden death. But Derek, waiting in his car outside The Surgery, was very alarmed when she came out and told him the doctor said she was suffering from pleurisy and pneumonia. Why, if it was so serious, had she been allowed to return home with nothing more than a prescription for antibiotics? Why hadn't she been sent straight to hospital, or at least given an injection of antibiotics at the surgery to start the treatment? These questions haunt Derek Steele, who has moved since her death to live in the neat little flat that Joan was so proud of, simply to feel closer to her.

Derek gave Joan and a friend of hers a lift back from the surgery, stopping to pick up her prescription and some Fisherman's Friends cough sweets for her sore throat, then went to his own home, returning as arranged to see her again at 5pm. He rang the doorbell, but when she failed to answer, let himself in with his key. At first sight he assumed she was deeply asleep, in an armchair with a cup of tea on the carpet beside her. His first reaction was surprise: Joan always sat on the settee by the window, never on the easy chair reserved for guests. But surprise soon turned to panic. When he touched her cheek it was icy cold, and she did not stir. It was inconceivable that Joan, so lively only a few hours earlier, could be dead. He did the obvious thing: he rang the doctor. When, within ten minutes, Dr Shipman breezed in, the only reaction he showed was one of surprise at Derek's presence. Without even examining Joan he told Derek that she was dead.

He was matter-of-fact to the point of being casual. Although all doctors are hardened to the sight of death, they know the impact on relatives and close friends, and act with the reverence and respect that should be accorded to the end of a life. But Joan was very near the end of Shipman's career, when he was perhaps growing tired of the pretence of being the perfect doctor. The woman was dead. He had killed her. As with so many others, the attentive doctor had made a house call, administered an injection of morphine and within twenty minutes to half an hour the patient quietly died, with a cup of tea next to her.

In Joan Melia's case, he was suspected of taking a considerable amount of money and jewellery from her flat. Joan was a squirrel. Throughout the last years of her unhappy marriage she had hidden money away, money she needed for her escape to independence. It was a habit she had not lost. She did not trust banks or building societies, and kept money in brown envelopes and old handbags hidden in cupboards around her flat. Nobody knows how much she had but Derek, who was closer to her than anyone, estimates it could have been as much as £20,000. After her death he and her nephew found

£1,100 in two separate hiding places, but this may only be a small proportion of what was there. Even the will was missing, with an old one, dated nearly twenty years earlier, being the only one found, and with all her possessions left to distant relatives she had not seen for many years.

Joan's reburial was a quiet affair: there was no religious service and only one member of her family was present. Derek Steele could not face being there – he was devastated at the time of her death and has found it very hard to cope with the realisation that it was a cruel, unnecessary end. To him, and to all other relatives and friends of the victims, these were warm, much-loved human beings whose bodies were being exhumed and re-buried; real people with lives, loves, aspirations and plans for the future.

'I have never felt so much pain,' says Derek, who was five years younger than Joan. 'First losing Joan, and then the police knocking at the door, and all the wounds reopening. I have never felt like this. After she died, I begged the council to let me have her flat, so that I could feel I was near her.'

He talks touchingly of a love affair that began twenty years before Joan's death, when they both worked together. 'As soon as I saw her I fancied her. She would wear a long black and white skirt. She had lovely legs. She was married at the time, but not happily. I was the organiser for the social committee at work, and she used to come to our bingo nights. I think she only came because I was there.

'Then one day she announced she was leaving her husband. She was a very strong-willed woman, and going out with me had shown her that it was possible to have a laugh and a good time. She realised there was another life for her. When I came up for retirement she suggested I get a flat near hers. I asked her to marry me, but she had been in one bad marriage and did not want to feel trapped. I saw her every day, and the last few years were the happiest of both our lives.'

Joan Melia had switched to Dr Shipman only two years before her death, when she moved to Commercial Street, in Hyde. Her previous doctor had diagnosed emphysema, a debilitating lung disease. She kept it under control, making sure she got antibiotics as soon as she suspected a chest infection. It gave Shipman an acceptable cause of death to fill in on her death certificate, along with pneumonia.

Winifred Mellor was the next victim to be disinterred and re-buried, and it is with her exhumation that we meet properly an important figure in the events as they unfold over the following weeks: Father Denis Maher, the priest at St Paul's Roman Catholic church. He was present at the exhumations and re-burials of five of the victims, and three of them were regular members of his congregation.

Win Mellor, seventy-three, was one of these. She had been the reader at Mass at Father Denis's church on the Saturday night, two days before she died on 11 May 1998. She was in church again on the Sunday, the day before she died, and when Father Denis began to organise a trip to the Holy Land for his parishioners she was the first to put her name on his list. At her funeral, one of the mourners paying tribute to her said that she had, in death, reached the Holy Land she longed to visit (and when the church group went on their pilgrimage the following November, they prayed for her every day). St Paul's Church was so central to her life that after the death of her husband Stanley, a lighting technician, she moved to Corona Avenue to be nearer to it.

She was a widow with five children, and she led a very active life. She visited the sick on behalf of the St Vincent de Paul Society, did shopping for housebound elderly people, walking everywhere, and went dancing at an Over 50s club. Shortly before she died she had been to Spain with the club. On the day before she died she spoke on the phone to her son, and one of her daughters called to see her. She seemed well and didn't mention any health problems. The following morning she was due at St Paul's Roman Catholic School, where she helped young children with their reading twice a week. She rang the school to say she had a chest infection, and did not want to pass her germs to the children. She said she expected she would be okay later in the week; she did not give the impression there was anything seriously wrong.

Later that morning she had two telephone chats with friends, making arrangements to go out to a dance later that evening with one, and after lunch went out to collect her pension and do some shopping at the market hall in the centre of Hyde. She told a 'hilarious' story to stall-holder Margaret Nickson, who was selling her some ham. By 3pm she was home: a neighbour, Mrs Gloria Ellis, saw her, and also saw the maroon Espace belonging to Fred Shipman – although, at the time, Mrs Ellis had no idea he was a doctor, and assumed he was an insurance agent. At 6.30 the same neighbour, Mrs Ellis, answered the door to Dr Shipman, who asked if she had a key to Win Mellor's house, as he could see Mrs Mellor through the window but there was no response to his knock at the door. Mrs Ellis and her husband Tony went with him to the house, where they found Win peacefully 'asleep' in her chair, her glasses askew and her sleeve rolled up.

Shipman told them it looked as if she had had a stroke. When Mrs Ellis said 'Do her daughters know?' he called her 'a stupid girl'. What the Ellises remember of his whole demeanour is a callous indifference: he flicked Win Mellor's eyes open and lifted her arm and let it drop. He made no effort to check for a pulse.

Shipman rang one of Win's daughters, Kathleen, and told her that her mother had died. She had angina, he said, but had refused treatment. He confirmed he had visited her at home at 3pm, and said that she had then phoned the surgery again to ask him to go back. The police were subsequently unable to find any trace of this alleged call.

After speaking to Kathleen for a few minutes, Shipman returned the key to Mrs Ellis. She told him that she had seen him there earlier in the day: he made no comment, but seemed to be irritated.

Mrs Mellor's three daughters, Kathleen, Susan and Sheila, all met at their mother's home, and they noticed that their mother's sleeve was rolled up, as if she had just had an injection. Father Denis appeared, having heard the unexpected news.

Tipperary-born Father Denis has been a priest in England for thirty-five years, although his Irish accent is still pronounced. He has thick, iron-grey, wavy hair, a fresh complexion and a slim figure, making him look years younger than his age – he was fifty-eight at the time of Mrs Mellor's death. Although he had only been in Hyde for two years at the time, he was already a well-accepted and popular priest, and it was natural for him to be there to try to comfort the three daughters.

Father Denis was shocked at the news of Mrs Mellor's death, having seen her so recently in such good health and good spirits. But he was even more shocked by the attitude of Dr Shipman, who came back to the house at 8pm to talk to the three daughters.

'I was the one who opened the door to him,' says Father Denis. 'His face registered surprise as soon as he saw me: I was aware that he resented me being there. I wasn't part of his plan. He was so scruffy that I was surprised when he said he was the doctor.

'I was amazed at his brusque and off-hand manner

with the daughters. Their mother was in an armchair, dead, and he had no words of compassion. He just said, "You know your mother had a heart condition. She wouldn't accept treatment or go to hospital, so it's her own fault. Have you got an undertaker? Because I can arrange that for you."

'I told him that I could help the family with all that. Advising and helping with funerals is one of the services I can offer to the bereaved: I was most surprised to hear a doctor offering to help with the arrangements. Those three girls were in shock. He could have persuaded them of anything.'

Shipman repeated to the daughters that their mother had called him. He told them there was no need for a post-mortem, and that they should call at The Surgery in the morning to pick up the death certificate. He put coronary thrombosis (heart attack) as the cause of death.

When the family checked, they could not find Mrs Mellor's pension money in her purse, probably about £50. She'd drawn her pension, done some shopping and had not put any money into her savings account, so the balance should have been in her purse. It was empty.

The news that their mother was to be exhumed was another shock for the grieving family, but they agreed to the police request. They asked Father Denis if he would represent them at the exhumation, and then be there to conduct a short service at the re-burial.

'I never imagined in my life I would ever attend a body coming up out of the ground, especially just a few months after I had buried her,' says Father Denis. 'It was a beautiful morning. I watched the men working at opening the grave, and I felt pretty upset, especially as I was the only one present who knew her.

'As they took her away, in a plastic body bag, the indignity of it hit me: there she was, driving back through the streets of Hyde that she knew so well when she was alive.

Winnie was such a lively, well woman, it was difficult to think about it all.

'The re-burial was at 2pm, and the weather had stayed fine. Her three daughters, one son and a daughter-in-law were there. I devised a special ceremony, largely based on the internment service, with some added prayers for the family. The police were very sensitive, very discreet. They stood back and let me get on with it.'

When Shipman was charged with the murder of Win Mellor on 5 October, he denied visiting her on the day of her death and denied telling family members that he had visited. There were extensive alterations to her computerised medical records which created a false history of angina: he denied making these alterations, although he had spoken to her family about her 'angina' on the day of her death. No trace of the phone call to Shipman, asking him to visit, could be found.

Six days after Win Mellor's re-burial, Father Denis, the police team and the exhumation specialists met again, this time for Bianka Pomfret. She was another stalwart of St Paul's Church.

The day of her funeral was very wet, the wettest day of the year, and for Father Denis that seemed somehow apposite.

'I felt guilty, wishing that I had been able to see her before she died. I heard about her death from the undertaker – they usually ask the next of kin if there is a priest or vicar they would like to be contacted. My first worry was that she had taken her own life; I knew how depressed she could get. It was almost a relief to find that she had died of a heart attack, although it was a terrible shock.'

Adrian Pomfret was on holiday when the news of Mrs Grundy's death broke, and he read about it in the *Daily Telegraph*. His initial reaction was that it was a case of sour grapes: Mrs Grundy's disgruntled family challenging her will because her estate had been left to the doctor. But within days he began to think about the strange circumstances of his ex-wife's death. He wondered why, if she was suspected of having angina, she had never been referred to hospital for tests to confirm the diagnosis. He also wondered why, as she was only forty-nine, no post-mortem had been held, despite the GP's assurances that it was not necessary.

'These are things you don't think about at the time,' he says. 'At the time I was distraught. It's bad enough when you've been through a divorce, that's traumatic, but then the person you divorced dies suddenly. It puts you through a rough period, your head is just not clear. But looking back, I found it odd that she had looked so relaxed: I've seen several people suffer heart attacks, three in all, and they have all clutched at their chests just before death.'

When he returned from holiday he contacted William, who told him that the police had already started making inquiries about Bianka's death. He rang them.

'I wasn't shocked when they told me she was a victim. I was expecting it. I'd braced myself, and warned the rest of the family. It took a long time for some people to accept it. It's had a devastating effect on everyone. There are certain people in life you are automatically wary of. In my profession, scrap metal and demolition, there are some characters. You expect hard cases and ruthless people in certain sections of society. But your local GP? No. You put burglar alarms in your house, your car, you warn your children not to go with strange men. But if somebody's sick you send them to the local family doctor for help.'

It is a thought echoed by DCI Williams: 'If a doctor tells you to stand in a corner and put your hands on your head to cure your ingrowing toenail, you would probably do it.'

# 11
# The Digging Continues

At the eleventh hour of the eleventh day of the eleventh month of 1998, Councillor Joe Kitchen laid a wreath at the cenotaph high up on Werneth Low, above the town of Hyde. It was hard to keep his sad thoughts on the millions of soldiers who died in two world wars. The vast grief of nations was overshadowed by a deeply personal anguish: in the early hours of the morning, his mother's body had been exhumed from Hyde Cemetery. That afternoon, at 2pm, he and his family would be laying her to rest for a second time, consoled at least by the fact that they would, they believed, have answers to all their fears and suspicions about the way she had died.

Alice Kitchen had eight children and twenty-one grandchildren at the time she died (more have been born since). Her family was the centre of her universe. Although she was in hospital recovering from a hysterectomy on the day of the local elections in May 1994 which saw her son Joe voted in as a Labour councillor, she stayed up late into the night listening to the results. She cut out every reference to him in the local papers, and she glowed with pride when he promised to take her to see him in action at a full council meeting. It was a promise he was never able to fulfil: a month later his mother was dead.

Alice Kitchen was seventy when she died, a fact that her children only found out when they tracked down a copy of her birth certificate. They do not think she even knew herself – it transpired that she celebrated her birthday on the wrong day each year. She came from a large Irish family where, in her childhood, the battle against perpetual poverty meant there was little time and even less money for frivolities like birthdays. She never had a holiday in her entire life, and she was generous in the way that people who have known real hardship often are: anything she had, she would share with others.

Despite a broken marriage and health problems, she had struggled to do her best for her own children. Two of her sons – Mick, the eldest, and Joe – spent chunks of their childhood in children's homes, when their mother was too ill to cope with all her brood. But she kept in touch with them, and although Joe Kitchen can look back on the stigma of being in a children's home ('People assumed you'd done something wrong, to be there. And nobody had much hope: I was told I would never make anything of my life'), he knows that there were always children worse off than him, children who had never known a mother's love at all.

She lived in a council house in Kirkstone Road, Hyde, with two of her grown-up sons, Mick and Bernard, both taxi drivers. She was recovering well from the hysterectomy, despite a panic when her heart stopped during the operation. The hospital doctors were very happy with her progress. Her angina was well controlled, and she was looking forward to what her son Joe describes as 'some of the best years of her life, with her children all grown-up and settled and her grandchildren to make a fuss of'.

On the day of her death Mick Kitchen, who had worked through the previous night driving his taxi, left the house at 1.30pm. His mother was her usual self, and did not complain of feeling unwell. Five hours later, when Mick walked in again, he found her dead on the settee. He also found a note from Dr Shipman saying that he had called at about 4pm, and found Mrs Kitchen slurring her words and dragging her foot, and it was clear to him that she had had a slight stroke. He said she refused to go to hospital and would not let him ring any of the family, as someone would be home at tea time, so he had left her. (Unfortunately, at the time, there was no need to keep the note and it was destroyed: it would be more than four years before suspicions were aroused about Shipman.)

Mick rang for an ambulance, and the control told him to ring the police, which he did. He then rang Dr Shipman, who told him there was no reason for the police to attend and that he would tell them not to bother. He explained that as he had seen her just a couple of hours before she was found dead, there was no need for a post-mortem or police involvement.

While he waited for the doctor and the rest of the family to arrive, Mick told a neighbour, a woman who had been very close to Alice for many years, about her death. The neighbour was shocked and upset that Dr Shipman must have walked past her door without telling her that Alice was ill, and asking her to pop in to look after her.

When he arrived, Shipman said Mrs Kitchen had phoned him that afternoon to say she was unwell, with a bit of a cold, and asked him to visit. He said that when he got there she had clearly had a slight stroke, and that she must have had a second one after he left her. Even if she had been found and taken to hospital, he said, she would have been paralysed.

The family were very unhappy, some of them wanting to take action against Shipman for neglect. They suspected nothing, but felt he had not fulfilled his duty by leaving her on her own.

'But because of what he said about her being permanently disabled by the stroke, we decided that it was a blessing in disguise that she had gone,' says Councillor Joe Kitchen. 'There are eight of us, and the consensus was that we should not pursue the matter.'

His sister Philomena, though, was determined to speak to Dr Shipman, and went to The Surgery expressly to question him about her mother's death. She wanted to know how he had got into the house if her mother had had a stroke. He told her that Alice was able to shuffle to the door and open it. He said he had to respect a patient's wishes: if she did not want to go to hospital, or have any of her family informed, he could not override her. Although the family accept that he could not have forced her into hospital, they do not believe she would have been unwilling to have her children phoned, or a neighbour brought in.

She was sorely missed, especially by her youngest son, Bernard. On the afternoon of her death she had made a couple of phone calls to friends of his, trying to speak to Bernard but always missing him. The effect on him was traumatic, and he is still badly affected by the loss of his mother. When, subsequently, the police investigated her death they carried out an audit trail of all the phone calls she made, and found the ones to Bernard's friends: they were unable to trace the call that Shipman says she made to his surgery.

When the news of the Shipman investigation broke, two of Alice's children, Angela and Mick, approached Joe and asked him to register her name with the police as a potential victim. A family meeting was convened. The initial feeling was disbelief, but as the circumstances of the other deaths began to emerge it became clear that their mother's death was highly suspicious. For Joe, the clincher came when the neighbour who had known Mrs Kitchen for so many years said that she couldn't understand why Alice was found sitting on the settee, as she always sat in an armchair facing the window.

'I hadn't thought about it – there is so much else to think about when someone dies,' says Joe. 'But when it was mentioned it seemed so odd. Our mum always faced the window, or if it was cold sat in a chair by the fire. She was the sort of person who had the door open and the kettle on before you got up the path to the doorstep.'

When the police decided to exhume Mrs Kitchen, the family had mixed feelings. They would have preferred it not to be necessary, but they were determined to get answers, and they felt that the greater cause of justice was more important than their own reluctance to have the grave opened. But they were in for a terrible disappointment. Although forensic tests did find morphine in the tissue samples taken from Alice Kitchen's body, the tissue had deteriorated so much after four and a half years in the wet earth of Hyde Cemetery that the police and Crown Prosecution Service eventually decided not to charge Dr Shipman with her killing.

'We are left in the same position as all those families whose relatives were cremated or who have not been exhumed: we suspect he murdered her, but, despite the terrible experience of having to have her dug up, we will never know the truth. We wanted it sorted out in a court. Now, unless Shipman tells all, we are in limbo,' says Joe.

Alice Kitchen was the eighth exhumation and re-burial, and by the time it happened the media were in full cry. Perhaps because of Joe's prominent position in the local community, the police prediction was that theirs would be a particularly difficult re-burial. To avoid the cameras, the police provided all the families with a minibus which picked them up at a rendez-vous away from their homes. In the event, because Shipman was appearing in court for remand on that day, the media presence was not intrusive.

It was an unhappy occasion, though. Father Denis Maher was there, but so, too, was an Anglican priest, and there was some confusion at the graveside over who was taking the re-internment service.

Relations with the police became strained, especially after the family were initially told that morphine had been found, and assumed that there would be a prosecution. When they learned that Shipman was not going to be charged with murdering their mother, they felt let down by a system with which they had done their best to co-operate.

From the police point of view, though, it was important to keep the charges against Shipman as strong as possible. In the cases of Alice Kitchen and the other two whose bodies were exhumed but with whose deaths he was not charged, Sally Ashworth and Elizabeth Mellor, they had been dead for longer and the vital muscle tissue was much more decomposed, making the morphine evidence weaker.

Mrs Ashworth, a 74-year-old company director, died in April 1993, five and a half years before her exhumation. Mrs Mellor had been buried for just over four years. None of the others had been in the ground for more than two and a half years. Like Joe Kitchen and his brothers and sisters, Lizzie Mellor's family are upset that they are left not knowing the full story of her death. Lizzie was a woman who had worked hard all her life, and despite the death of her husband Sam, a bricklayer, six years earlier, she was making the most of her retirement. Sam was a popular figure at some of the local schools, where he would give talks to the children about the 'old days' in Hyde: Lizzie, too, enjoyed reminiscing about life in her youth, when there was a pawn shop in the centre of Hyde, and a stand selling cups of hot Oxo next to the bus station.

Lizzie, who worked most of her life as a cleaner at the

Senior Service cigarette factory, lived for twenty-nine years in one of the upstairs flats in a block of four in Sidley Place. Pride of place on the mantelpiece was a photograph of her son, who died when he was eight years old: she kept fresh flowers next to it, and would often talk about him. Her other child, a daughter, Shirley, is married and Lizzie was very close to her, doting on her two grandchildren.

A year before she died she suffered a stroke. Her close friend and neighbour, Joyce Harrison, popped up from the flat below her and found Lizzie, and immediately contacted Shirley. Before the stroke, Lizzie was very active: despite rheumatism in her feet she would go to the pensioners' club to play bingo and have a meal, and potter round the market in the town centre. Sometimes, with friends, she'd visit a spiritualist, hoping for messages 'from the other side'. She was proud of her appearance, always neatly turned out in a smart jacket, blouse and skirt, with gold earrings and just the slightest trace of make-up. Her clothes were immaculate and so was her flat; if she wasn't going out, she was doing housework or gardening.

When the Harrisons moved in, she asked them if they minded her doing the garden, which was under their front window.

'Every Tuesday, without fail, she'd be in the garden from 9am to tea time, and I'd be bringing her cups of tea,' says Joyce. 'She listened to all the gardening programmes on TV and radio. She loved primulas, they were her favourites, but she also loved the lilac bushes. She would get large-print gardening books from the library, and spend hours on her balcony reading.'

After the stroke her life changed. She was unable to get out at all until a campaign for a handrail alongside the fourteen steps to her flat was launched, backed by her doctor, Fred Shipman. Councillor Joe Kitchen took up the cause and after an article about her, headlined 'Lonely Life of a Frail Widow' in the local paper, the rail was provided. Her daughter Shirley took on all her shopping, washing and prepared her meals, popping in to make breakfast, leave a sandwich for lunch, and returning in the evening to cook a meal.

Joyce Harrison, who was ten years younger than Lizzie but always enjoyed her company, remembers the day of her death, 30 November 1994, very clearly.

'She lived above us and we heard her moving about and running the taps, so we knew she was up,' says Mrs Harrison, who lives with her husband Keith. 'I was sitting in my kitchen with my daughter and granddaughter, when the man from the chemist's came to the door. He said he had a prescription for Lizzie but there was no reply when he knocked, so he left the package with me. At about 1pm I sent my granddaughter Charlotte to see if Lizzie was in.'

Ten-year-old Charlotte got no reply, and later Joyce's daughter Lyndsey also tried. Joyce assumed that Lizzie must have gone to a friend's, as she occasionally did. But when she was not back by four o'clock, and it was dark, Joyce rang Shirley.

'I knew she did not like being out after dark. Shirley and her husband Ken came, and we went up to the flat and Shirley unlocked the door. Lizzie was sitting in a chair, with her glasses on and a book that had fallen down at the side of her legs. God, I can still see her now. Shirley thought she was asleep, but when her husband said she was dead, Shirley ran out screaming.

'Me and my husband came away. I was good friends with Lizzie, but this was a private family matter. I gave Shirley Dr Shipman's number, and he came shortly after. I remember him saying, "What's the matter? She was all right when I left her." I hadn't seen him come that day, but I know now that he was there earlier.

'He came about once a month since her stroke. He had been her husband's doctor, and she was so impressed with him that she changed to be his patient. She knew she was at risk of having another stroke, but she thought that if she could survive a year after the first one she'd be all right. She used to say to me, "If I can just get through to the end of November." But she died on the last day of November.

'I miss her. We got on well. She was a good neighbour and a good friend.'

Sally Ashworth, also a widow, was one of Shipman's wealthiest victims. She was a director and shareholder of J. H. Ashworth & Son Ltd, a long-established textile firm in Hyde, a company with assets of over £1 million and annual profits of more than £400,000. She lived in a £150,000 modern bungalow in Bowlacre Road, Gee Cross, a secluded, tree-lined road where neighbours tend to keep themselves to themselves. A habitual smoker, she was seventy-four when she died. Shipman put heart disease and hypertension on her death certificate. She did not have much social contact with her neighbours, but was a familiar sight locally as she walked her small dog Lucy. Despite her wealth, she drove a small car and dressed inexpensively. As well as the bungalow, she had a seaside home at the upmarket resort of Lytham St Anne's. She had two sons and two daughters; it was to her daughters that she left her entire estate, apart from bequests of £7,000 each to her grandchildren.

Coroner John Pollard formally opened inquests on all the exhumed bodies, and for the three where no charges were initially laid against Shipman – Alice Kitchen, Elizabeth Mellor and Sally Ashworth, the inquests will be resumed after the trial.

In the vestry of St Paul's Roman Catholic church a huge three-foot-high cream-coloured candle from the shrine of

Medjugorje near Mostar, in the former Yugoslavia, has pride of place. Father Denis Maher looks at it every time he puts on his vestments to conduct a service, and every time the sight of the candle reminds him of the unhappiness the town of Hyde has suffered over the past few years. The candle was given to Father Denis by Marie Quinn, after she and a small group of other devout Catholics made a pilgrimage in 1996 to the shrine where it was said that the Virgin Mary appeared to a group of children. By the end of the following year, 67-year-old widow Mrs Quinn had become another of Fred Shipman's victims.

The descriptions given of Mrs Quinn by those who knew her echo the words of friends and acquaintances of both Kathleen Grundy and Winnie Mellor: 'human dynamo', 'always whizzing about', 'busy doing something for somebody', 'always on her way somewhere'. She was not old, she was not ill, she should never have died.

On the day of her death she rang her only son John, thirty-five at the time, in Japan, where he works as an English teacher, and then rang a friend of his, a Roman Catholic priest who also works in Japan. She was cheerful and sounded well. It was early afternoon in England, and evening in Kobe, on the southern coast of the main Japanese island. She also had a chat with a friend the same day: she gave neither her son nor her friend any indication that she felt even slightly off-colour. Yet that evening Dr Shipman arrived at her home in Peel Street, and she died while he was there.

He phoned the undertakers, Frank Massey & Son. Unusually, the Masseys were unable to go within the half-hour they pride themselves on normally attending the scene of a death, and it was after 7pm on a cold, dark, wintry evening before Debbie Massey and her husband David Bambroffe arrived at Mrs Quinn's home. As they pulled up outside, Dr Shipman was also arriving, with his wife Primrose. Primrose was carrying a cat basket, presumably to take Mrs Quinn's cat away, which a neighbour was already looking after.

He told them that he had received a phone call asking him to make a house visit because Mrs Quinn was experiencing pain down her left arm. He said he told her to leave the door on the latch for him, and that when he arrived she was dying, and that nothing could be done to help her. He said that if she had not died then she would have had another stroke.

The Masseys were accustomed to being called by Fred Shipman to the scene of a death: it happened about five times in the last five years he was practising in Hyde. Yet they can hardly remember it ever happening with any other doctor. On two occasions he told them there was nobody in the house with the deceased, and that he would leave the door on the latch for the undertakers to get in.

As with every other investigation, the police carried out an audit trail on Mrs Quinn's phone, and although they found the calls to her son and to her friend, there was no record of a call to The Surgery, nor was the call logged by Shipman's staff. When John Quinn contacted the GP after his mother's death, Shipman said she had rung him to say she had had a stroke and was partially paralysed. He told her to leave the door unlocked for him, and when he got there said he found her 'breathing her last'. In a later discussion with John Quinn, Shipman told him that if his mother had survived she would have been paralysed.

Seven months before Mrs Quinn died, he murdered 58-year-old Jean Lilley, another woman far too young to be bracketed as elderly – tragically, she died just days before the birth of her first grandchild. Unlike many of the others, Mrs Lilley had a genuine medical condition: she suffered from angina. In the week before her death she had a heavy cold and was having breathing difficulties, so before he left at 5am for his lorry-driving job, her husband Albert persuaded her to ring The Surgery and ask for a home visit. Dr Shipman was only too happy to oblige. On the morning of her death, Elizabeth Hunter, who lived in a flat above, had visited Mrs Lilley, and found her in good spirits although full of cold.

The two women often spent the morning together, and Mrs Hunter described her friend as 'full of zest, full of life'. They spent a couple of hours together 'nattering and drinking tea'.

'I left her laughing, we were laughing and joking,' said Mrs Hunter. 'She was looking forward to going shopping with her husband for clothes for her grandchild.'

At lunchtime the neighbour saw Dr Shipman arrive. He was with Mrs Lilley for between forty and fifty minutes, and she became concerned. She called around to see if her friend was all right, seeing Shipman as he left.

'I went into Jean's flat. We had a signal for each other: we always shouted, "It's only me, missus." I didn't get a response.'

She found Mrs Lilley on the couch, not only dead, but cold, with a blue tinge appearing around her lips. She tried giving resuscitation, and then called an ambulance. The crew pronounced Mrs Lilley dead, and said she seemed to have been dead for some time. When Shipman reappeared Mrs Hunter accosted him, accusing him of knowing that Jean Lilley was already dead when he left her flat. He denied it. He told Albert Lilley, when he phoned him at work, that when he saw his wife she was very poorly but had refused to go to hospital – yet another of Dr Shipman's patients who, according to him, rejected hospital care.

His treatment of Elizabeth Hunter was brusque – he told her it was no good crying, because Mrs Lilley was dead. He seemed inexplicably concerned about the Lilleys' pregnant daughter, Odette, coming to the flat while he was there; both the paramedics who attended the scene remember him becoming agitated at the mention of Odette, and being remarkably unsympathetic towards her when she arrived.

Mrs Lilley's death was in one way an anomaly: she was not a widow, or a spinster, or a divorcée living on her own. Her husband Albert was at work when she died and heard about her death in the phone call from Dr Shipman – a 'bizarre and circuitous' conversation, it was later described at the doctor's trial. Shipman told Albert Lilley that he had been with his wife for quite a while, trying to convince her to go to hospital, but she had refused because Mr Lilley was not home. He went on to say that he would return that evening when Mr Lilley was home, but that it was 'too late'. It was only with those two words that Albert Lilley began to take in what was being said.

'I asked, "What do you mean?" He said, "You're not listening carefully, you don't understand." Then it clicked and I said, "Why – has she died?" I put the phone down and came home. I couldn't believe it.'

Irene Turner, who died nine months before Jean Lilley, was, more typically, a widow. She was only sixty-seven years old, the widow of an insurance broker, who had worked before retirement as a secretary. She was a smartly dressed, active, cheerful woman who coped well with being diabetic. In the week leading up to her death on Thursday 11 July 1996, she was suffering from a cold, and feeling sufficiently under the weather to ask for Dr Shipman to visit her at home – although she was well enough to have a cheerful phone conversation with a friend. At 1pm her son-in-law called round, and although she was in bed she was in good spirits and gave him a list of shopping to collect.

Shipman turned up at 3.15. After visiting Mrs Turner he called on a neighbour and asked her if she would help

Mrs Turner pack some things as she was going into hospital. He told her not to go immediately, but in about five minutes. He said he had to go somewhere to carry out some tests, and drove off.

The neighbour, Sheila Ward, went to Mrs Turner's home and found her lying on the bed, dead. Shortly afterwards, Shipman returned, confirmed the death, and said that it would have been too late for the hospital to have saved her, and added that the diabetes 'was all through her body'. He was holding and studying a sheaf of papers, which Sheila Ward assumed were the test results.

But when Mrs Turner's son-in-law arrived later, Shipman contradicted himself, saying, once again, that she had refused to go into hospital – despite having told Mrs Ward that he had arranged a bed for her.

As usual, he told the family there was no need for a post-mortem. He put heart disease and circulatory failure as the main causes of her death. When a post-mortem was eventually carried out after her body was exhumed, there was some evidence of heart disease, but there were also massive levels of morphine in her body. There was also no record of Shipman ringing a hospital to organise a bed for Mrs Turner.

Muriel Grimshaw was murdered in July 1997, a year before Shipman's killing spree ended. The widow of an office clerk, 76-year-old Mrs Grimshaw was a proud, smart woman, whose hair was always immaculately set. She lived in a small, one-bedroomed ground-floor flat, keeping herself to herself apart from a close friendship with her next-door neighbour, Barbara Ryan. The two would go shopping together, and on trips out. Mrs Grimshaw was a regular member of the congregation at Holy Trinity Church, Gee Cross, although she was not actively involved in any of the church's social activities.

Her son-in-law, Laurie Brown, is reconciled to seeing

his name in headlines: he is the former physiotherapist to Manchester United Football Club, whose first wife Mary left him in the full glare of the public spotlight when she moved in with (and subsequently married) soccer boss Tommy Docherty. After the break-up, Laurie Brown also remarried, to Mrs Grimshaw's daughter Anne.

Anne was her only child, and close to her mother. They had been to church together the day before her death, and made arrangements to go out for lunch three days later. No problems with her health were mentioned, and Anne left her mother cheerful and happy.

It was Anne who found her mother dead, after a phone call from Mrs Ryan, who had called at 9am for the usual shopping trip they made together but failed to rouse Mrs Grimshaw by knocking or shouting through the letter-box. She went home and tried to telephone her, and when there was no reply she rang Anne. When Mrs Grimshaw's daughter let herself into the flat, she found the doors open, the curtains pulled back, the television switched on and her mother laying fully clothed on the bed, as if asleep. She had died the previous day.

Shipman arrived twenty minutes later, after a call to his surgery. He had with him a young woman, dressed in white overalls and white shoes, whom Anne Brown assumed was a nurse – although she has never been traced, the police believe she was a trainee nurse assigned to The Surgery.

According to the death certificate supplied by Dr Shipman, Mrs Grimshaw had suffered a stroke: her perfect composure made this, with hindsight, an unlikely cause of death, as stroke victims are usually contorted by spasms immediately prior to death. When the computer records at The Surgery were examined, there was evidence on the hard drive that Shipman had inserted an entry for the day before, to create the impression that she was at risk of having a stroke, but he did not tell her daughter about this visit to her. Nor, even more surprisingly, had Mrs Grimshaw herself rung her daughter to discuss the doctor's visit. There was no corroboration of this visit from The Surgery diary, there were other falsified entries, and the death certificate had been altered from 15 to 14 July.

There was one more exhumation that Greater Manchester Police wanted to carry out, another death they wanted to add to the list of charges Shipman faced. But they failed: the victim was buried in Malta, and because of a legal anomaly they were unable to get permission to exhume her. In Britain Marie Fernley's next of kin were her children, and they were as keen as the police for the exhumation to go ahead and the truth of their mother's death to be revealed. But under Maltese law her mother and brothers and sisters were her next of kin, and they refused to give permission for the grave to be opened. In Britain the coroner's warrant would override any relatives' objections, but in Malta the Manchester police would have had to go to court to establish a right to retrieve the body, which would have been time-consuming and costly. In the end, reluctantly, they decided to leave the case of Mrs Fernley on file, along with the many others that they could not investigate fully.

Marie Fernley was one of the younger victims – she was only fifty-three at the time of her death, an attractive, dark-haired woman who had two daughters. She lived in a small, one-bedroomed upstairs flat in a complex for single and elderly people in Darwin Street, and mixed well with her neighbours. She joined a residents' club and went on coach trips to Southport, Morecambe, Knutsford and Etherow Country Park in Stockport.

She was Maltese by birth, but had come to England when she married, and had run a hardware shop with her husband in Royton, near Oldham, and also worked as a secretary. When they separated she returned to Malta, but felt that her roots were in England, with her daughters. She moved in with her daughter Julia Gregg, Julia's husband Mel and two children, Christopher and Samantha, in Denton, until she got the council flat just a couple of miles away. She had another granddaughter, Chantelle, who is her daughter Loretta's child. They live in Cambridge.

The grandchildren were the centre of Marie's world, and the other residents at the complex were used to seeing Christopher and Samantha with their grandmother. She also doted on her cat and her two budgerigars. She is remembered as an active, busy woman, always ready to help others. When she was not physically on the go, she read: 'She always had a book in her hand,' said one neighbour.

Three days before her death she came home from Tameside Hospital, having spent a few days there having her blood pressure monitored. She was not feeling well, and for the first day and a half her daughter Julia stayed with her. But the following day, a Sunday, Julia's husband was due home from Spain, and so Marie's best friend, Doreen Armitage, said she would look after her.

'She told me the hospital said she had to look after her diet, and if she did that she would be fine. We joked about all the things she was not allowed to eat. She was quite weak, and stayed in her nightie and dressing-gown because she kept taking naps. I took her Sunday lunch and we had a good laugh about whether everything I had cooked was on her diet sheet. I spent the evening with her talking about Malta: she said she wanted to show me all the beautiful places there, and that we should go on holiday there together in November. She said she had enjoyed the evening so much it felt like she had been back to Malta for a short trip. She was a real daddy's girl: she was very upset when her father died about two years before she did, because she thought the world of him.

'The next day I called in at 9.30am. I was going shopping with my husband, and wanted to know if she needed anything. She said she'd love some fresh strawberries – I told her she'd be lucky, as they were out of season in March. We didn't find any.

'I went back to see her about 4.15pm. I let myself in and I always shouted, "Marie, it's only me, Doreen." She would usually say "Come up" but there was no sound, so I crept upstairs in case she was asleep. She was lying on her bed, in her nightie and her flowery dressing-gown, propped up on a pillow. She had a book on her lap with a pencil on top of it. I thought she had dropped off, so I went to the kitchen to tidy up.

'When I went back into the bedroom she hadn't moved, and she looked so still that I thought something must be wrong. I went over and touched her hair, saying her name over and over, but she didn't move. I felt for a pulse in her neck, but I couldn't find it. I went downstairs and called my husband Frank, and he came up. He said, "I'm sorry, love, I think she's gone."

'She wasn't cold; she can't have been dead long. I can't help thinking that if only I had gone to check on her as soon as I got back, instead of putting my own shopping away first, things might be different.

'I knew the doctor had been because there was a prescription on the side on a chest of drawers. I think there was a note that said he had given her a blood-pressure tablet and that she had to have another one later. She hadn't seemed that poorly – it was all a shock. I rang the doctor and her daughter. Julia was so distressed that Dr Shipman had to give her a sedative to calm her down.'

After her death, her body was flown to Malta for a funeral service at the Sacro Cuor Church, where her family worshipped, in Silema. She was buried at the Santa Maria Addolerata Cemetery. The police were planning to bring the body back to England – they worked out that it would be cheaper to do that than to fly the pathologist out there and hire a mortuary. In October 1998 two detectives, DCI Williams and WPC Jackie King, flew out to liaise with their Maltese counterparts, but their plans were scotched by Marie's brother, Alfred Falzon, who objected to the exhumation, saying it would 'desecrate' the family grave, leaving her relatives in Britain feeling sad and disappointed that they would never know the cause of her death.

Her neighbours and friends at the complex of small flats where she lived have the cards, made for her funeral, to remember her by: a photograph of the dark-haired, smiling woman they knew, and a quotation from St Ambrose: 'We have loved her in life, let us not forget her in death.'

Ten days after he was arrested, Shipman's lawyers applied to a judge in chambers at Manchester Crown Court for bail. They produced a list of friends who were prepared to put up substantial sums of money as surety, including the Shipmans' close friends Robert and Jayne Stokes (Primrose's partner in the 'Jayne and Prim' sandwich shop), who offered £16,000; the family's GP, Wally Ashworth, who offered £25,000; and Bill Walsh, a self-employed carpet fitter, who offered £16,000.

Primrose orchestrated the bail offers, ringing round their friends asking for volunteers. There was no shortage, as the charges had come so unexpectedly and there was, at the time, such strong support for Fred Shipman among his friends and patients. There was a meeting at the solicitor's office, with Primrose and all four of the Shipman children present. Despite the bail offers, the judge had no doubt that he should remain in custody. The police were relieved, but not surprised – they never expected him to be granted bail, in the light of the evidence they were accumulating.

In the first week of his arrest they downloaded everything from his surgery computer system. There were
seven computers at The Surgery, one of them an independent machine and the other six what computer buffs
call 'a master with five slaves', in other words one system
with five extra terminals that could log on to it. The practice had been computerised since 1993, with medical
records pre-dating that kept in the traditional brown enve-
lope folders that doctors use, known as Lloyd George
folders. The computer system had been updated in 1996,
a fact that Shipman lived to regret, because under the
old system it would have been impossible to trace the
dates and times that he made the false entries. The software program he used, Microdoc, was designed
specifically for GPs. After his arrest, the hard drive
revealed its treasure, allowing Detective Sergeant Ashley
to see exactly when extra entries had been made on
records, and dates changed.

It was this evidence, which Shipman had not anticipated the police ever finding simply because he himself
did not realise it existed, which brought him closest to
breakdown in the months of imprisonment before his
trial. When he was charged with the murders of Joan
Melia, Winifred Mellor and Bianka Pomfret on 5 October
he said nothing, but when the police began to interrogate
him about the computer entries, he collapsed on the
floor, sobbing and gibbering.

Ann Ball, his solicitor, intervened and a doctor who
was summoned by the police agreed with her that the
interview should be suspended because he was 'in a distressed and emotional state and unfit for interview'. The
more cynical among the police believe it was a calculated
ploy to give himself time to think: he had discovered that
the police knew far more than he expected, and he was
stalling in order to work out how to handle it. Others
believe he was genuinely broken down by the realisation

that he was not only going to stand trial for Mrs Grundy's murder, but at least three more, and that the evidence against him was more than just the morphine levels found in the bodies.

It was not the first time he had played for time. At his initial formal encounter with the detectives, when he was charged with the murder of Mrs Grundy plus fraud and forgery charges, he demanded time to discuss what the caution meant with his solicitors, which gave him a twenty-five-minute breathing space to assemble his thoughts. He also demanded an adjournment when he was going through his curriculum vitae with the police, and when they reconvened he refused to answer any more questions about his background. Significantly, at this point the police knew nothing about his previous forgery conviction from his Todmorden days, and he naïvely thought that by refusing to give any more information he could prevent them finding out. Similarly, he refused them permission to look at his own personal medical records.

But on that first day of interviews he was cool and calm, even though the questioning lasted for about six hours. He appeared to be well rehearsed. He was anxious for the police to examine Mrs Grundy's medical records, confident that his forgeries would not be detected. He told the police that he did not have to keep a controlled-drugs register because he did not keep drugs in his surgery.

But the computer evidence shattered his composure. After a reprieve for the rest of the day on which he had his 'breakdown', a prison doctor at Walton Prison in Liverpool, where he was being held, felt that he was fit to be questioned again the following day. There were two teams of police interrogators, one DS Mark Wareing with DC Marie Snitynski and the other DS John Walker and DC Mark Denham. The detective constables were chosen deliberately: 'Shipman would have liked to be interviewed by the Chief Constable,' says Bernard Postles. 'He didn't like taking questions from a DC, let alone from a woman. He had an air of arrogance about him. He knew best – he felt intellectually superior.'

All the interviews were audible in an adjoining room, where the senior officers listened in. When Shipman was told that the police had enough evidence from Winnie Mellor's computer records alone, regardless of the morphine, to charge him, he was, according to Postles, 'floundering'.

'I believe he was on the verge of confessing,' he says.

'It's the moment a detective dreams of,' says DCI Williams. 'You have the victim in front of you and then – wallop. You produce the piece of evidence that floors him.'

Once again the solicitor insisted the interview be stopped, and Shipman was taken to a cell where he flopped on the bed and held his head in his hands.

The following day, Wednesday 7 October, he cried again, at Tameside Magistrates' Court when he was formally charged with the three murders. He appeared looking pale and drawn, wearing a navy blue round-necked sweater and flanked by two Group 4 security guards. He shook his head and swayed from side to side, sobbing, throughout the fifteen-minute hearing, and had to be helped from the dock by the guards.

Back in prison, he was put on 'suicide watch', with officers checking on him every few hours. His original prison home, Strangeways, had proved temporarily too dangerous: other prisoners are never happy about those who are charged with harming children or old people ('After all, everybody's got a mum,' as one Strangeways prisoner said).

His police interrogators were seeing a different side to Fred Shipman. At the initial interviews, after the death of

Mrs Grundy, he was arrogant, rude and unhelpful. He even managed to suggest that Stan Egerton, renowned among his men for having the voice of a sergeant major, was talking too softly for him to hear – guaranteeing that in all future encounters with Stan Egerton he would be addressed at a decibel level that made him recoil. He would answer facetiously (although without great wit). For example, when asked if anyone apart from his wife and youngest son lived with him at the house in Roe Cross Green, he once replied, 'The cat.' He would object to the standard procedures the police are compelled to follow, like asking him his name at the start of an interview – 'You know my name.' And he could be downright insulting, once describing the blunt Stan Egerton as 'stupid' – a serious miscalculation ('stupid' is one of Shipman's worst terms of abuse for anybody: he has since described the prison staff as stupid, and it was always the accusation he levelled at any member of staff he chose to bully).

But it did not take long, after his 'breakdown', for him to recover this arrogance and confidence, at least in public. Three days after sobbing in front of Tameside Magistrates' Court when he first faced charges over the deaths of Mrs Melia, Mrs Mellor and Mrs Pomfret, he was in court again for a further committal on the charges relating to Mrs Grundy, and this time he was calm and composed, and he winked and smiled at Primrose in the public gallery.

From then on, the police did not interview him further. 'There was no point dragging him from prison to find him a gibbering wreck,' says Postles.

At each fresh batch of charges, he was given the chance to reply, but he gave a set response: 'I treated them appropriately for their medical condition at the time.'

Dr Richard Badcock, a psychiatrist from Wakefield, was brought in to examine him at length, and was satisfied that he understood what was happening to him.

From the beginning of the police interviews, Shipman was suspicious of his interrogators, behaving on one hand in an arrogant, contemptuous way, and on the other being paranoid about his own safety. He refused to eat any food supplied to him by the police, bringing his own apples along to the interviews. He would drink tea and coffee only because he knew it came out of a machine which was used by everybody else at Ashton Police Station.

What was he afraid of? For someone who had killed so many people so easily, perhaps it was not surprising that he was paranoid about being poisoned. But did he, the man who called other people stupid, really believe that the senior ranks of Greater Manchester Police were conspiring to murder him?

# 12
# Ashes to Ashes

When Tony Nuttall arrived home at 2pm on a cold Monday afternoon in January 1998 from his shift as a council workman, his mum Norah had not had time to go shopping for anything for his tea. She'd had a persistent cough all weekend, and had spent the morning queuing to see her doctor, Fred Shipman. It was an open surgery, so she did not need an appointment, but it meant that it had taken a couple of hours. She'd returned home before lunchtime to the house in Baron Road, Gee Cross, she shared with Tony, with a bottle of medicine and instructions from the doctor to stay inside for a couple of days. She rang a friend for a chat, and said she was under the weather, but certainly did not sound critically ill. When her son got home she was cheerful.

Tony told her not to worry about the meal, as he would go up to the field to feed his horse, and would later pop to the fish and chip shop to get them both some supper. It was the last time he spoke to her. When he came back from attending to the horse, Dr Shipman was at the open front door, and he told Tony: 'She's not well. She's got chest pains. I've phoned for an ambulance.'

Tony went past him into the house, unable to believe

that his 64-year-old mum, who had been chatting to him just half an hour before, could have become ill enough to need to go to hospital in that short time. He saw her, slumped in a chair, as if asleep. He knelt in front of her, gently shaking her hands to wake her.

'Oh, she seems to have taken a turn for the worse,' said the doctor.

Checking her pulse, he turned to Tony and announced that his mother was dead. The doctor went to the phone, saying that he was ringing to tell the ambulance service they would not be needed. Tony heard him saying words to this effect.

The ambulance service, who meticulously log calls, have no record of either the summons or the cancellation of an ambulance by Shipman. Nor have detectives been able to trace any call from Mrs Nuttall summoning the doctor: she had not booked a home visit when she was at The Surgery, nor had she told her friend or her son that she was expecting the doctor. There is no record of a home visit in the practice diary. But Shipman told Tony that he had been driving in the area when he got a call saying he should get to Mrs Nuttall as soon as possible.

Even more distressing for Tony was the fact that the doctor did nothing to revive his mother. If, as Shipman suggested, she had died in the brief moments that they were talking on the doorstep, then surely it would have been possible to do something for her?

Norah Nuttall was a big woman, clinically obese despite successfully losing eight stone a few years previously with the help of a hospital dietician. She was well known in Gee Cross: her father, Walter Mansfield, used to be landlord of The Hare & Hounds pub at Werneth Low, a local beauty spot. For years Norah worked in the pub, and was a popular figure behind the bar – much friendlier than her father, who was renowned for the notices all over the bar: No Kissing, No Holding Hands,

No Potato Chips to Be Eaten on These Premises.

She was, in the words of a neighbour, 'a real country lass' – at her funeral, the local farming community packed out Hyde Chapel. She loved dogs and horses, and passed her love of country life on to Tony. He was upset by the police investigation into her death, and talked about it to his friend Frank Arrowsmith; at the time of their conversation, Frank had no idea that his own mother, Winnie, would also become entangled in the investigation.

On the day she died, Fred Shipman updated Norah Nuttall's medical records to say that she had 'wheezy bronchitis'. Because of her size, her history of high blood pressure and heart disease, her health was undoubtedly at risk, and with the added complication of a chest complaint it would have been feasible for her to have had a heart attack at any time. When an independent doctor was invited by Greater Manchester Police to look at Shipman's medical records he concluded that Mrs Nuttall's death was consistent with her medical history: in other words, at face value, it appeared to be a natural death.

Unlike the other cases, where the bodies were exhumed and the pathologist and toxicologist could find the real reasons for the death, Mrs Nuttall's body was cremated. There will never be any way of proving from forensic tests whether or not she was murdered with an injection of morphine.

So it was a significant moment for the police – and for Fred Shipman – when he was charged on 22 February 1998 with the murder of Mrs Nuttall and five other women whose bodies had also been cremated, just thirteen months after Norah Nuttall's death.

The decision to charge him with some cases where the bodies were not available for post-mortems was made by the Crown Prosecution Service, who persuaded the police that it was important not to limit the case to the more easily-provable burial victims.

In other words, they wanted to establish beyond challenge, in court, that Shipman was an indiscriminate killer, and careless enough to be convicted not just on indisputable forensic science but also on circumstantial evidence. The police had known, from their first involvement with Mrs Grundy's death, that most of Shipman's victims had been cremated: in his crude forgery of Mrs Grundy's will he had elected for her body to be cremated. As 70 per cent of all deaths in Britain result in a cremation, it was always logical to assume that at least this percentage of his victims were reduced to ashes, taking with them into the furnace the evidence of the final, fatal morphine injection.

Initially, though, they assumed they would never get enough evidence to convict in the cases where there was no body. Being buried scored a point on their original five-point assessment of which deaths they would investigate. But that did not mean they did not keep evidence on the cremation cases they came across, and they soon found they were unearthing computer evidence of records being tampered with for these victims as well as those who were buried.

It was this, the computer evidence, that prompted the prosecution service to push for the inclusion of cremation victims in the list of charges against Shipman. As a result, six of the fifteen murder charges he faced initially were of women whose bodies were no longer around for analysis. Nor was it only computer evidence that the prosecution could rely on: they also had the damning telephone records, where he claimed he had been summoned to visit his victims by calls to the surgery, or claimed to have requested ambulances, and yet no trace of these calls could be found. There was also another, very powerful, strand of evidence – the testimony of witnesses who saw him at the scene of death, and who had conversations with him in which he contradicted what he had said to others.

There was such a solid body of evidence against him that the prosecution barrister, Richard Henriques QC, told one of the police officers involved in the case that in all his long and distinguished career he would have loved it if every case he was asked to prosecute was as strong as any single one of the Shipman charges – let alone the added strength of there being so many of them, with a well-established pattern running through them.

There was another advantage to charging Shipman with cases where the bodies had been cremated: the lack of good forensic evidence in the cases of Mrs Kitchen, Mrs Ashworth and Mrs Mellor, whose bodies were exhumed but with whose murders he was not charged, demonstrated that it was not possible to go back more than two years with the exhumation charges; further back than that, and the remains tended not to be in good enough condition for adequate evidence of morphine poisoning.

With cremation charges, which did not depend on the existence of bodies, it was possible to go back further, and establish that Fred Shipman had been murdering innocent victims for many years.

Marie West was killed in March 1995, the earliest of any of the deaths that Shipman was charged with. Mrs West, who was christened Maria but always known as Marie, was a widow of eighty-one, and for two weeks before her death she was having regular visits at home from Dr Shipman because she had pains in her legs: she had had both her hip joints replaced twenty years earlier. She also had breathing problems and used an inhaler.

She was well known in the Gee Cross area of Hyde because, while her motor-mechanic husband John was alive, she ran a children's clothing shop. She lived in a pretty £80,000 terraced house, with the nameplate 'Marie's Cottage', in Knott Fold, in the smart Dowson Road area of the town. Despite her age and the pain from her legs, neighbours described her as 'bright and bubbly', always with time for a chat. She loved travelling, and before her hip problems used to visit different parts of Britain every year. Five years before her death she went on a *QE2* cruise to New York, flying back on Concorde: it was the realisation of a long ambition, and she was thrilled by the whole experience.

On the day of her death she was expecting a visit from Dr Shipman. He had seen her three times in the previous eight days, because the medication he prescribed for her pain was making her feel unwell. Four days before her death he wrote in his surgery diary: 'Pains in the hip, no better, can't sit.' Unlike many of Shipman's entries made after the death of a patient, this one genuinely summed up Mrs West's condition.

Early in the afternoon of the day she died, her friend Maria Hadfield called round to see her, and Mrs West explained that she was waiting for the doctor. The two women watched TV together, and had tea and cakes. Mrs West was well enough to make the tea. Then Mrs Hadfield was getting ready to go, and went upstairs to the bathroom. The stairs to the bathroom led off the kitchen, and when she came down Mrs Hadfield could hear a man's voice, so assumed that the doctor was with Mrs West. Rather than disturb the consultation, she waited in the kitchen.

After several minutes there was silence. Everything stayed quiet for a few more minutes, and then Dr Shipman walked into the kitchen. He was startled and confused when he saw Mrs Hadfield and said ingenuously, 'Oh, I didn't know there was anyone else here.' He said he was going upstairs to see if Mrs West's son was there, but he neither went up nor called up (and he gave no explanation as to why Mrs West's son, who did not live with her, would be upstairs in the middle of the afternoon).

After a brief pause he seemed to regain his equilibrium, and said calmly to Mrs Hadfield, 'She's collapsed on me.' Mrs Hadfield asked if he could do anything, and he replied, 'No, she's gone.' He made no attempt to resuscitate Mrs West, nor to call the emergency services.

As Mrs Hadfield followed him into the living room she saw her friend in the same chair she had been sitting in all afternoon, but her normally animated face was now resting on her shoulder and her eyes were closed. Shipman went across and lifted the lids, saying, 'See, there's no life there.'

He then said to Mrs Hadfield that he had been expecting this: 'But not so soon. She did have hardening of the arteries, you know.'

He did not ask for a post-mortem, and when he filled in the death certificate he put the cause of death as a cerebro-vascular accident (a stroke) and arteriosclerosis (hardening of the arteries).

When he later spoke to Mrs West's son Christopher he gave a different account of her death. He said that he had turned away from Mrs West to put his things back in his case, and then taken the bag outside to put it in the car. On his return he found she had had a massive stroke and had collapsed. He told Christopher West that he had taken his mother's blood pressure, but no record of the reading was found.

One of the standard questions on the cremation form is: 'Have you any reason to suspect that the death of the deceased was due, directly or indirectly, to a) violence; b) poison; c) privation or neglect?' It is unlikely Fred Shipman ever paused for even a second before filling in 'No' on all the many cremation forms he made out over the years. On Mrs West's, at the section on who was present at the death, he wrote: 'Myself and a neighbour.'

Mrs West's medical records were among those found in a Kleenex box at the Shipman home, in Roe Cross Green. When they were examined by Dr John Grenville, the GP who gave evidence for the prosecution, he observed that they were 'less than detailed' and that he would have expected the blood-pressure measurement, if taken, to have been recorded. He also said that death from a stroke would not have been silent, that there would have been muscle stiffening and that Mrs West would have collapsed on the floor. While she was dying, he would have expected the doctor to have tried to resuscitate her, and to have called for an ambulance.

Lizzie Adams enjoyed life. She may have been seventy-seven years old, but as far as she was concerned, getting old was no excuse for slowing down. The retired machinist taught dancing regularly, with her good friend and dancing partner Bill Catlow, until six months before her seventy-seventh birthday. She and Bill had known each other for years, and after the death of his wife and her husband they decided to give dancing classes together, and were still dancing regularly at the time of her death.

'She was a very lively and intelligent person, proud of her appearance. Because of the dancing classes, she was well known locally, and well liked,' says Bill, a retired driver.

Lizzie was well qualified as a dance teacher, and she and Bill gave lessons at evening classes in local community centres and church halls, including the community centre at Hattersley and the British Legion in Hyde.

'Her main interests were dancing and travel,' says Bill. 'She was a great dancer, with a lovely, light step. I danced with her twice a day, every day. She could dance as well as any youngster. And she was well travelled: she had been to China, Australia, the USA and the Caribbean.'

Lizzie and Bill had just returned from a holiday with an

Over 50s group to Malta at the time of her death. She had mild diabetes, the type that comes on later in life and can be controlled by eating a wholefood diet, and she was prone to chest infections, but she was rarely seriously ill.

Perhaps it was the contrast in the climate, from the mild temperatures in Malta to the bitter February weather back home, but the day after she got back from holiday she began to feel unwell. Both her daughters, Sonia and Doreen, visited her, and although she told them she wasn't on top form, she was in good spirits and neither of them felt there was anything seriously wrong. On the day before her death, Doreen collected a prescription for antibiotics which she had obtained by phone from The Surgery, and afterwards they went to Stockport, spending two and a half hours shopping.

The next day, Friday 28 February 1997, Doreen rang her mother. The phone rang longer than usual: Lizzie was out in the garden hanging out the washing. She did all her own laundry, without a washing machine. She told her daughter that the tablets Dr Shipman had given her did not agree with her – although he knew she was allergic to penicillin, he had prescribed Cephalexin, a penicillin-related antibiotic (10 per cent of all people who are allergic to penicillin will react badly to Cephalexin). Lizzie said she felt they 'nearly blew her head off'. Doreen advised her to get a different prescription. At 12.10 she rang The Surgery and reported her symptoms (green phlegm, irregular pulse and chest infection) to receptionist Alison Massey, who wrote them down and arranged for Dr Shipman to visit Mrs Adams at home. It was not, according to the receptionist, an urgent visit.

Less than two hours later, at 2pm, Bill Catlow arrived at Mrs Adams' home and found the front door open: unusual, because he knew his friend Lizzie was normally very security-conscious. Walking in, he encountered Dr Shipman, who was admiring Lizzie's treasured collection of Royal Doulton figurines and cut glass, displayed in a china cabinet. The GP was alone in the room.

'Are you Bill?' he asked, and then told Bill Catlow that Mrs Adams was very ill, and that he had ordered an ambulance. Alarmed, Bill ran through to the living room where he saw Lizzie in a chair. He held her hand, which was warm, but she did not respond when he spoke to her.

Shipman said, 'She's gone. I'd better cancel the ambulance.'

Bill challenged him: 'Are you sure? She's warm. She looks as if she's asleep.'

Shipman talked into the phone, with Bill Catlow assuming he was cancelling the ambulance – in fact, he had never called for one in the first place.

Just after 2.30 Shipman called Mrs Adams' son-in-law, Doreen's husband, to say that Mrs Adams was very ill and that he was sending her to hospital. Doreen, who had started work at 1pm, rang and was told by Shipman that her mother had pneumonia: she dashed round, running all the way, to find her mother peacefully stretched out in her armchair, legs crossed and mouth open, as if she was asleep. Her top button was still fastened, despite Shipman describing her as fighting for breath when he arrived.

As Doreen sobbed and struggled to accept the fact of her mother's death, the doctor said: 'You should come and see old people more often.'

'It was as if I hadn't seen her for a while and she had been very ill,' said Doreen. 'I told him, "Well, I saw her yesterday, and we were walking around Stockport." He didn't say anything.'

Shipman then addressed her in an abrupt and patronising way, prefacing his remarks with, 'You've got to just sit down and listen to me, I have got to know that you know what I am saying.' He said that her mum had died from chronic pneumonia, and that a post-mortem was not needed because he had been there at the time of death. He told her to contact the funeral directors, and to call at his surgery the next day for the death certificate.

Doreen and her sister Sonia were not only saddened but also astonished at their mother's death. Doreen had been chatting to her on the phone earlier, and felt sure that her mother would have rung her if she had suddenly felt unwell. She had been doing the washing, the ironing board was set up ready to use, there were pans on the cooker as if she was going to prepare a meal: none of it was consistent with Shipman's description, given to Sonia the next day when she went to The Surgery to ask him about her mother's death, of Lizzie Adams being so ill that she could barely get to the door to let him in, and that he had to help her back to her chair.

He told Sonia that he could see there was no air getting into her lungs, and went on to say that some people walk around with pneumonia without knowing it for weeks. He said that Mrs Adams had been struggling to breathe, but that she looked peaceful and had colour in her face. Sonia accepted it when he told her it was not necessary to have a post-mortem.

In fact, according to Dr Grenville, if she had died through lack of oxygen she would have been distressed, not peaceful. Lizzie Adams' medical records were among others found in a Tesco carrier bag in the garage of Shipman's home, and when the computer records on her were examined there were two entries, made within a minute of each other, one registering her as very poorly and needing to be admitted to hospital, the other record-ing her death. They were both made the day after her death.

There are quite a few women in Hyde who believe they may have been 'the one that got away'. There is a woman who saw Shipman just before going on holiday, and he told her he would call on her when she returned and 'try out a new medication'. There is another who was told to stop taking the medication prescribed for her by a previous doctor, and who discovered after Shipman's arrest that she should never have been taken off it. There are others who tell tales of his frequent home visits, one who tells of his efforts to persuade her to liquidise the assets of her home, of his excessive interest in their financial affairs.

But among them all, there is perhaps one who really might be classified as the one that got away: Mrs Ann Royle. Tragically, her possible reprieve may have been at the expense of another much-loved local woman, Kathleen Wagstaff.

Ann Royle wanted to thank her GP and his staff for all the care and attention they gave to her. The 74-year-old widow knew from her years of running a busy chemist's shop with her pharmacist husband just how off-hand and overworked many family doctors are, so she was determined to show her appreciation for everyone at The Surgery, where looking after patients seemed to be top priority for the doctor and all his staff.

On 9 December 1997 Ann, who moved to Hyde to be near her daughter after her husband died, took a bottle of gin for Dr Shipman and some wine for his staff to the reception desk at The Surgery – Christmas presents donated early so that the staff could enjoy them.

Shipman was, as usual, busy with a long list of patients, but he said hello to Mrs Royle. That afternoon, to Ann's astonishment, her daughter Angela turned up at her door in Baron Street, Gee Cross, almost hysterical.

'You're alive, you're alive,' she kept repeating. 'Dr Shipman just told me you were dead.'

Shipman had driven up to the school where Angela is a teacher, Dowson Primary School, and she was called from her class to see him.

'I hope it's not bad news,' said Angela, whose whole

family was registered with him.

'I'm afraid it is. Your mother is dead,' he said. He told Angela her mother had called The Surgery, and that he had received a message to visit her. He was already in the locality, but she had then had a coronary and died quietly and painlessly. He told Angela to meet him at her mother's home, but when Angela and a friend, another teacher from the school, arrived at Mrs Royle's house there was no sign of him. Frantically ringing the bell, Angela bent to look through the letterbox – and became almost hysterical when she saw her mother walking along the hall to open the door.

Mrs Royle said she had not seen Shipman since she dropped the Christmas presents off at The Surgery earlier that day.

Confused, Angela soon discovered that it was, in fact, her mother-in-law, not her mother, who had died. Her husband Peter's mother, 81-year-old Kath Wagstaff, was 'found dead' at her home, a first-floor flat in Rock Gardens just one street away from Ann Royle's address.

Mrs Wagstaff, the widow of a retired garage manager, had been well enough that morning to have a chat with gardener Andrew Hallas, who was working on the communal gardens, offer him a cup of tea and to have gone out at midday to the Bradford & Bingley building society. At 2pm both the gardener and Mrs Wagstaff's neighbour, Margaret Walker, saw a man arrive and Mrs Walker heard Mrs Wagstaff say, 'Fancy seeing you here,' as if she was both surprised and pleased to see him.

He went inside her flat, and when Mrs Walker returned from shopping she was told by her husband Donald that Mrs Wagstaff was dead: the man who called, Dr Shipman, had knocked at the Walkers' door and told Donald that he had been to see her and that she was dead.

He told Mr Walker that he had called an ambulance,

but had cancelled it: Greater Manchester Ambulance Service have no record of either call.

For Angela Wagstaff, there was a short-lived relief when she realised her own mother was not dead, superceded by the grief of discovering that the deceased was her mother-in-law. She and Peter, a company director who has lived in Hyde all his life, went to see Shipman to discuss Mrs Wagstaff's death, and he told them that when he arrived at her flat her pulse was erratic, and that he called for an ambulance, then went to get his bag. On his return she was dead. He told them that she had heart disease, which came as a surprise as she had never mentioned it.

Shipman also told them that Mrs Wagstaff had phoned the surgery asking for a home visit and that he had been paged by the reception staff. There is no record of her calling the surgery, nor does the receptionist remember paging him. On the death certificate he recorded that he and a neighbour had been present at the death. This neighbour, too, has never been found.

At the time, though, Peter and Angela Wagstaff, and Peter's brother John, accepted the doctor's version of events. Peter and Angela had always been very satisfied with their GP – he had turned out on a bank holiday to treat their daughter when she came back from abroad with a nasty skin infection. Angela's mother Ann had twice gone to him with health problems, once with an ovarian cyst and another time with a duodenal ulcer, both of which he had diagnosed before sending her on to the right specialist for treatment.

In fact, when the first news of the suspicions about Kathleen Grundy's death came to light, Angela, whose pupils have included the Shipman's oldest child, Sarah, phoned the *Manchester Evening News* complaining that Dr Shipman was the victim of a witch-hunt. She was one of the many people in Hyde who took flowers and cards to The Surgery after his arrest.

She knew his wife Primrose: having teenage children of roughly the same age gave them common ground for gossip about the problems of parenting adolescents. Primrose had even told Angela about her stern upbringing in the Oxtoby household, of the big age gap between her and her sister Mary, of her feeling that her mother had not wanted another girl. She told Angela that the Shipmans spent Christmas quietly, but made more of a celebration of New Year . . . the normal, low-level exchanges that oil the wheels, and made Angela feel she was close to the Shipmans.

During the time between Mrs Grundy's exhumation and Shipman being charged, Peter Wagstaff went to The Surgery for a health check to coincide with his fiftieth birthday. He asked the GP what was happening. Shipman shrugged and commented that it would be a while before the results were known, because the pathology labs were overloaded with work because of the Omagh bombing. 'I just hope they don't find a single trace of aspirin in her body,' he said, with an insouciance which convinced Peter Wagstaff of his innocence.

His belief in the doctor was reinforced by Carol Chapman, Shipman's loyal receptionist. Giving her a lift home Peter asked her what she thought about the police allegations. Her reply was crude and forthright: 'It's a crock of shite,' she said.

At the time, Peter and Angela Wagstaff would have endorsed that opinion. Now they know otherwise. For Ann Royle, the emotions are mixed: she will never know whether it was her he intended to kill that day, the same day that she took him a bottle of gin for Christmas. There is relief that she escaped, and deep sorrow not just for her son-in-law and daughter, but for all the other countless relatives and friends of victims in Hyde.

It took just six minutes for Fred Shipman to add six new

entries to the medical records of 68-year-old Pamela Hillier. He did it on the afternoon of her death, and he did it to build up a medical history of her having out-of-control blood pressure, leading up to the stroke he claimed she died from on 9 February 1998.

Mrs Hillier had suffered from raised blood pressure, but it had always been well controlled. After her death, Shipman inserted the six new entries (and created and deleted two more) to suggest that for the final month of her life her blood pressure had gone up considerably.

He added the new records just two hours after he had visited her at home and ended her life. She had been a loyal patient of his for over twenty years, ever since he arrived in Hyde, and during that time she had presented him with few problems: she was a fit, active woman who, only a couple of weeks before her death, stripped the wallpaper off two rooms in her house in Mottram, close to the Shipmans' own home. Her husband Cyril, a financial consultant, died almost exactly one year before her, from stomach cancer. After his death, she devoted herself to her grandchildren and to her little black Scottie dog, Trudy.

Just over a week before her death she caught her slipper in the carpet, tripped and damaged her knee, which meant that she had been to The Surgery to see Dr Shipman a couple of times – genuine visits whose records he altered to establish the pattern of dangerously high blood pressure.

On the day of her death she was expecting a home visit from him. Her daughter Jackie Gee, who lives in Glossop, visited her in the morning, and then rang shortly after 1pm. Getting no reply she assumed the doctor had called and her mother had then gone out. Getting no reply again at 4.30pm, she rang the neighbours, Peter and Katherine Elwood, who had a key. Mr Elwood found her fully clothed, on her back on the bedroom floor. Some blood pressure tablets were on the bed.

Mr Elwood called an ambulance and tried to resuscitate Mrs Hillier: she had no pulse but there was no *rigor mortis*, so she had died relatively recently. Shortly afterwards Jackie Gee arrived, and the ambulance crew, who also tried to resuscitate her, and later Dr Shipman.

The GP told Mrs Gee that her mother had died from a stroke, and that this was apparent from the way she was laying on her back. He said he'd called at 1.30pm, and told her to go upstairs and take another blood pressure tablet. He said that because of her history of headaches and high blood pressure, it was not an unexpected death.

But to Mrs Hillier, it obviously was unexpected – downstairs in the house it was clear she had been preparing her meal, and working on accounts which were spread across the dining-room table. It was also unexpected for Mrs Gee and her brother Keith, who drove up from Loughborough as soon as he heard the news. The following day they went together to see Shipman, and Keith Hillier argued that a post-mortem should be performed: he was not happy with the inconsistencies in Shipman's explanation of his mother's blood-pressure problems.

Most of the relatives of Shipman's victims, unaware of his involvement in the deaths, were relieved and pleased to find that there was no need for a post-mortem: the vast majority of families prefer not to have their dead loved ones cut open. But there are others whose attachment to the person is not compromised by a detachment from the physical body, and who simply want to know the truth about a death, especially a sudden one. Keith Hillier and his sister felt like this.

In the end, they were convinced by Shipman that it was not necessary to have a post-mortem. He told them that he was absolutely certain about the cause of death, and that a post-mortem would be unpleasant. He must have heaved a sigh of relief when they finally accepted it, and

Mrs Hillier was safely cremated – he had come perilously close to having his hand forced by them.

When Dr Fred Shipman typed the details of Maureen Ward's brain tumour into his computer records, she was still alive. She was about to die, but only he knew that. Shortly before her death he typed in three false entries to suggest that for the previous two months she had been seeing him because of headaches; after all, he was planning to put down a brain tumour as the cause of her death and he needed to back up that diagnosis with some symptoms.

Then he left his surgery, drove a quarter of a mile to Miss Ward's home, and killed her. It was at 5.30pm on 18 February 1998 that the warden at the old people's complex at Ogden Court, where Maureen Ward lived, answered a knock on the door to Dr Shipman, who said: 'It's Maureen in number 41. Can you come across? I found her dead on the bed.'

The warden, Christine Simpson, was shocked. Ogden Court was designed for the elderly, but Maureen was only fifty-eight – she had been living there to care for her elderly mother, who had died three years earlier at the age of eighty-seven. Maureen was planning to move out a few weeks later and spend her retirement years in Southport. In the immediate future, she had a Caribbean cruise booked with a friend, Mary France – she'd even contacted the taxi driver, John Shaw, to make sure he could take her to the airport.

It's true that she had had more than her share of health problems. She was treated for breast cancer in 1992, and for stomach cancer and skin cancer in 1994. But she had been remarkably well ever since, and check-ups in the previous months had shown there was no recurrence of the cancers. On the day before her death she visited The Surgery, and as she came out of the consulting room with the doctor he told the receptionist about her plans for the cruise and the move to Southport. That evening, Maureen had a long phone chat with a close friend, Christine Whitworth, in which she mentioned her visit to the doctor's but gave no indication that there was anything seriously wrong.

On the morning of her death she went shopping in the town centre, had a coffee with her friend Mary, and carried a bin-liner full of washing to the complex laundry for Mary. The various friends and neighbours she saw said the retired teacher – she lectured in child health-care – was well, cheerful and looking forward to her holiday.

Christine Simpson was also surprised when the doctor said he had told Maureen to 'leave the snip' on the door so he could get in – the flat had a push-button system that allowed Maureen to open the door without going downstairs, and she was so security-conscious that it was out of character to leave the door on the latch.

The warden was usually one of the first to know if any of the residents had health problems, so it was another shock when Shipman said to her: 'She did have a brain tumour, you know.'

Shipman said he was calling to deliver a letter, which he claimed was an appointment to see a consultant at Stepping Hill Hospital. He said it had been difficult to get the appointment, but he had managed it. Yet there is no record of any letter being written at his surgery, nor of a request for an appointment being made to the hospital.

Inside number 41, Christine found Maureen stretched out on the bed, fully clothed, with her eyes closed. She appeared relaxed and peaceful. A tin of cat food was open on the kitchen work surface with a spoon still in it, and there was an empty cat bowl on the floor. It appeared she had been disturbed in the middle of her normal routine.

When he got back to The Surgery at 4pm Fred Shipman gave his receptionist Carol Chapman a different version of events that afternoon. He told her Miss Ward had died, but that he had been passing the end of the road when he saw an ambulance there and went to enquire. No ambulance had been called, nor were there any in the vicinity that day.

Maureen's close friend Christine Whitworth went to see Shipman to discuss the death, and he repeated that the cause was a brain tumour, and that this could cause someone to pass out. He said that Maureen had been to see him before Christmas because she was distressed to find she had wet herself in the night. He had referred her, he said, to the opticians, and there was blurring in her eyes. He said he had been trying hard to get her a quick referral to hospital, and had been taking the details of the appointment to her when he found her dead. When Mrs Whitworth asked him if her friend would have suffered he replied that it would have been a very quick death because 'when cancer is secondary in the brain it can cause the patient to pass out, and she would have laid down on the bed feeling unwell and died'.

On the cremation form he falsely claimed that the warden was the person who found her, and that the warden had been present at her death. He also stated that the warden found her on his own computer records, made before she died. He put 'cancer in the brain' and 'breast cancer' on the death certificate.

However, when consultant neurosurgeon Andrew King was asked to review Maureen Ward's medical history before the trial, he concluded that Shipman's assertion that she had breast cancer with a secondary tumour in the brain was completely at odds with the clean bill of health she had been given at her last breast cancer check-up, and that it was impossible to state she had brain cancer without a post-mortem. He also said that, had she been dying of cancer, she would have been unwell, not out shopping and gossiping with friends.

Dr John Grenville, the independent GP consulted by the prosecution, agreed with the neurosurgeon that there would have been other symptoms of a brain tumour, and it is unlikely that Miss Ward would have been as well as she was on the morning of her death, or in the weeks leading up to it. Friends of Maureen Ward are left with another uncomfortable thought: could her mother also have been a victim of Fred Shipman's?

# 13
# On the Morphine Trail

The words that Dr Fred Shipman used when Jim King went in for an early morning appointment on Saturday 19 July 1997 were: 'You've won the lottery.' He went on to tell Jim, who was fifty-five at the time, that he did not have cancer. Not only did he not have cancer, he had never had cancer.

For Jim, the immediate feeling of relief was quickly followed by one of shock, and then of anger. For eight months he had been receiving heavy doses of morphine from Dr Shipman, to help him cope with the pain and anguish of his 'terminal cancer'. Shipman had twice told him that he had no more than a few months to live. Jim had lost his job, his home and very nearly his marriage.

But he did not blame his GP. He blamed the hospital which had originally diagnosed cancer, and had subjected him to a twelve-week course of chemotherapy. It was not until months later, as he and his wife Debbie battled to make sense of the whole experience, that they discovered that three weeks after discharging him from the chemotherapy treatment, the hospital had written to Dr Shipman saying that Jim King did not have cancer.

For eight months, Shipman kept up the pretence to Jim

that he was dying – and continued to prescribe massive amounts of morphine for him, turning him into a junkie. At the same time, Shipman may also have used Jim's name to procure even more morphine, which he was using to kill other patients.

Horrifyingly, Jim's own father was probably one of Shipman's victims: and Jim now has to live with the realisation that it could have been morphine prescribed in his name which was injected into his own father.

The enormity of the suffering that Fred Shipman has imposed on this one family defies belief. As Jim's life collapsed around him, his father, also called Jim King, was one of his main supports. When the old man died, Jim already knew that his cancer had been misdiagnosed, and was embarking on a complicated claim for compensation against the hospital and against Dr Shipman. He was distraught when his father died, on Christmas Eve 1997, but, like all the other relatives of possible victims, had no clue that there would be a suspicion that he had been murdered – until Shipman's eventual arrest.

Also among the list of suspicious deaths on the police files are two aunts of Jim's, one of whom died three months after his father.

Jim King was born and brought up in Hyde, but for many years had been living and working in America. His marriage to his first wife, an American, had collapsed, and he was looking after his two teenage children, a girl called Jamie and a boy, Jimmy. At the same time his second wife, Debra, who comes from Independence, Missouri, was also recovering from a failed first marriage, and living with her daughter, Melissa.

They met when Debbie put a lonely hearts ad in a Florida newspaper, asking to meet an Englishman. She had visited England, loved the country, and thought it would be fun to date an Englishman. It was the first time she had advertised, and the only time Jim had responded to an ad. They clicked immediately. Before long, they had both given up their jobs and flown to Britain with young Jimmy and Melissa. It was a tentative arrangement: if they didn't settle, they would go back to the States.

They went to Hyde, because Jim's father and sister lived there. His mother, also a patient of Fred Shipman's, had died a few years earlier. Debbie loved it: England was everything she had dreamed of, and the couple had a fairytale white wedding on 4 May 1996 at Flowery Field Church, with their delighted children Jimmy and Melissa, both fifteen at the time, in attendance. Jim found a job as a sales engineer, and they rented a house in Newton which they were negotiating to buy.

Two weeks after the wedding, Jim began to suffer backache. He dismissed it, thinking it was caused by moving a wardrobe. But he also started to pass blood in his urine, and when Debbie found out she made him go to see his GP, Fred Shipman. (Jim had been registered with Shipman before moving to America, and his father recommended him highly.) Shipman took a urine sample to send off for tests, and Jim and Debbie asked him to arrange an appointment with a specialist.

Two days later, on 17 May, Jim woke up in such chronic pain that Debbie put him in the car and took him directly to the hospital casualty department. He was admitted, tests were carried out, and Jim was told that he had tumours in his urethra, the tube from his bladder to the end of his penis. It was a terrible time for the Kings: not only were they coping with the shock of Jim's diagnosis, but Debbie had to fly back to America to the death-bed of her mother, who also had cancer.

Jim was admitted on 2 July for his first dose of chemotherapy, and was given another five doses, every other week until the end of September. He was very sick, and could hardly walk when Debbie collected him. They carried a bucket in the car for him to throw up into, and frequently had to stop for him to be ill at the side of the road. He managed to carry on working, arranging the chemo sessions for a Friday, so that he had the weekend in which to recover, but eventually he was so ill that he could no longer work. After his last session the hospital told him he was 'all clear', but he did not understand whether this meant he was better or that he did not need any more chemotherapy at that time.

He was still in pain, and on 1 November, Dr Shipman prescribed morphine for him, for the first of many times. He continued to prescribe it, telling Jim that he had received a letter from the hospital.

'He said, "I'm sorry to have to tell you that at the rate the cancer is spreading – it's in your kidney, urethra, prostate and bladder – I'm afraid you've only got about eighteen months to live,"' says Jim.

Unknown to the Kings, the letter that Shipman received from the hospital on 22 November made it clear that Jim did not have cancer. It was an in-patients' discharge summary from the consultant, and it read: 'My house surgeon's diagnosis is wrong. Mr King has no evidence of prostatic cancer. Indeed, the papillae are no longer present within the cystoscopy. I intend requesting an anteriogram of the right kidney.'

In other words, although Jim was still in pain, he did not have cancer – and Shipman surely appreciated this. But he continued to pump Jim full of morphine, telling him that he could have as much as he liked to ease his final few months.

Having lost his job, Jim and Debbie were unable to keep up with the rent on their house, and the benefits system would not recognise Debbie, Melissa or young Jimmy, because they were all American citizens. Jim's father helped out as much as he could, from his old age pension: he would walk three miles to their home with food for them and then walk back again. Jim's car was a company car, so they lost it, and Debbie's car was being paid for on hire purchase, and was repossessed. Even Jim's claim for disability allowance was held up, because Shipman, who had to authorise that Jim was terminally ill, twice claimed to have sent it off even though it was never received by the benefits agency. Eventually, Jim's father collected it personally from The Surgery and hand-delivered it to the agency in Manchester.

Jim took more and more morphine, partly to kill the pain and partly because he was, by this stage, desperate. He and his new bride, who is eleven years younger than him, were living in very difficult circumstances. They had pawned the video, Debbie pawned her wedding ring to pay an electricity bill, and on one occasion young Jimmy was reduced to eating peanut-butter spread on lettuce leaves because that was all the food they had. Once Jim collapsed and had to be rushed to hospital: he was delirious, blacking out, unable to breathe. In retrospect, the Kings know that the morphine induced these symptoms, but at the time they put it down to his serious medical condition – the cancer. Over Christmas 1996 he was so ill that Debbie rang his daughter in America and told her that she feared he would not make it. The family managed to get through Christmas on £300 awarded to them from the Cancer Relief Macmillan Fund – Debbie and Jim did without presents, young Jimmy got socks and Melissa two candles.

In January 1997, with the help of the Macmillan nurse, Jim was referred to another hospital to see a different consultant; Debbie had insisted on having a second opinion. More tests were carried out under general anaesthetic, and once again the consultant wrote to Shipman saying that Jim did not have cancer. Once again, Shipman did not pass this on to Jim, but told him that the cancer had been confirmed and he was, indeed, terminally ill.

Soon afterwards, there was another blow: Jim's son, Jimmy, was arrested for committing vandalism at his school which cost £6,000 to repair.

'He was so disturbed by what was happening to me,' says Jim. 'He'd been born and raised in America, and he has no relationship at all with his mother. I'd brought him to a foreign country, a new school, a new stepmother – and then, out of the blue, he finds out that I am dying. I was the only thing he had, all his life. We tried to talk to him, but I was out of it half the time on morphine, at that stage he wasn't close to Deb, and he was living in near poverty. He just exploded.'

Despite all the mitigating circumstances, Jimmy was expelled from school and appeared in court. He was sentenced to do community service in Oldham (which cost the Kings a precious £5 a week in fares). At this stage their weekly income had risen from £55 to £125, but for two adults and two teenagers it was very tight.

Within a month of Jimmy's outburst, they lost their battle to stay in the house. They were eventually moved into a council house, which when they arrived was without carpets, a cooker, light-bulbs, curtains or any furniture. With the help of a £1,000 social loan, which they are paying back out of their benefits, they bought some essentials.

'I have never bought anything second-hand before in my life,' says Jim. 'I just could not believe what we had come down to – but while I was desperately worried for Debbie and the kids, I thought I was dying, and there was nothing I could do to help. I lived from one dose of morphine to the next, it was all that was keeping me going.'

They faced another problem, too: their relationship. Had they been a married couple of many years' standing they would have had a bedrock of shared experience to fall back on, and to keep their love for each other strong. But they were newlyweds, at the start of their life together, and neither of them had bargained for this. Jim, mortified that he had reduced Debbie to living in such awful conditions, tried to persuade her to leave him and go back to America permanently. Debbie was sure they could see it through, although it was very difficult for her. To make matters worse, their sex life, which had been new and exciting, had stopped completely: the morphine, Jim's depression, and the after-effects of the chemotherapy had annihilated his libido. He had lost four stone in weight and barely had the energy to climb up the stairs to bed, often sleeping all night on the sofa.

In a final attempt to salvage their love life, they asked Fred Shipman to refer them to a sexual dysfunction clinic, which one of the nurses had told them about. When they told the clinic consultant their story, and the psychological effect on Jim of living with a terminal illness, he looked puzzled, and said he would need Jim in hospital for yet more tests under general anaesthetic. He also said that it was vital for Jim to come off his high doses of morphine. After the tests, he told Jim that there was no sign of cancer. Jim assumed that the chemotherapy must have worked.

'But by this stage I was so addicted to morphine that I could not take in a lot of what was said to me, or remember it afterwards: I have suffered permanent memory loss through it.'

The consultant told Jim he would be writing to his GP, and within days Jim received a letter from The Surgery telling him to meet Shipman on Saturday 19 July, before normal surgery hours.

'When I arrived there was nobody there but him. He unlocked the door to let me in, and took me into his consulting room. Then he told me I had won the lottery, that I didn't have cancer – and what's more, that I had never had cancer. He told me I might like to get myself a lawyer – he said he had consulted his, and was probably in

the clear. He said, "If not, I will have to suffer the consequences. Go home and talk it over with your wife. If you
don't want to sue, I will do everything in my power to
help you."

'I was stunned. I didn't know how to break the news to
Deb. I didn't believe I could have gone through all this for
nothing.'

Debbie was equally astonished. She, too, initially
believed that it meant Jim had been cured: she was horrified
to hear that he had never had the disease in the first place.

'What should have been a joyous celebration of the fact
that he was going to be well again, was completely overshadowed by all the misery we had been put through,' she
says.

They both initially assumed that Shipman was blame-
less, that he had been misinformed by the hospital about
Jim's condition. It was only when they managed to get
access to Jim's records, after they started a medical negligence claim, that the full extent of his guilt became clear.
They switched to another GP, and Jim has gradually been
weaned off a very heavy morphine addiction. But getting
him off was hell: he changed from a peaceful, gentle man
into an angry, difficult husband who would storm out of
the house in the middle of the night; who hid caches of
morphine in the toe of his shoe or in his glasses case,
where Deb could not find it; who lived 'for nothing but
my next dose of it'. As the dosage was reduced, he would
shake uncontrollably. He had shivers, sweats, palpita-
tions – classic heroin withdrawal symptoms. Eventually,
he decided to give it up completely; the following few
days were hell.

'It felt as if someone was scratching the bottom of my
feet with a needle. I would walk for miles, in the middle of
the night. I would plunge into cold baths, anything to
dull the pain. It took about a week, and then it all began
to gradually dull down.'

The legacy of the addiction is still with him – he has times when his memory blanks completely, and he cannot remember his way home, or why he is at a certain place. He says that however ill he is in future, he will always refuse morphine, because he knows 'the sheer horror of being a drug addict'.

Christmas 1997 was going to be good for Jim and Debbie. Although they were still very poor, and Jim was still battling his craving for morphine, life was a great deal more hopeful than it had been the previous Christmas, when Debbie was convinced her husband would not pull through. They were planning to enjoy it, and drink a toast to their new future.

Jim's father was very angry with the way Shipman had treated his son, and intended to change to another GP, but he never had the chance to get round to it. A retired truck driver, he was a very fit 83-year-old. He walked five miles every day, and just before Christmas he wallpapered his flat from top to bottom. On Christmas Eve Jim rang him to see if he wanted to meet for lunch, but he told Jim he was waiting for the doctor to call, to give him a flu jab. At 2.30pm, when Jim rang again, Shipman had still not been, but while they were talking on the phone the old man said, 'Here he is, hang on while I let him in.' He put the phone down, and when he picked it up again Jim told him to give him a call after the doctor had gone.

An hour and a half later Jim rang again. There was no reply. He assumed his father had gone shopping. He rang again later, and then phoned his sister Margaret, who said she would pop down to see their father. Half an hour later she called to say he was dead.

'When we got there he was sitting in a chair, his hand hooked in his collar and his sleeve rolled up. He had his slippers on. It wasn't his favourite chair, it was a recliner my mother always sat in. We rang for Dr Shipman, and for an ambulance. Shipman arrived and felt for a pulse in

Dad's neck, then announced that he was dead. I asked what he died of and Shipman shrugged and said, "Old age?"

'I said, "Old age? He's just papered the house."'

Shipman told them that old Mr King had had high blood pressure. Then he asked a curious question: 'What would you like me to put on the death certificate?'

Jim King replied he'd like him to put the cause of death. Shipman put cerebro-vascular accident, or stroke. 'But there was no distortion of the body. He looked just as though he was asleep,' says Jim.

Debbie Massey came out to organise the funeral: Jim King's father's death was the one that Shipman had predicted when she told him earlier in the day that she wanted a quiet Christmas.

Despite their own problems with Shipman, Jim and Debbie never suspected that Jim's father may have been murdered. They questioned Shipman's competence as a doctor, but they never dreamed that he was a serial killer. Even when Jim's aunt, Irene Berry, was found in similarly suspicious circumstances three months later, they accepted it.

'We didn't like him and we were very angry about what he had done to our lives. But we thought he was an incompetent bungler, not a multiple murderer,' says Jim. 'I realise now that he was lucky to get away with it as long as he did with me. Maybe he was hoping the massive amounts of morphine I was taking would kill me. As everyone, including me, thought I had terminal cancer, nobody would have been surprised. When I was ill with flu he asked Debbie if he should give me a shot of antibiotics, but she said she would prefer a course of tablets. If he was trying to kill me, I now think, he could have killed me then, because the more doctors I insisted on seeing the more likely he would be found out.'

Debbie and Jim were as amazed as anyone when

Shipman was arrested. Debbie immediately raised the question of Jim's father, but before the family had time to take in the implications, the police arrived on the doorstep as part of their investigation of all deaths connected with The Surgery. Jim's aunt Irene Berry, and another aunt, Molly Dudley, who died in 1990, are also on the list of suspicious deaths.

'We believe that he forged prescriptions in my name to obtain morphine for his own use. I have to live with the possibility that my own father and my own aunt may have been killed with morphine he acquired for me. It is just one more terrible thing that happened to this family.'

Jim King's prescriptions were just one source of the vast amount of morphine Fred Shipman pumped into the arms of unsuspecting patients in the last years of his career. As his death toll escalated, so did his need for the drug, and he was obtaining it both by forging prescriptions and by over-prescribing it for terminally-ill patients with genuine need: he would personally collect their prescriptions, and then deliver to their homes less than he had obtained from the pharmacist. He would also, after the death of a terminally-ill patient, keep the 'returns', the morphine left over at their home, which should be destroyed by the doctor or pharmacist.

Then, with a syringe full of at least 100ml of morphine, he would visit the homes of unsuspecting patients, none of whom would question the doctor's wish to give them an injection – he would probably explain it away as a flu jab, or antibiotics, or a vitamin injection.

The amount of morphine it takes to kill someone varies from person to person. The terminally ill, who grow accustomed to it, can build up enormous tolerance, and can be taking very large doses to control pain without it killing them. Jim King reckons he was on the equivalent of almost 500ml a day, a phenomenal amount that would certainly have killed someone of a less sturdy constitution. (A 55-year-old man recently survived being given ten times the amount of morphine prescribed for him as he recovered from a hip replacement operation – but only because, at 19 stone and 6 feet 2 inches tall, his body was big enough to absorb the excess.)

To kill the average person within three hours, a minimum of 60ml is needed, 100ml to be sure, injected into the tissue. The patients who died while at The Surgery obviously had sufficiently large doses injected straight into a vein to die much more quickly than this; others, who died while Shipman was still in their homes, must also have been injected intravenously, perhaps to enable him to snoop around their homes, looking for cash or jewellery. For all of his victims, the end was pain- and distress-free: morphine travels through the blood to receptors in the brain, damping down all pain and slowing down breathing, eventually to the point of stopping it completely. The peaceful old ladies, sitting in comfortable armchairs, were the hallmarks of a Shipman killing.

It is likely that the drug he actually administered was diamorphine (heroin), which is simply double-strength morphine. Because it is more fat-soluble, it travels more quickly to the brain. It rapidly decomposes and turns to morphine, which is what was found in the tissues of the exhumed victims. Diamorphine can be diluted in a very small amount of water, and can be injected through a small-bore needle. If injected under the skin, there would be no easily detectable injection mark, but it would take between an hour and two hours to kill the victim. Given intravenously it would kill almost instantaneously.

In the words of Professor Robert Forrest, Britain's leading forensic toxicologist, 'They would die on the end of the needle, virtually. They would take a few breaths and be gone.'

With every suspicious death they investigated, a crucial

question the detectives asked was how soon before the body was found had the doctor been there. Occasionally it was twenty-four hours earlier, but in those cases it was always also clear that the victim had been dead for some time. With all the others it was astonishingly consistent: two hours, two and a half hours, immediately, three hours, twenty minutes, half an hour. It is rare, although not unknown, for a patient to die so soon after a doctor's visit, unless they are known to be terminally ill. Normally, a doctor will dispatch a very ill patient to hospital. Shipman's defence, made to so many relatives, of his failure to admit patients to hospital was that they refused to go, a reaction completely at odds with the normal character and behaviour of many of his victims (some of whom, according to friends and families, were positive hypochondriacs who would have revelled in a trip to hospital).

Not that he was infallible. When Renate Overton died in Tameside Hospital in April 1995, she was only forty-seven years old, making her Shipman's youngest possible victim. The final fourteen months of her life were spent in a persistent vegetative state on a hospital ward. Family and friends visited and chatted to her, but Renate never responded. Her daughter Sharon spent every free evening and weekend at her bedside, hoping for the miracle that never happened.

A bubbly, friendly woman, who was an expert on all the comings and goings of the characters in *Coronation Street* and *EastEnders*, Renate, like Bianka Pomfret, came originally from Germany. She was separated from her second husband, but had plenty of friends and family. Sharon lived with her, and her son Douglas used to visit and spend time with her.

On the day she died Sharon came home to find Shipman attending to her mother. He was actually administering an injection. Renate passed out and never

recovered consciousness. Renate's neighbour and friend
for nineteen years, Carol Batho, was devastated.

'She was a smashing person. There was a strong sense
of community in our street, and Renate was the core of it.
She would do anything for anybody. She was like a sister
to me, and my children got on well with her. She used to
have a broomstick hanging on the wall, and she told my
children she was a witch, and if they looked into the sky
on Bonfire Night they would see her flying on the broomstick. When she died, my daughter Nicola kept looking up
in the sky, hoping to see her.

'Sharon gave me the broomstick, and I've got it in my
bedroom. When I think about Renate, I think about the
happy times. I don't like to think of the last terrible
months of her life – it is too sad.'

Shipman's choice of victim helped shield him from suspicion for years. To target elderly women, who lived alone,
made easier both the execution of the crime and the
acceptance of it without question. Of course, there were
questions: time and time again, relatives queried him not
sending the victim to hospital, not telling them the victim
was ill, his apparent carelessness about what he wrote on
death certificates, and his cavalier and often brusque attitude at the scene of a death. But time and time again
they accepted, if reluctantly, that he knew best: after all,
he was the doctor.

It would be wrong, though, to think that he only targeted elderly women. The youngest woman he was
charged with killing was only forty-nine, and plenty more
were in their fifties and sixties – hardly old. Men may
have died, too – possibly Jim King's father. There was also
Harold Eddleston, who had lung cancer and died the day
before his seventy-eighth birthday, and only a few days
after his wife's death. A neighbour, knowing Harold was
taking his wife's death hard, met Dr Shipman in the street

and suggested the doctor call in to see Harold, to give him some help over his depression. Shipman called that afternoon and Harold died while he was there.

But over and over again, the victims were women living on their own. There are far too many stories than can be told here, but that does not mean they are less important, less poignant, than any of the others. To most families blighted by Shipman's needle, their relative was the most remarkable, the most missed. Sadly, in a few cases, the old lady who died was scarcely mourned, but for the vast majority, there are children, grandchildren, friends and neighbours whose lives are poorer for the unnecessary deaths.

Joel Lane, only a mile and a half long, stretches from the main Hyde-to-Stockport road upwards to the local beauty spot of Werneth Low, which commands a sweeping view of Greater Manchester. On one side of the ridge lie the built-up areas of Tameside, the view punctuated by the high-rise flats of the Hattersley overspill estate, and on the other lie the posher suburbs of Romiley, one of the better areas of Stockport. And all around are budding hills, the beginnings of the Pennine range, adding natural power to what would otherwise be an urban, industrial landscape.

Even without looking at the properties themselves, it is easy to see why prices and desirability rise as the road winds upwards. The view alone must add thousands. The houses themselves acknowledge the climb in their status, with the neat terraces at the lower end expanding to semis, then detached houses and eventually to the individual one-offs with large gardens and drives for several cars which hide behind high hedges at the top of the lane, and which sell for as much as £200,000.

Joel Lane deserves a particular place in the history of Dr Fred Shipman because it was from this road alone that he is suspected of involvement in the deaths of six old

ladies in the space of four and a half years. Two of them
lived next door to each other, in numbers 55 and 57, terraced houses with the front doors not six feet apart, and
two others, Alice Kitchen and Norah Nuttall, though no
longer living in Joel Lane at the time of their deaths, had
both previously lived there.

It must have come as a great shock to Marion Higham
when her neighbour of many years' standing, 82-year-old
spinster Joan Harding, died in January 1994 while on a
routine visit to Dr Shipman's surgery. Hers was one of the
five deaths on the doctor's own premises. There had been
no clue that she was seriously ill, but equally there was no
reason to suspect a doctor who said his patient had tragically had a heart attack while he was examining her.

It was two and a half years after Joan's death, on 19
July 1996, that her neighbour, 86-year-old widow Marion
Higham, died in the house next door. Again, she was
being attended by Dr Shipman. He simply wrote 'natural
causes' on her death certificate.

Prior to Marion's death, two more widows, both good
friends of hers, also died in Joel Lane – one of them just
three days before Marion. Mrs Carrie Leigh, who was
eighty-one, died suddenly at her new £50,000 semi in
the lower end of the road. She was slim, smart, active, still
driving around the town in her little Vauxhall Nova. She
and her husband, Noel, used to own a shop in Union
Street, in Hyde, which sold the unlikely combination of
bikes and tobacco. She had been widowed for many years,
and her three daughters were all living away from the
area, but Carrie was not short of friends. Every Sunday
afternoon she would provide cups of tea and cakes for a
regular circle of visitors, which often included Marion
Higham and Hilda Hibbert.

On the day she died she had been due to attend a function at Hyde Chapel: she was not a punctilious
church-goer, but went often enough to be regarded as

part of the congregation. When she did not turn up, a friend went round to check on her, and found her dead in her armchair, fully clothed.

Six months earlier, on the day after New Year's Day, Carrie's friend, 81-year-old Hilda Hibbert, died a few doors higher up Joel Lane. She and Carrie used to go together to the local Townswomen's Guild meetings: they had plenty in common, as Hilda's family had also owned a bike shop. On the day of Hilda's death a young workman from the council arrived to fit railings on the steps to her front door, because her arthritis was making it difficult to climb them. When he found the old lady's door ajar he went to the home of Elsie Barrow, next door, because he did not want to walk in and startle Mrs Hibbert. Elsie went in with him, and they found Hilda in her chair, as if asleep. When they realised she was dead the young man phoned the police.

After three deaths within six months, the next eighteen months were quiet for Joel Lane. Then came the death of Joan Dean, who lived higher up the lane, where the terraced houses have given way to neat semis. Number 58 is spacious and well maintained, with a garage alongside the house. Joan died two weeks after her seventy-fifth birthday in February 1998, and her death was an unexpected tragedy for her two sons and her friends. She, like so many of the others, was a very active woman, the widow of a company director, herself a former professional actress who had once appeared in *Coronation Street*.

On the day she died she spoke to her gardener in the morning, and seemed her normal, bright self. She had her weekly hairdressing appointment in the afternoon, a fixture she never missed, and which she would certainly have cancelled had she not felt well enough to go. At 4pm the salon rang her home when she failed to turn up, but there was no reply. She was probably already dead.

On the day of her death she visited Dr Shipman at his

surgery, complaining of dizziness. After her death, he told her son that the cause of death was 'probably' a stroke, but when Brian Dean asked if there would be a post-mortem Shipman replied brusquely, 'She doesn't need one of those. I will speak to the coroner, leave it to me.'

The death certificate said she died of coronary thrombosis, heart disease and high blood pressure, but she was not being treated for any of these conditions, and without a post-mortem Brian is left wondering how the doctor knew she had heart disease. As his mother was covered by private medical insurance, he cannot understand why she was not referred to a specialist.

Brian's brother Terry flew over from New Zealand for their mother's funeral, and it was while he was sorting out her belongings that Terry discovered there was jewellery missing, including a watch worth more than £1,000 and an engagement ring valued at £5,000. The £300 she had taken from her bank account that afternoon was also never found. Her sons made sure that she was as glamorous in death as she had been in life: in her coffin she wore the mink coat that her father had bought for her many years before.

Further up Joel Lane is number 79, the attractive stone-built detached home of Kathleen Grundy. She died six months after Joan Dean, and was the victim of the final murder committed by Fred Shipman.

Less than a hundred yards from the imposing Magistrates' Court in Ashton-under-Lyne, where Fred Shipman appeared regularly to be remanded on an increasing number of murder charges, is the office of the Tameside Victim Support Group. From here, trained volunteers are dispatched to offer comfort and advice to the 8,000 victims of robberies, assaults, muggings and criminal damage that the police, health workers, social workers and hospitals refer to them every year.

Here, the shockwaves of the Shipman case were felt with full force, as more and more families of victims and potential victims turned to them for help. Helen Ogburn, a pretty woman in her mid-thirties, is the full-time co-ordinator of the group and therefore the co-ordinator of one of the biggest operations the Victim Support organisation has ever had to undertake. Not only have the support volunteers helped the families of the fifteen victims with whose deaths Shipman was charged, they have also found themselves helping 144 other relatives of patients who died unexpectedly.

With only two volunteers out of the ten in the Tameside area who are specially trained in dealing with the families of murder victims, Helen had to draft in another ten from the rest of Greater Manchester. 'We have, in a way, had to write our own blueprint for how to deal with the victims,' she says.

Helen, the wife of an electrical engineer, has been born and bred in Hyde, and from childhood has been immersed in helping others: her parents, both councillors, were instrumental in setting up the first battered wives' refuge in Tameside, and she has vivid childhood memories of her father loading up the women and children who appeared on their doorstep in the middle of the night into his Reliant Robin and taking them, with their carrier bags of possessions, to the refuge.

From leaving school she has worked for Victim Support, and has seen the devastating effect of crime on victims. Yet she, like everyone else, had never dreamed of anything as vast as the Shipman case, with tentacles spreading throughout the community.

'In the beginning, the Shipman case didn't seem such a big thing, but as there were more exhumations and murder charges it was obvious it wasn't going to be simple. The police approached us and said they felt the families of the murder charge victims needed help, and then we also had contact with the relatives of other families, where there was a suspicious death but no charge.

'It was such an unusual case. Grieving for a murder victim is different from grieving for any other kind of death. If an old person has died from illness we come to terms with it, knowing that they have had a good long life, and grateful that they did not suffer a lingering illness. When birthdays and other anniversaries come around, we remember them with affection, tinged perhaps with a little sadness.

'With murder, a life has been taken unjustly. You are hit in the face with the raw emotion of it all. Many people go to pieces, they just can't cope. The death is on their mind all the time. They don't sleep, they can't work, some lose their jobs. It is appalling for them.

'But with the Shipman deaths we have something different: the normal grieving process has taken place, they have learned to live without this person, only for the whole thing to be resurrected by the police knocking on the door and gently telling them that their mother, father, aunt may not have died of natural causes after all, but may have been murdered.

'For a lot of them, there wasn't even the knock on the door: they came forward themselves after reading about the case. They have been putting two and two together, and starting to work out that their relative might be a victim. The majority of them are not at the screaming, ranting stage where you feel actual physical pain, which we encounter after a "normal" murder. Don't imagine this is like anything we've ever done before.'

Helen would brief each of the support workers with a bare outline of the case, without giving too many details, to avoid the volunteer having preconceived ideas. 'It is then up to the person we are visiting to tell us what they want to do. That way the family don't think we are taking over,' she says.

The Victim Support organisation fights shy of the word 'counselling', preferring to see themselves as giving support and information. They know how the police work and how courts work; they can prepare the families of victims for the ordeal of giving evidence.

'We stay with a family for as long as they want us, usually trying to make sure they see the same volunteer. We might see them every week for a month, and in some cases the support will last eighteen months. We are available on the end of a telephone, when they simply need an ear to talk to.

'When we offer our services, it is one of the chances the family have to get back into control again. When the police or a court case is involved, the victims' families can feel sidelined – it is not for them to say "I want him charged" or "I don't want to be a witness." That is all out of their hands. But they can choose to see a Victim Support worker, and just being able to make that choice helps.'

The one question asked by all the Shipman victims' families was, 'Why?'

'We can't answer that question,' says Helen. 'People think we must know, because we are working with the police. But we don't. There have always been pieces of the jigsaw missing. People want to know why there were only fifteen murder charges. Well, there had to be a ceiling, even on cost grounds alone, and we have had to break that gently to some of the families of other victims.'

The families who opted for Victim Support tended to be those who were convinced of Shipman's guilt – those who were still in denial did not ask for help.

'There is a complete split among the families of the victims, a 50/50 split about whether he should have been charged with more murders. Half are relieved that they are not in the spotlight, the other half want him to be charged so that they can have a resolution to their case.'

The case has strained the financial resources of the Victim Support Group. Each separate Victim Support scheme is an independent charity, with 75 per cent of funding coming from the Home Office, approximately another 10 per cent from the local authority, and the rest coming from fund-raising.

'We are always strapped for cash and the Shipman case has put an enormous strain on our budget,' says Helen Ogburn.

The case is also set to place a huge financial burden on the Criminal Injuries Compensation Authority. Under the government-funded scheme, a minimum payment of £10,000 is made to the close family of a murder victim (a husband or wife, a long-term partner, a parent or a child). In the case of a widow dying and leaving several adult children, each would qualify for a payment of £5,000. The scheme is open to all victims of crime, not just those cases in which the perpetrator has been convicted. This means that in the Shipman case all the families where there has been a suspicious death can apply, and the potential payout could be as much as £2 million.

# 14
# The Trial

**P**rison life was a lot like doing a junior housemanship, Fred Shipman wrote to one of his doctor friends from Strangeways jail in Manchester. He was whistling in the dark: the effects of prison life were etched starkly into his face when he appeared, thirteen months after his arrest, in the dock at Preston Crown Court. He was noticeably thinner and greyer than when he went into custody. Never looking young for his age, he now looked positively old. His pre-prison clothes hung off his shoulders, his thinning hair was combed forward. He had lost two stones in weight, shrinking from a 36-inch waist to 32 inches. He was fifty-three years old, but anyone who did not know would guess he was in his late sixties or even seventies.

He was originally held at Strangeways (properly known as Manchester Prison) but there were genuine fears for his safety there, in an environment where staff and other prisoners could possibly have relatives in Hyde. Because of the seriousness of the charges against him, he was a Category A prisoner, and was initially kept under close observation because of the suicide risk. Any first-timer in jail is a potential suicide: the noise, the smell, the attitude of other prisoners, and the endless indignities that come with the loss of liberty, push those who are unfamiliar with the regime to despair. And there are some, like Shipman, facing such serious charges that suicide must offer a seductive alternative. Every fifteen minutes, a warder would flip open the spyhole in his cell door, to check that he was still alive, and random searches of his cell were carried out to make sure he had no potential weapons. The embarrassment of Britain's most recent prisoner of equivalent notoriety, Fred West, killing himself in prison in Birmingham while still on remand, haunted the prison authorities, and they were determined that nothing similar would happen to Fred Shipman.

He would eventually have a single cell, but initially he shared with another man on remand for serious crimes, and who was also regarded as a serious suicide risk. Peter Hall, a 34-year-old heating engineer, was arrested five days after Shipman. He had brutally murdered his girl-friend and her two children, leaving a callous note for her ex-husband which said: 'You are welcome to your family back.' It was a particularly horrific murder: he bludg-eoned Brazilian-born Celeste Bates, then used her car to collect her seventeen-month-old son from nursery, bat-tering him to death with a pick handle. He then collected her eight-year-old son from school and killed him the same way.

Whether the two murderers, both new to life in prison, were able to offer each other any comfort is debatable. Hall was racked with remorse and self-pity; Shipman was still keeping up a determined assertion of innocence, behaving as though he had been grossly wronged. Hall, who Shipman described in a letter to a friend as 'a decent cellmate', came to trial in March 1999, six months before Shipman, and was given three life sentences. (The need for suicide precautions was dramatically underlined when, just a month before Shipman's trial, another man accused of killing five elderly women hanged himself in his cell in Strangeways. Stephen Akinmurele, a 21-year-old homosexual with a hatred of old people, had a history of violence and mental illness.)

Because of the fears for his safety, Shipman was transferred initially, in the autumn of 1998, to Preston Prison, and then moved to Walton jail in Liverpool. After a few months he was returned to Strangeways, after checks had been made that none of the staff with whom he would come into contact was related to any of his victims. It was much more convenient for his visitors for him to be held in Manchester.

His family remained steadfast throughout the remand and the trial. In her new red Ford Fiesta, bought after her Ford Sierra was crashed by joyriders, Primrose went to and from the prison, often accompanied by one of her children, or by friends. Jayne Stokes, who set up the sandwich business with her, and Jayne's husband Robert were a constant in the Shipman family's life, both visiting Fred in prison and supporting Primrose during the trial. If they ever doubted his innocence they did not show it: before the trial Robert Stokes described himself and his wife as the people closest to the Shipmans.

Fred's daughter Sarah moved to a new home within a mile of the prison, and his sons Christopher, David and Sam were also regular visitors. He received many letters, and replied at great length to most of them, sometimes writing letters out of the blue to old colleagues and friends. He wrote almost compulsively, as if letters were his grip on the outside world: he even replied to an old school friend who had written wishing him luck even though it was clear Shipman could not remember him.

The letters were generally bullish: the theme was always that he was the centre of an appalling mistake, and that as soon as he came to trial the truth – and his innocence – would be revealed. He even joked about the armed police from the Tactical Support Group who transported him between prison and court.

'We had a lovely drive at greater than the speed limit, lights on, flashing blue lights, the lot,' he wrote. But he also described feeling 'very, very lonely' when he sat in the dock at remand hearings: 'You get the dry mouth, fast heart rate and sweating.'

But there were also moments of realism in his letters: He talked about William Hill, the bookmakers, offering odds of 9/5 on for a guilty verdict, 15/1 not guilty. He himself assessed his chances of ever being freed as 'possibly ten per cent. The amount of evidence is enormous. Perhaps all the jury are dead from the neck up but that is unlikely.'

As well as writing copious letters and legal notes, he found time for a new pastime: writing poetry. One poem, sent to Primrose, was entitled 'Despair' and summed up his feelings about being held prisoner, stating that only his wife could now help him.

He took tranquillisers, joking in a letter to a colleague: 'Me, well I keep taking the tablets – only once a week now that I sit in a corner and cry.' He described the routine as very ordered: 'go there, come here, do this and do that'. There was lots of time, but he was filling it, he said, with preparation for the case. He claimed that the only evidence the police had was that he practised as he always had done: without spelling it out, he meant that he was only guilty of being a good doctor. He also claimed that the police were withholding evidence from the defence.

Apart from complaints about the case, the letter was assured and chatty, giving news about his own family and starting and ending with a personal comment about his friend's life.

As far as the overcrowded prison system allows, prisoners held on serious charges are housed in single cells, especially if, as in Shipman's case, there are large amounts of paperwork to be dealt with, and it was soon apparent that he needed to be housed alone. By the time he came to trial, the mound of papers in his cell was ten feet high, covered in stickers with notes on for his lawyers: there was no room for a cellmate.

He took part in prison social activities, playing Scrabble, chess and pool. When he joined a quiz team his arrogance prevailed, and his fellow prisoners booted him off the team for being a know-all.

Despite the seriousness of the charges against him, he kept his status within the prison – he was always known as 'the Doctor', and held unofficial surgeries for prisoners and even, occasionally, for prison staff, giving them precise instructions as to which medication to ask for when they saw their own doctors. He even gave his expert opinion on medical evidence being used in other prisoners' cases, and helped them write letters.

For his friends and family, there was a new experience: the media spotlight. Immediately after Shipman's arrest, the town of Hyde was under siege to reporters and camera crews. Bewildered and unprepared to even contemplate his guilt, friends, family and patients of the doctor closed ranks. All inquiries were referred to Primrose, and Primrose stolidly refused to comment, glaring angrily at any journalists who dared to visit the house in Roe Cross Green. Sam, living at home, was the one who came in for the worst treatment, being attacked in the street on one occasion. But his confidence never wavered: until a week or two before the trial he was assuring his friends that it was all a ghastly mistake, that his father would be released and that the family would even take possession of Mrs Grundy's house in Joel Lane.

In Nottingham and Wetherby, too, the families of both Fred and Primrose encountered reporters and cameramen on their doorstep. All inquiries were greeted with a polite refusal to talk. In Wetherby, friends closed ranks around the elderly Mrs Oxtoby and her disabled daughter Mary, the family from whom Primrose had for years been estranged, and with whom the arrest and trial brought no reconciliation.

There was, naturally, speculation about the trial. Many serial killers, when confronted with the enormity of evidence against them, plead guilty: their time in court becomes a legal argument about their sanity, which determines whether they will go to prison or to a secure psychiatric hospital. But there was little doubt among those who knew Shipman well: he would make the most of his appearance in court, dragging the case out as long as he could, and insisting on giving evidence himself – and proclaiming his innocence to the last.

Preston as a venue was decided upon after legal arguments from the defence that it would be difficult to empanel an impartial jury in Manchester. Thirty-five miles from Hyde, the town of Preston is a bigger version of the Manchester satellite town, its prosperity also built on the cotton trade, its criss-cross of terraced housing also thrown up during the Industrial Revolution to accommodate factory workers. Historically, though, unlike Hyde, it existed as a town long before the nineteenth-century explosion of mills. In the eighteenth century it was a smart, chic place to live, with many rich and landed families settled around it, and a social round of balls and parties and assemblies. It was dubbed 'Proud Preston'. The famous Preston Guild, set up in medieval times to regulate trade, still meets every twenty years and has for hundreds of years now been a focus for a great pageant and celebration of the town.

By strange coincidence, one nineteenth-century ex-mayor of the town, Thomas Monk, has had his name removed from the inscription under a statue to Robert

Peel in the town centre: Monk was a doctor who brought shame and disgrace to the town when he forged the will of a patient and was sent to prison.

The court at Preston is known as the 'Old Bailey of the North', with some justification. It is architecturally similar to the most famous criminal court in the land, both inside and out. And because it is not as hemmed in by modern development as the London court, it looks, set among grandiose Victorian buildings, more imposing. The statue of Justice, blind and carrying scales, which tops the London court is reproduced here in the Public Assembly hall, where she stands in a large niche. The court building was opened in 1904, having cost £65,000 (it was renovated in 1995 for £1.2 million). At the turn of the century, two courtrooms with eight cells beneath them were ample (although the cells were, according to the architect, deemed to be able to hold seventy-five prisoners). A third court was added in 1965, and nowadays Preston also has another ten courts in a modern building half a mile away.

Court One, where Fred Shipman stood in the dock, is decorated with the sort of shiny green tiles you only see in municipal buildings, with rich oak panelling and intricately carved plasterwork above, and a stained-glass centre to the curved ceiling to allow in light. Hanging from the walls are stern portraits of past chairmen of Lancashire Quarter Sessions.

Across from Court One, Court Two was transformed into a media room, with an audiolink to allow the overflow of reporters who could not get seats in court to follow the proceedings. The thirty-eight press seats in court were allocated on application, and included three for the BBC, two for ITN, *Pulse* and *Doctor* magazines and, improbably, Rock FM, as well as all the national dailies and local newspapers and radio stations. Extra power points for laptop computers were installed in Court

Two for journalists, and a room was set aside for court artists.

Outside the building, Harris Street, named after a nineteenth-century philanthropist, was closed off between the court and the Harris Library for days at the beginning and end of the trial, forming a bay for all the outside broadcast vans of the television companies. Thick electricity cables led from the library to the vans. Preston is familiar with such a huge incursion of media: it was in the same court, six years earlier, that the two schoolboys who murdered the toddler James Bulger stood trial. That case, even more than the Shipman trial, attracted media interest from all over the world.

It was on Tuesday 5 October 1999 that Harold Frederick Shipman first appeared in the dock, facing sixteen charges, fifteen of murder and one of forging Mrs Grundy's will. The fifteen women he was accused of killing were Kathleen Grundy, Joan Melia, Winifred Mellor, Bianka Pomfret, Marie Quinn, Ivy Lomas, Irene Turner, Jean Lilley, Muriel Grimshaw, Marie West, Kathleen Wagstaff, Pamela Hillier, Norah Nuttall, Elizabeth Adams and Maureen Ward.

The leading prosecution counsel was Richard Henriques, who also prosecuted in the Bulger case. Henriques, fifty-five years old at the time of the trial, is the leader of the Northern Circuit of barristers, making him the most senior barrister in the north-west – and the most respected. He comes from a legal background: his Madeira-born father was a celebrated divorce lawyer. The year before the trial Henriques was named as one of Britain's 'fat cat' lawyers, reportedly earning legal aid fees of £500,000 in one year. Yet the Oxford-educated QC lives unostentatiously near Blackpool, and is in chambers in Manchester. His junior counsel, Peter Wright QC, is also based in Manchester.

By contrast, Shipman's defence team were not local to the area. Leading for the defence was Nicola Davies QC, forty-six at the time, who specialises in medical cases. From South Wales, she read law at Birmingham University, but worked for a time in the City as an investment analyst. She has been involved in several high-profile medical cases, including the Bristol heart surgery inquiry, the Cleveland child abuse inquiry, and the BSE inquiry. She was on holiday in Brazil when she took the call from Ann Ball, Shipman's solicitor, offering her the case. Slim, fair-haired and smartly dressed, her clipped style seemed at odds with the case and she did not come into her own until the trial reached the stage of dissecting expert evidence. Her junior, Ian Winter, seemed equally uncomfortable with the parade of elderly, working-class witnesses.

The judge was 61-year-old Thayne Forbes, who had been presiding judge of the Northern Circuit for two and a half years at the time of the trial. Of Scottish descent, he was born on the Isle of Wight and educated at Winchester College, then at a grammar school in Surrey, before getting his law degree at London University. His reputation is of being scrupulously fair and meticulous: none of his trials has ever seen a successful appeal against conviction. His owlish, patient and occasionally amused expression came to characterise the proceedings for the regulars in court.

The first day in court brought a small crowd to the outside of the building, mostly women shoppers, who told reporters they were waiting to see Primrose. She, flanked by all her children, had arrived early, and they were already in the public gallery. Later, as they left, they were pursued to the nearby multi-storey car park by photographers and film cameras, but they neither hurried not showed any reaction. There were one or two shouts from the crowd, and a couple of young boys yelled obscenities.

But it was a low-key protest, and the police crash barriers looked surplus to requirements. Inside the courtroom, the officials had not needed their 'Public Gallery Full' sign.

To the frustration of the assembled media, the start of the trial was delayed for four days by legal arguments, not getting into full swing until the following Monday. On 11 October, however, a jury was finally sworn in. A panel of sixty possible jurors were warned that the trial could last for five months, and asked if there was any reason why they could not serve for that long. More than twenty put their hands up. The judge excused a single mother, a woman who regularly suffered from bronchitis in the winter, a man who had planned a fortieth wedding anniversary holiday. Others, like a man who was planning a trip to Disneyland, were not given permission to leave. Eventually seven men and five women, ranging in age between their mid-twenties and late fifties, were sworn in. Several times Mr Justice Forbes stressed how important the case ahead of them was.

If they had any doubts about its importance, these were instantly dispelled by Richard Henriques' opening address. For eight hours the prosecution QC went through the nature of all the charges in detail. But it was his very first remarks which offered the only explanation put forward by the prosecution as to why a respectable family doctor should become a serial killer.

Talking about the fifteen victims, he said: 'None of them were prescribed morphine or diamorphine; all of them died most unexpectedly; all of them had seen Dr Shipman on the day of their death. There is no question of euthanasia or what is sometimes called mercy killing. None of the deceased were terminally ill. The defendant killed those fifteen patients because he enjoyed doing so. He was exercising the ultimate power of controlling life and death, and repeated it so often that he must have found the drama of taking life to his taste.'

For the first few days of the hearing Shipman struggled with a large pile of papers on his lap, making copious notes to pass to his lawyers: a table was eventually installed in the dock to allow him to spread them out.

The first witness to give evidence was Angela Woodruff, Kathleen Grundy's daughter. As a solicitor, she should have been less in awe of the panoply of the law than the many others who would follow her, but she looked drawn and distressed throughout her time in the witness box.

For Shipman, the prosecution evidence gave him the opportunity to see again many of the patients who had hobbled in and out of The Surgery. But now, as friends and relatives of the victims, they were struggling to and from the witness box: elderly women with their hair freshly permed and given a silver or blue rinse for the occasion, wearing their smartest coats with brooches on the lapel, and with silver- or gold-rimmed spectacles. Several of them were hard of hearing, and the barristers had to shout their questions to them. Often, when asked an obvious but necessary question, the old ladies would answer with ill-concealed impatience. 'Was Mrs X a friend of yours?', for example, and the reply would be 'Of course she was', delivered in a tone which suggested, 'What a bloody stupid thing to ask.'

Alongside the elderly friends came the middle-aged sons and daughters of the victims, telling the court how fit and well their mothers had been. 'She always played football with my kids,' one of the daughters of Winnie Mellor told the court. If, from the prosecution opening, any of the jurors had had the impression they were going to hear a recital of boring details about the deaths of old women, the witnesses dispelled this: from their testimony all the victims were portrayed vividly, became real, important people who had led full and rewarding lives.

It was against these witnesses that the defence team really struggled, trying to make old ladies admit that their memories of events might be confused, that they may have talked among themselves and stories may have changed. There was a stoical dignity about the witnesses, who refused to be flustered or trapped into admitting confusion. The defence could not capitalise on their age or the unreliability of their memories: every attempt to do so lost them the sympathy of the courtroom.

The prosecution case lasted twenty-five days, punctuated by two breaks of a few days. There were a few laughs: Richard Henriques brought smiles to the jurors' faces when he asked the pathologist Dr John Rutherford to explain his medical evidence more simply by saying 'Can you put that in layman's terms, bearing in mind that we are in Preston, not a city?' There was consternation in the local press: could he possibly be suggesting that people in Preston were not as bright as those who live in cities? It gave the reporters the chance to remind local inhabitants that they had narrowly missed out in the bid for city status in 1992, and they hope to be declared a city as part of the Millennium celebrations.

The dignity of the court was punctured on Monday 8 November when a local drunk took refuge from the cold in the public gallery, somehow escaping the watchful eye of the good-natured security guards. Twice during evidence he drifted off to sleep, snoozing off the effects of the empty cans of lager he left outside the courtroom. Both times, when he awoke, he muttered the word 'Murderer', loud enough for those in the gallery (including Primrose) to hear, but not audible to the bench. Eventually he shouted 'Murderer!' and everyone, except Shipman, turned to look at him. The jury and the judge left the court while security guards tried to cajole the drunk to leave. He refused to go, gripping the side of his seat. Eventually one of the policemen working on the trial and a burly security guard manhandled him out of the room. He shouted 'Fucking murderer!' as he went.

A bomb scare closed the court on Day 22 of the trial. Ushers shepherded the jury to a nearby hotel as the bomb squad from Liverpool was summoned and a police helicopter hovered overhead. After the initial excitement, the reporters headed for the nearest pub. Three hours later, after the court had been searched, the judge decide it was not worth resuming. It was Friday lunchtime, so everybody got an early start to the weekend.

As well as the friends and families of the victims, the prosecution produced a parade of experts, including one from Germany and one from America, to describe the amounts of morphine needed to kill, and the effects of morphine. The German expert, Dr Hans Sachs from the University of Munster (coincidentally, Bianka Pomfret's home town) told how he found morphine in hair samples. When Julie Evans, the toxicologist who analysed the tissue of the exhumed bodies, was questioned by the defence about the existence of morphine in over-the-counter medicines such as codeine and the kaolin and morphine diarrhoea treatment, she told the court that Kathleen Grundy would have had to have drunk a litre and a half of kaolin and morphine to achieve the level found in her body.

Three pharmacists from Hyde gave evidence about dispensing morphine and diamorphine on prescriptions issued by Shipman, and then the court heard the details of twenty-six patients, some living but many dead, in whose names the doctor had written prescriptions. The widows, daughters and sons of some of these patients gave evidence about the last days of their dying relatives, and the medication prescribed for them. The daughter of one old man who died from lung cancer said he had never been treated with diamorphine, despite prescriptions being cashed in his name at the chemist for the drug.

Lilian Ibbotson, a patient of Shipman's for twenty years, and in whose name he had prescribed morphine, appeared in court in person to say the only injection she had ever been given was for tennis elbow. Asthma sufferer Leonard Fallows also told the court that he had never been treated with morphine – despite a prescription in his name having been dispensed.

Two witnesses made reappearances to give more evidence against him. The district nurse, Marion Gilchrist, to whom he said shortly before his arrest, 'On the evidence they have, I would have me guilty,' told the court how she had challenged Shipman about a discrepancy in the amount of diamorphine logged as having been provided for a dying cancer patient. Shipman told her he had 'borrowed it' for another terminally ill patient.

One of the most moving moments in the trial was when Ann Brown, the daughter of Muriel Grimshaw, returned to the witness box. She had already given evidence about the last days of her mother's life: now she talked about the death of her first husband, Raymond Jones. In the autumn of 1993 her husband was diagnosed with cancer, and was prescribed morphine tablets. When the pain became worse a syringe driver was set up. He died in the early morning of 27 November. Dr Shipman attended soon afterwards, and took away two or three boxes of diamorphine. The court was hushed as Mrs Brown gave her evidence, as the awful thought that her mother might have been killed with morphine stockpiled after the death of her husband crossed everyone's minds. In fact, Mrs Brown's mother did not die until almost four years later, no doubt with morphine obtained from another terminally ill patient.

In police interviews Shipman had insisted that he did not keep stocks of morphine at his surgery or his home, and had not done so since his drugs problem at Todmorden. But in a white plastic C & A carrier bag found in an upstairs rear bedroom at the house in Roe Cross Green the police discovered a stash of ampoules and tablets of morphine.

In one of the few mistakes made in the second police investigation, the contents of the carrier bag, which was seized when the house was searched on 14 August 1998, were not properly examined until an audit of evidence was taken nearly a year later. Then, six weeks before the trial started, they discovered inside an orange Zantac (an anti-ulcer drug) box fifty-four slow-release morphine tablets prescribed for Mrs Maureen Jackson. There were another thirty-nine similar tablets prescribed for Mrs Lena Slater, and a white Nozinan (an anti-psychotic drug) box contained four ampoules of diamorphine.

All in all, the prosecution had assembled an impressive collection of evidence, and the defence had scored very few points in cross-examination. What fascinated everyone with an interest in the case was what kind of defence the doctor could possibly produce.

It was on a blustery, wild day, Thursday 25 November, that the defence case started, and the moment that the public gallery and the press had been waiting for arrived: Shipman himself went into the witness box. He took the stand just after noon, looking frail and nervous, diminished. His light grey suit was hanging loosely on his hunched shoulders, and he wore a white shirt and grey striped tie. Even his voice seemed small: he spoke in low husky tones, having to be gently reminded by the judge to speak up. He apologised, saying, 'I slur my speech sometimes. It's the tablets I'm on.' The first part of his evidence took the court through his training and the details of his career. Then he described the weekly routines of The Surgery, explaining how he did administrative work on Mondays and minor operations on Fridays.

'Removing warts or ingrowing toenails,' he said, with a smile. 'Nothing glamorous.'

He talked about making home visits and how, if he had time he 'might pop in and have a word with the wife'.

Just fifteen feet away, Primrose, 'the wife', sat impassively on one of the black plastic chairs in the public gallery which were permanently reserved for her and her family, wearing a voluminous dark-blue cotton suit patterned with gold motifs. Her middle son, David, sat next to her, much of the time with his head in his hands.

In the lunchtime recess Primrose, who had become so used to the rhythms of the court, smiled and nodded amicably to the familiar faces of the reporters and the court officials, but in court, although she kept her eyes fixed on him, her husband of thirty-five years did not glance up at her.

The news that the doctor was on the stand brought queues for the forty seats in the public gallery, with a gaggle of women sitting on the steps outside Court One, eating biscuits and sharing cans of soft drinks.

In the afternoon, Shipman began to get into his stride. The initial nervousness had evaporated, his voice was stronger, and there were glimpses of his usual hauteur: he frowned when his QC shared a joke with the judge, making it clear that in his opinion this was no laughing matter; and when he told the court he did not like using a word-processor he slipped unselfconsciously into the present tense.

'I'm one of the few doctors in the area who still hand-writes letters,' he said, as if he had just popped along from his surgery for half a day to talk to the court.

Going through the evidence about Mrs Grundy's death, he told the court he believed she was taking drugs not prescribed by him.

'I had a suspicion she was taking an opiate: codeine, pethidine, perhaps morphine.' There was an almost imperceptible pause before he spoke the word 'morphine', as if it took extra effort to utter it. Then he said Mrs Grundy looked 'old and going downhill'. He fiddled for ten minutes with a piece of A4 paper, folding it and refolding it to demonstrate the way in which he claimed Mrs Grundy presented her will to him to be witnessed.

While he spoke, Angela Woodruff, Mrs Grundy's daughter, watched intently from the gallery, making notes. When his QC, Nicola Davies, asked him the all-important question, 'Did you murder Kathleen Grundy?' he batted the answer back emphatically: 'No, I did not.'

It was a question he would hear, with only the name varied, another fourteen times over the following few days, and each time the answer would be the same. No, according to Shipman, he definitely had not murdered anyone.

As he left the court building at the end of his first day in the box, a Sky television crew filmed him being led to the prison van which would transport him back to Strangeways. He looked as he had done in his first few minutes in court: exhausted, defeated.

But by the next morning he had rallied again, and was ready to answer questions about the next three victims, Bianka Pomfret, Winnie Mellor and Joan Melia. In each case, according to him, the deaths had been entirely natural. His only admission was to backdating his computer records – done, he said, to bring his files in line with when the patient said they had first noticed the symptoms.

He said that Bianka Pomfret told him, on the day of her death, that she had chest pains which sounded to him like angina.

'I had to politely tell her off. She was a regular visitor, but she had not mentioned the chest pains. I was upset she hadn't trusted me enough to tell me about the pains.'

He alleged she told him she had had the pains many

times before, so he backdated his computer records for six or eight months to show progression of an illness.

He did the same backdating for Winifred Mellor, because again he said he had not been given the information about her 'angina' until the day she died. Twice he told the court how, faced with a patient 'dying in front of me', he decided not to attempt resuscitation. Marie West, he said, had been walking and talking moments before she died, but she collapsed as he was looking in his bag for a stethoscope. Marie Quinn had collapsed before he found her, he said. In both cases, he told the jury, he did not try to revive the women because he felt their lives would be impaired. With Mrs West, he said, he was 'bothered' by 'what we would end up with'.

'In my experience, you would not get someone who is able to live independently and enjoy life like she did.'

When he went into her kitchen, looking, he said, for the telephone, he met her friend Marion Hadfield. He did not know she was there. But later, when he filled in the death certificate, he said she was present at the death, defending this in court by saying she was in the house at the time.

With Mrs Quinn, he again said he did not try to resuscitate her because 'patients who survive often have a loss of personality and a loss of use of their body, and end up in a nursing home'.

Kathleen Wagstaff also, he said, died in front of him: but in her case he claimed to have tried resuscitation for ten minutes, although he did not call an ambulance. It was while giving evidence about Mrs Wagstaff that he started to cry, slumping down in the witness box with his head in his hands. He explained his distress in a cruel and unnecessary way: 'It was one of the few times when possibly I was more upset than the relatives.'

Kathleen Wagstaff's family did not deserve any suggestion that they were not caring. It was her daughter-in-law who had had to endure the double shock of first being told that her mother was dead, and then discovering that this was a mistake: it was really her mother-in-law. Forgiving him this mistake, the Wagstaff family were supporters of Dr Shipman in the early days of the investigation. Again, on Kathleen Wagstaff's death certificate Shipman said that a neighbour was present at the death, but this time there was no one even on the premises: he told the jury that his only explanation for this mistake was that he was so upset about the death.

As well as three patients dying while he was in the same room, he also told the court about two who died while he was attending them but briefly out of the room. He made what he called 'a cold visit' to Norah Nuttall after seeing her earlier that day at his surgery. There was no request for a visit: 'This was me calling to see how the patient was coping.'

He claimed he found her much worse, and decided to get a drug from his car. He met her son outside the house, followed him back inside, and found her dead. Similarly, when Lizzie Adams died he claimed to be in the next room, looking for the telephone number of a relative, when Mrs Adams' friend Bill Catlow went through to her and called him back in. She, too, was dead.

Three others died within minutes of him leaving their homes. In the case of Pamela Hillier, who was found dead half an hour after he left her, he admitted backdating her medical records on the day she died, using, he claimed, information she had given him on earlier visits to his surgery.

Irene Turner died, he said, in the ten minutes between him telling a neighbour to pack a bag for her admission to hospital and his return to her home after, he claimed, carrying out a test on her urine at his surgery.

Talking about the death of Jean Lilley was, for the doctor, the highlight of his defence. Mrs Lilley, who was found dead fifteen minutes after he left her, had several genuinely serious medical complaints, and had been referred to hospital consultants on a few occasions. This gave Shipman a chance to explain her medical history to the jury, and he warmed to the task. He delivered a mini-lecture on lung disease, defining terms like cryptogenic alveolitis, idiopathic fibrosis and vascular necrosis as if he were addressing a group of medical students. It was Shipman the doctor, slightly patronising but very much in control, who addressed the jury about Mrs Lilley's medication: 'I'm sure you all know people who, when they have an angina attack, put a tablet under their tongue – this is a souped-up version.'

'Aspirin, as you are all aware, has had lots of publicity, and I expect everyone knows that it is what we give to make the blood less sticky.'

Muriel Grimshaw was another victim to whom he made 'a cold visit', prompted, he said, by her asking for a repeat prescription. The day after his visit she was found dead, fully clothed, on her bed. Despite the suddenness of her death he said he felt there was no need for a post-mortem.

'With hindsight, I would have had it done, but at the time I thought I didn't need to.'

Nicola Davies, his counsel, asked: 'With hindsight?'

'If I had had it done, I would not be stood here today,' he said.

Ivy Lomas was the only one on the indictment who died at his surgery. He admitted in court that he joked about putting a plaque up in his surgery because she came to see him so often, but said it was a joke he made about all regular attenders – and he denied cracking it to the policeman who called at the surgery after Mrs Lomas' death.

He said he did not ask his receptionist to help him resuscitate Mrs Lomas because he did not want 'to disrupt the surgery'. He claimed that, because of his years in the St John Ambulance Brigade, he did not need help. He said he carried out heart massage and mouth-to-mouth resuscitation for fifteen minutes. He did not tell the receptionist that Mrs Lomas was dead, but carried on seeing other patients, 'because to tell her in front of three other patients I thought was inappropriate'.

The final death that he told the court about was that of Maureen Ward, who he claimed to find dead when he called at her home to give her a letter for an urgent specialist appointment. After briefly explaining how he found her lifeless on the bed, for the fifteenth time his QC asked him the familiar questions: 'Did you administer morphine or diamorphine?' and 'Did you murder Maureen Ward?' The answer, as ever, was: 'No, I did not.'

After the final question Nicola Davies sat down, to the apparent surprise of Fred Shipman. He seemed to be expecting her questioning to go on beyond the outline of his dealings with the fifteen victims. His shock was so great that when Richard Henriques stood up to start the cross-examination he broke down, telling the judge he was unwell. He was given a fifteen-minute break, and returned to court composed, but still looking uncomfortable.

He would remain uncomfortable throughout the cross-examination, which was relentless. For another seven days, Shipman remained in the witness box while Henriques picked over the bones of his evidence, constantly hitting on the inconsistencies in Shipman's records of the deaths, and the uncanny similarities between the deaths.

The doctor admitted 'a bad habit' of prescribing very large amounts of morphine for patients in need of it, claiming that he had no idea what subsequently happened to it. He said the morphine found at his home was 'an oversight'.

He offered no explanation for the morphine found in

the bodies of the exhumed victims, other than to reiterate that he suspected Mrs Grundy of drug abuse. The others, he said, showed no signs of drug abuse, and he could not say how morphine got into their bodies within minutes of him visiting them. His failure to offer any explanation was particularly marked in the case of Ivy Lomas, who died in his surgery. He conceded that, despite writing 'heart disease' on her death certificate, in the light of the toxicology evidence she must have died from morphine poisoning. He agreed that the morphine level was so high that it would have taken effect within five minutes.

'If this lady died at 4.10pm she must have been administered or administered to herself the drug between 4pm and 4.10pm, mustn't she?' Richard Henriques asked.

'You could put the evidence that way and, yes, I would agree,' Shipman said, wearily. He went on to say that he had not seen her administer the drug to herself, he hadn't left her alone in the surgery, and nobody else had been present.

'I don't know of any explanation,' he said.

'There is no sensible explanation, save and except your guilt,' Henriques retorted.

'That's what you're saying and I disagree with it strongly. I didn't administer anything to this lady and I have no idea how it got into her body,' said the doctor.

In the case of Norah Nuttall, Richard Henriques spoke of the 'spectacular coincidence' of Shipman making an unexpected and unscheduled call at her home, only to find her minutes away from death. Shipman said he called to see how she was getting on in her 'new' house – in fact, as Henriques was happy to point out, she had lived there for eight years.

'The family doctor comes off the street, having not done so in the preceding eight years, at the very moment when Norah Nuttall's pulse is thready and difficult to feel. That is a chance in a million, isn't it?'

'I wouldn't know,' Shipman replied, sullenly.

On 10 December, the thirty-seventh day of the trial, the cross-examination finished, with Richard Henriques reminding the GP of what he had told Nurse Gilchrist, in the early days of the police inquiry: 'I would have me guilty on the evidence.' Back then, as the QC pointed out, the evidence then was 'nothing compared to the evidence now'.

'Not once in all these cases did you call an ambulance . . . Not once did you admit any patient to hospital . . . Not once did you permit a post-mortem . . . The simple explanation for all the evidence in this case is your guilt.'

To the surprise of the reporters in court, only one other defence witness was called, a fingerprint expert who talked about the fingerprints found on Mrs Grundy's will. There was no expert toxicology evidence: by this stage of the trial it was clear that Shipman was conceding that morphine was the cause of death for all the victims whose bodies were exhumed. His defence was virtually non-existent, and consisted only of his determined insistence on being not guilty.

On Monday 13 December, with all the evidence heard, the judge wished the jury members a merry Christmas and a pleasant holiday, telling them that he would see them again on 5 January 2000.

When the court reconvened it was Richard Henriques' turn to address the jury again, with his closing speech. He spoke calmly and incisively, reminding them that they had heard the evidence of more than 120 prosecution witnesses. He spoke about the way in which Shipman had abused the trust that the victims and their families put in him, as a doctor.

'They trusted him to care for them, their relatives trusted him to tell the truth about the circumstances in which the patients died, and the community trusted him to complete records with honesty and integrity.

'We submit that he breached that trust. He did not care for those fifteen patients, he killed them. He did not with truth relay the circumstances of death to grieving relatives, he duped them to save his own skin and falsified medical records to cover his tracks. He took advantage of their grief and lesser knowledge of medicine. As they grieved, this determined man deployed any and every device to ensure that no post-mortem took place. He would overbear, belittle, bamboozle and disadvantage relatives until they accepted the doctor's word that they should not "put their mother through it".'

The reason why no post-mortem was called, said the prosecuting counsel, was because 'the poisoner fears pathology, ambulances and hospitals'.

Shipman, wearing a familiar charcoal grey suit, white shirt and striped green and red tie, listened to the résumé of evidence against him, taking, as he did throughout the trial, notes on a foolscap pad. But many of the marks he made on the paper on the desk in front of him were doodles: he sketched a Christmas tree, a lectern with a heavy book on it and what appeared to be a church window behind it. He also drew in a grid of squares which he filled with crosses and dashes, as if he was playing a game of his own creation with himself, making the marks frantically and repetitively. He seemed to be sitting lower in the chair, and every so often his shoulders heaved and he sighed audibly. His solicitor, Ann Ball, glanced at him frequently, as if she was unsure that he would survive the day.

Just feet away from him in the well of the court sat Stan Egerton, the Detective Inspector who started the inquiry and who retired from the force halfway through the investigation. A larger-than-life character, wearing a club blazer and a vivid red Disneyworld tie, the contrast between the two men could not have been more marked. Had they both leaned forward and stretched out their arms, they could have shaken hands. But Shipman never once glanced at the policeman who first charged him with murder. He was no longer the arrogant, patronising doctor who dismissed the police as 'thick': he looked cowed, defeated and greatly diminished.

The prosecution summing-up was over by lunchtime the following day, with Richard Henriques ending with Dr Shipman's own summing-up of the case, as given to the practice nurse before his arrest: 'I read thrillers and I would have me guilty on the evidence.' Then it was the turn of Nicola Davies to address the jury on behalf of the defendant. She painted a portrait of a dedicated doctor, describing him as 'caring if idiosyncratic', a GP who went beyond the call of duty in his care for his patients. He was not, she said, a doctor who stood on ceremony, and often went calling on patients who had not summoned him – but not for a sinister purpose. Keeping records was not his forte, she said, because he was 'more interested in the patients than the paperwork'.

She dismissed the fact that friends and families of victims found him cold and unsympathetic as nothing more than a doctor bringing 'a calm and professional attitude' to the deaths.

She homed in on the fact that the prosecution had failed to find a motive for the killings, dismissing the 'power complex' as an amateur psychological theory. And she described the stockpiling of morphine by the GP as 'a red herring'.

'Here is a doctor on occasion going the extra mile for a patient, anticipating the pain and the medicine,' she told the jury.

On the charge of forgery, she pointed out that the Grundy will and accompanying letters were, in the opinion of handwriting experts, 'crude and clumsy simulations'.

But Dr Shipman was a skilled letter-writer because he ran a one-man surgery.

'Are these letters the sort a devious, clever and cunning man would write?' she asked.

She said that the toxicology evidence was not safe, because of the decomposition of the bodies, and because the prosecution toxicology expert, Julie Evans, admitted she had broken new ground in carrying out some of the tests.

'The scientific evidence in this case is inherently unreliable, these are uncharted scientific waters,' the defence QC said. 'The prosecution case stands and fall on the toxicological evidence.'

Mr Justice Forbes began his lengthy summing-up of the case on Monday 10 January. He described it as a deeply disturbing case.

'The allegations could not be more serious: a doctor accused of murdering fifteen of his patients. Inevitably in the course of this case you will have heard evidence that will have caused anger, disgust, profound dismay and deep sympathy. They must not be allowed to cloud your judgement. You must consider the facts dispassionately.'

He stressed that each of the sixteen charges had to be considered individually. 'They do not stand or fall together,' he said.

For two weeks the judge painstakingly went over all the evidence that the jurors had heard. The fourteenth of January, the fourth day of his summing-up, was Fred Shipman's fifty-fourth birthday: the day passed unmarked in court, as did the birth of the judge's fifth grandchild.

It was on Monday 24 January that the jury retired to consider their verdicts. Thirty relatives of victims watched from the public gallery as they were shepherded out of the courtroom. But there was to be no conclusion that day: after five hours of deliberating, they were sent home for the night. It was a week later, after six days of increasing tension, that the jury came back with their verdicts, on Monday 31 January. It was late in the court day: the sixty media people who were waiting were expecting the jury to once again be sent home for the night. Then a whisper went through the ranks that the jury had asked for another ten minutes.

At 4.33pm they came back into the courtroom and the foreman announced in a clear, strong voice that all their verdicts were unanimous. Not that there was any need to speak up: the court was so quiet that a whisper could have been heard. Guilty, guilty, guilty . . . sixteen times, fifteen murders and the forgery of the will.

Shipman remained stock still and emotionless. Primrose, wearing a black suit, sat next to her son Christopher, with David behind her. She, too, showed no sign of the turmoil that must have been crowding in on her mind; but both the boys lowered their eyes and shrank in their seats, and David visibly winced.

There were gasps from the public gallery, full of the victims' relatives, as the court was told about Shipman's previous conviction for forging prescriptions. Defence counsel, Nicola Davies, then rose to ask for sentence to be passed immediately.

For three full minutes Mr Justice Forbes addressed the doctor, who slightly bowed his head and twiddled his thumbs around each other.

'You have finally been brought to justice by the verdict of this jury. I have no doubt whatsoever that these are true verdicts. The time has now come for me to pass sentence upon you for these wicked, wicked crimes.

'Each of your victims was your patient. You murdered each and every one of your victims by a calculated and cold-blooded perversion of your medical skills for your own evil and wicked purposes. You took advantage of and grossly abused their trust. You were, after all, each victim's doctor. I have little doubt that each of your victims smiled and thanked you as she submitted to your deadly ministrations.

'None realised yours was not a healing touch, none knew in truth you had brought her death, death disguised as the caring attention of a good doctor. The sheer wickedness of what you have done defies description. It is shocking and beyond belief. You have not shown the slightest remorse or contrition for your evil deeds and you have subjected the family and friends of your victims to having to re-live the tragedy and grief you visited on them.'

After passing fifteen life sentences and a four-year sentence for the forgery, the judge then broke with the usual tradition of sending his recommendations about the length of the sentence to the Home Secretary in writing.

'In the ordinary way, I would not do this in open court but in your case I am satisfied justice demands that I make my views known at the conclusion of this trial. I have formed the conclusion that the crimes you stand convicted of are so heinous that in your case life must mean life. My recommendation will be that you spend the remainder of your days in prison.'

As Shipman was taken from the dock he did not glance at his wife or his sons. Mr Justice Forbes then paid an emotional and very moving tribute to those involved in the case. To muffled sobs from the public gallery, he spoke directly to the relatives, his own voice cracking and tears welling behind his glasses as he addressed them.

'I would like you to know how much I admire the courage and quiet dignity you have shown. Your evidence was at times intensely moving and touched the hearts of all who heard it. Your contribution to the course of justice in this terrible and tragic case will stand as a moving memorial and tribute to your loved ones.'

He then spoke to the police, commending particularly Detective Superintendent Bernard Postles and DCI Mike

Williams, but also naming the whole of the team, as well as the legal teams.

'This has been a deeply disturbing trial and the significance cannot be understated. This has also been an historic trial.'

Finally the judge thanked the jury, many of whom themselves looked close to tears as he addressed them: 'On a personal note, I would like you to know that I count myself privileged to have had you as my jury in this dramatic and significant trial.'

As the judge finished speaking, there was a spontaneous, if unconventional, smattering of applause from the public gallery. Red-eyed but relieved, the relatives of the victims filed out of court, leaving Primrose and her family to be escorted away by security guards.

The marathon fifty-seven-day trial was finally over, but the reckoning had only just begun. How many other victims are there? Could he have been stopped before? What lessons can be learned? Within minutes of the verdict the rhetoric began. The government announced an inquiry, the West Pennine Health Authority held a press conference and suspended the doctor who had advised the police on the first, abortive, investigation. The police announced that Shipman would be charged with another twenty-three murders. Television channels re-ordered their schedules, the next morning's newspapers contained acres of coverage, and Fred Shipman's picture was beamed across the world.

No doubt procedures will change: disposal and prescription of drugs will be monitored more effectively; single-handed doctors will come under closer scrutiny; cross-checks on doctor's death rates will be instituted.

Had these changes been in place, it is likely that Shipman would have been stopped earlier, and the death count would have been lower. But he would still have murdered, because it was a deep need within his own personality that led him to inject lethal doses of morphine into his patients. In the words of the coroner, John Pollard: 'Shipman was quite clearly an evil man, and it is extremely difficult to legislate against evil.'

# 15
# Expert Opinions

One day in March 1999, just before he retired after thirty years in Greater Manchester Police, DI Stan Egerton walked into St Luke's Church in Dukinfield and sat for a time, on his own, in one of the pews. Then he lit fifteen candles, one for each of the victims that Fred Shipman was charged with killing. It was, he felt, a very small gesture: he had spent months working on the case, directing detectives, sifting evidence, but he had never lost sight of the fact that, at its heart, were sad families who had lost wives, mothers and grandmothers they loved. As a policeman he had occasionally had to trespass on their grief, and this was his private way of atoning for that.

It will come as a surprise to some of those who have worked with Stan over the years to know that underneath his bluff, straightforward, no-nonsense exterior he is a sensitive man with a deep religious belief. He is not a church-goer, but he is a committed Christian who, from time to time, finds solace at St Luke's, the church of the divisional chaplain, Rev. Denis Thomas. Stan Egerton has lit candles here once before, for a mother and two of her children who died in a house fire in Dukinfield, after petrol was poured through their letterbox.

Like everyone else who worked on the Shipman case, in the early days it was impossible to take in the enormity of the crimes: what started as a forgery case quickly became murder, and then multiple murder, and eventually the biggest case ever in British criminal history (and world history, if genocide and political murders are discounted). While grappling with the huge scope of Shipman's crimes, Stan Egerton was also dealing on a regular basis with their perpetrator. The doctor treated the policeman 'like something that had been brought in on his shoe'. It was an arrogance he could ill afford.

Because he believes in God, and good, DI Egerton also believes in evil. Despite his long career working with criminals, he believes he has rarely, if ever, encountered true evil before: but that is how he classifies Fred Shipman.

Evil is the verdict given by others who have had to deal with the consequences of Shipman's actions, especially the families of the victims. The simplest definition of evil is 'finding pleasure in harming others'. Most people – certainly most of the victims' families – regard it as an absolute, and that is how it has been accepted for much of man's history. But in the latter half of the twentieth century a great deal of work has been done on the nature of evil (particularly as a result of the Holocaust) and there is a consensus among experts that the capacity for evil may exist in all of us, but that it takes more than a predisposition to turn someone into a sadist or a serial killer. There is a trigger, a defining moment, usually in childhood, when the way of thinking about others becomes fixed.

'Evil is a state of mind, a state of relating to other people. It is always dynamic, but in some people the capacity to relate becomes fixed and distorted,' says Gwen Adshead, a clinical psychotherapist at Broadmoor Hospital, a secure hospital for the criminally insane.

'We can usually find some trauma in childhood from which it stems (although there is some evidence now, from work done with Vietnam veterans, that adult trauma can also release a capacity for evil). But there are a few individuals in whom it is very hard to find any defining moment.'

Accepting this definition, Fred Shipman is certainly evil, but it is necessary to look deeper to understand the dynamic element, the point at which his capacity for evil was allowed to thrive, and why it continued to thrive for so long.

Surprisingly little work has been done on the characteristics of serial killers, and what has been done is mainly American research. In most ways, the Shipman killings are very much at odds with the usual run of serial killings. He is much older than the typical profile of serial killers (under thirty-three), although this could simply be a function of him having managed to escape detection for very much longer than most.

Most serial killers are alienated from society, unable to function well in social settings, and come from dysfunctional backgrounds. Examples are Jeffrey Dahmer or Dennis Nilsen, complete misfits who found most normal social relationships difficult, if not impossible. They were both able to hold down jobs – Dahmer killing 17 young men in Milwaukee while he was working shifts at a chocolate factory; Nilsen murdering and dismembering fifteen youths in North London while holding down a Civil Service job at an unemployment centre. But they failed conspicuously to establish or hold normal relationships with family, friends and sexual partners.

Fred Shipman managed, superficially at least, to have a 'normal' life, with a wife and children, with colleagues who, while perhaps not liking him much, did not find his behaviour bizarre or alarming. He made social contacts, although perhaps in a rather contrived and unsatisfactory way, always on his terms: his sudden enthusiasms for the Rochdale Canal Society, the St John Ambulance, the school PTA, the Family Practitioner Committee, were all-or-nothing affairs, where his interest waned as rapidly as it was generated.

He maintained a job, and did it well by most accounts. All his failings as a doctor are to do with his murders. To those patients he was not killing he was a marvellous GP, caring, attentive and always prepared to prescribe expensive drugs.

Unlike most serial killers, the murders he committed were not violent. He does not, we can assume, fantasise about violence, because his killings have been remarkably violence-free. Whatever fuelled his obsession with killing, it was not a sadistic pleasure: he gave his victims a gentle, pain-free death, almost as though he was bestowing a blessing.

Nor did he choose victims at random (although there is a certain randomness, a randomness of opportunity, in his pattern of killing). Serial killers may have themes – sexual killers may kill young girls, killers like Peter Sutcliffe, the Yorkshire Ripper, may become fixated on a certain group of individuals (Sutcliffe believed, though not always correctly, that he was killing prostitutes). Most serial killers do not know their victims, but Shipman knew all of his.

There does not appear to have been any overtly sexual motivation (by far the most common motivation for serial killers), although the relationship between power and sex is an intricate one (rapists do not single out old, frail pensioners because they are sexually aroused by old women, it is because the act of rape is an act of domination and power, and it is this element that arouses them). If Shipman derived any sexual pleasure from his murders, it was private: he never interfered with any of the bodies nor did he, when found at the scene of a killing, appear to be excited (although the witnesses, themselves shocked and distressed, were not aware that they were in the presence of a murderer or a murder victim, so would be unlikely to take much notice of his behaviour).

But there is one way in which his attitude to his victims does seem to have been consistent with that of other serial killers. At the point of death, he no longer saw them as human beings. He was distanced from them: they were not real people with families, hopes and fears. He was able to pull down a blind between the old ladies he knew, and 'twinkled at' when he chatted to them about their cats and their aches and pains, and the bodies he dispensed to death. He was never completely remote from what he was doing (he was perfectly capable of holding a reasonable conversation with anyone who came upon him at the scene of a crime), but he was able, possibly because of the job he had chosen, to regard those bodies separately from the individuals who inhabited them.

We will explore the desensitising effects of his chosen profession later, but to return to Gwen Adshead's definition of evil as a dynamic state of mind which can, in some people, become fixed, we must look for a defining moment in Fred Shipman's life. It is most likely to have been the death of his mother (although this came later than most clinical psychologists would expect to find a trauma triggering such a capacity for distancing himself from other people's feelings). He was already isolated: his childhood and adolescence were spent on the fringes of his peer group, always the outsider, watching the others. His participation – and accomplishment in – rugby and athletics gave him a great opportunity for redemption, a key to being accepted and accepting, and both a physical and emotional bond with others. But he rejected it: he played no sport after leaving school, to the surprise of those who knew him as a talented rugby player.

He is certainly not psychotically ill – or at least was not at the time of the killings. Psychosis is rarely an explanation for serial killing. It can be the cause of single murders, or of spree murders, when a killer like Michael Ryan (the perpetrator of the Hungerford massacre) goes on the rampage and kills several people within a short space of time. There is some suggestion that the Yorkshire Ripper was schizophrenic, and was being told by God to carry out his crimes, but psychosis is rarely as regular or organised as that: it is, without medication, an erratic and ungovernable state, and most acute schizophrenics would be showing signs of their illness in all areas of their lives, not just when they went out on the streets at night to kill.

What Shipman is suffering from, as all serial killers are, is a personality disorder – a pernicious and untreatable aberration of personality. The Home Office is currently vexed over how people with personality disorders can be restrained before they have committed crimes, to prevent them doing so (because they are technically 'untreatable' they are released from mental hospitals and prisons even though those around them, and often they themselves, know that they are dangerous). But Dr Shipman's crimes could never have been anticipated. As Gwen Adshead says: 'We associate personality disorder with high levels of dysfunction, but it is possible to be an effective and functioning person on one level, and have a personality disorder on another. The work that has been done on serial killers, mainly in America, finds that they usually are chaotic and dysfunctional, but that is not a prerequisite.'

There are various elements within his personality that have almost certainly contributed, to a greater or lesser extent, to making him a serial killer. They include:

## Grandiosity

The god-like regard in which most of his patients held him is perhaps the greatest clue to the warp in his character that turned him into a serial killer. He has grandiose ideas about himself: as we have seen, his greatest insult to anyone is to call them 'stupid', because in his own estimation he is cleverer, superior, above them. His mother, who died before he was mature enough to question her judgement, worshipped him, and brought him up to believe that he, the boy who went to the best grammar school in town, was, indeed, clever and superior. She died at a time in his life when he should, quite naturally, have been distancing himself from her; her death took her away from him completely, but paradoxically meant that he. could never, emotionally, loosen the bond with her. Just at the stage when most adolescents are realising that their parents are fallible and flawed human beings, his mother became seriously ill and eventually died, putting herself beyond reproach, beyond criticism, and enshrining her views and opinions for ever in him. And her view was that Freddie was the clever one, better than everyone else.

His experience at school conflicted with this. He was no academic slouch – he did get into High Pavement Grammar School, after all. But once there, he was by no means brilliant; he was a C-stream boy who stayed into the sixth form among the A- and B-stream boys, boys who coped easily with the A-level workload while he struggled to and from school under an enormous weight of books. It is interesting to note that he did not go back to the big bicentennial reunion held for the school a few years ago, nor does he have any contact with the thriving Old Paviors' Rugby Club, yet he always went to the Leeds Medical School reunions. His old school friends' assessment of him as an earnest plodder, who got where he did through sheer hard work, does not fit in with the view of himself that Shipman promulgates (and, on one level at

least, believes in). At medical school his application and
doggedness were the greatest of virtues: everybody there
was overwhelmed by the amount of work they were
expected to do, and brilliance and natural ability came a
very poor second to determination and sweat. He did not
stand out in any way, but very few did, so returning to the
reunions only reinforces his status.

His choice of medicine as a career appears to stem
entirely from his mother's protracted death, and the contact it gave him with the medical profession (and perhaps
a realisation of the reverence in which doctors are held).
It also began his life-long love affair with morphine, which
has to be an intrinsic part of his urge to kill. He could
have found better, less easily-traced drugs had he simply
been setting out to kill and rob a large number of patients.
For many years he showed considerable skill in covering
up his crimes (we may be astonished, in retrospect, about
how careless he was with circumstantial evidence, but the
truth is that had he not alerted the world, with his crude
forgery of Mrs Grundy's will, to what he was doing, he
could have been killing yet), but he certainly did not set
out to commit perfect murders or he would never have
chosen morphine: his relationship with that particular
drug derives from seeing it used on his mother, and, possibly, administering doses of it to her himself, to ease her
pain.

Making sure that everyone he encounters recognises
his importance and his superiority has been Fred
Shipman's quiet crusade all his life. He has done it by bullying those he regards as his inferiors, and who are
ill-equipped to defend themselves – the surgery staff, the
drugs company reps. Latterly, when his self-belief was
total, he would even try to score points off eminent pro-
fessors and consultants, deluding himself always into
imagining that those around were as impressed with him
as he was with himself. He bullied his children: easy meat

for a parent. If Primrose resisted his bullying, and she did (in some ways, she held sway over him), it was because she was forged of Oxtoby steel, made strong by her own strange childhood – but not strong enough, in intellectual confidence, to ever challenge his grandiose delusions about himself.

His own family doctor, Dr Wally Ashworth, points out that it is easy for all doctors to see themselves as God, especially single-handed practitioners who do not even have other GPs with whom to discuss their diagnoses. But even in a group practice, inside the confines of the consulting room the doctor enjoys an exalted position, invariably looked up to by his patients (and especially by the elderly, and by women). Patients go to a doctor because they are in need, and he, hopefully, satisfies that need. It puts him in a position of power, and his patients in a position of dependence. Unless he levels this with a healthy pinch of self-knowledge, with an understanding of the peculiar nature of the job, and comes down off his pedestal the minute he leaves the surgery, he has problems.

Pamela Taylor, Professor of Psychiatry at Broadmoor Hospital, also believes that his self-reverential attitude could have a persecutory element. 'What starts out as a useful defence mechanism can gradually turn into paranoia. A neurotic defence evolves into an illness. The paranoia would not necessarily show in other areas of his life: it can be well masked, especially within a slightly withdrawn existence.'

It is possible to imagine the young Fred Shipman, aware of his place within the pecking order of the intellectual elite at High Pavement Grammar School, developing just such a neurotic defence. He needed to believe in himself: he was, in the sixth form, surrounded by brighter boys, and his main support system, his mother, had been taken from him. It was necessary, for survival in a society in which he was ill at ease, to believe himself better, cleverer, special. It worked well on one level: it made him work hard to establish himself as that clever person (he was prepared to sit his A-levels twice to get the results he needed); it made him persevere with the grind of medical school, even though he had a wife and child to look after.

But eventually, his quest to be above others made him dispense drugs freely (he was the god-figure, handing down the blessings); and eventually it gave him the power of life and death, a power which all doctors have but very, very few have the urge to exercise: the ultimate manifestation of his god-like qualities.

## Aspberger's Syndrome

It is possible – although only a possibility – that Shipman suffers from a mild form of Aspberger's Syndrome, which is a mild form of autism. Many Aspberger's children are hyperactive, lack concentration, and fail to achieve their full potential. But there are some high-achieving Aspberger's cases where the sufferers are the opposite of hyperactive: they are devious, intense, quiet, yet they have failed to internalise the normal rules of society. They do not relate well to other people. The fact that Shipman has held together a marriage, a family and a job for so many years makes it unlikely that he is, in fact, an Aspberger's case, but there are some interesting parallels.

'Isolation is part of the Aspberger's profile, which may explain his choosing not to work in a group practice,' says psychologist Lisa Blakemore-Brown. 'He may want to be with people, but spoils it by behaving inappropriately and ultimately becomes isolated.' (Shipman's various attempts at hobbies and interests outside work invariably ended dramatically and suddenly although, in fairness, he did maintain some of them for a number of years. But there was an all-or-nothing commitment to them.) 'Aspberger's victims are often obsessive, like a hamster in a wheel, running and running but never getting anywhere, being secretive and being driven further and further into what they are doing.'

Dr Susan Bailey, a forensic adolescent psychiatrist, agrees: 'A very small number of high-achieving Aspberger's cases are dangerous. One typical characteristic of them is their aloofness. They get fixated about things, and although they may have intelligence and common sense, these do not prevail over the fixation. For example, he used morphine to kill: not a very intelligent choice, because it is traceable in the body. But you have the morphine thread running through his life – his mother's death, the conviction for forging prescriptions, the fact that when he was training he experimented with morphine. There is a pervasive interest in morphine almost certainly triggered by his mother's death.

'I can only speculate, but I think his mother must have been a very controlling influence on his life. She set about isolating him, not letting him play with the other children. He went to grammar school, which isolated him more from those around him. It is unusual that he was good at sports; this should have given him a bridge to cross to get close to other people.

'His marriage is interesting: it was a different time and there would be more pressure on them to get married because his girlfriend was pregnant. But even if there was pressure to marry, if the relationship was not good, you didn't have to stay married. Yet his attitude is "If I've done it, I'll stick by it," which is very much the Aspberger's mind-set.'

## Desensitisation

Doctors, by nature of the work they do, become adept at distancing themselves from the people they care for. Dr

Ian Napier, who worked with Shipman at Donneybrook, makes the point that it is hard, when dealing with patients every day, not to see them simply as part of the job, bodies to repair.

'Being a doctor is a very numbing experience, it requires detachment. You couldn't be a good doctor if you cared too much,' he says. 'When I had been a GP for about a year I had three patients die in one week. I felt I didn't want to carry on, but that feeling passes quickly. When I was a houseman, I had a patient who was a young man, about the same age that I was. He was married with a little daughter, and he had leukaemia. I was with him when he died. I'd been called out, and I was in evening dress, watching him die. It hurt, but it becomes less hurtful. It's not that you don't care, but you have to remove yourself from hurt and pain or you'd go crackers.

'Think about surgery. It goes against every instinct to stick a knife into flesh and cut a real, living person, even though they are anaesthetised. It is a hard thing to do the first time. My first post-mortem was on a two-year-old child who had been hit by a bus. He looked perfect, and then the pathologist started cutting him up. At that moment you think, "I can't be a doctor." But after a bit you can watch anything.

'I don't think Fred Shipman saw his victims as human beings. He was completely desensitised.'

At face value the desensitisation theory may sit ill with the picture of the good doctor Shipman who gently flirted with the old ladies, who spent ages chatting about their cats, who remembered each of them personally: he hardly appeared to treat them as though he had no regard for their humanity. Yet, perhaps more significantly, he was able to carry out very callous robberies of the dead, pocketing their engagement rings and pension money and the valueless bits of jewellery they had accumulated over their long lives, which suggests he had ceased to regard them as human beings. The chatty, personal way he dealt with them was nothing more than the scientist being nice to the laboratory animal, to inspire trust. He actually told Pamela Turner, whose mother Edith Brady he subsequently killed, that 'the old are a drain on the health service'.

## Obsession

People who suffer from obsessive-compulsive disorder (OCD) have intrusive thoughts, which they may try to resist, and even develop strategies to resist (OCD sufferers may persistently wash their hands, or have to follow exact rituals to get through each day). For some serial killers (and this possibly explains why the Yorkshire Ripper believed 'God' was telling him to kill) the intrusive thought concerns killing, and creates a need to kill to damp down the obsession. Professor Pamela Taylor believes that Shipman's crimes could be the product of an addiction to the thrill of killing (see next section), or of an obsessional drive, leading to an almost ritual urge to murder.

'Either or both of these hypotheses goes a long way to explaining why the pathological behaviour is repeated,' she says.

## Addiction

'Addiction' used to mean alcohol, drugs or tobacco, where a physical dependence is created. But now the meaning has widened to embrace patterns of behaviour which appear to be addictive, but in which no physical dependence is present. John Hodge, the head of the psychology department at Rampton Hospital, another secure establishment, has long been interested in the application of research on addiction to criminal behaviour. In a book entitled *Addiction to Crime* he writes: 'The idea that addiction or addictiveness is a property of substances is losing ground . . . there is increasing consensus that addiction can be demonstrated where no substance is involved, e.g., gambling, exercise, sexual behaviour.'

One chapter of the book, co-authored by Clive Hollin, consultant forensic psychologist at Rampton, and Mark Greswell, a clinical psychologist and forensic psychologist, is devoted to the study of multiple murder as an addiction. While not claiming that there is an addictive element in all serial killings, they see it as part of the drive to kill again for some murderers.

'With serial killers, the first murder tends to be unplanned: the murderer is in the frame of mind to do it, the opportunity arises, he does it. Once the taboo is broken, he can do it again, and he may start to engineer the opportunities,' says Mark Greswell. 'After that, he can become addicted to the adrenaline rush, the excitement, that the murder creates for him. Then he follows the classic addiction pattern. The more he does it, the more he wants to do it, to re-create the buzz. Often, the "high" is never as high as he hopes it will be, so he needs to do it again, and again, to try to achieve that peak.'

In Shipman's case there is a very clear picture of the frequency of the crimes increasing: from the occasional one during the Donneybrook years, to one every couple of months, to one a month and possibly even to six or seven a month. He was addicted to killing, it was the most dominant force in his life, and it seemed he needed to repeat his 'fix' ever more frequently.

The pathology of the killing career of Fred Shipman cannot be considered in isolation, as those of the solitary, dysfunctional killers can. He had one long-standing and apparently successful relationship from the age of nineteen, with Primrose. As a result, he had ongoing relationships with his children. He may have distanced himself from other members of his family, and certainly from his wife's family, but there remains a central core of human involvement in his life.

Their early relationship underlined his mother's view of him as cleverer than everyone else. While other medical students were going out with girls of equal intellectual ability, Fred's defining romance was with a girl who, although by no means unintelligent, was, by his standards, poorly educated. She is only three years younger than him, which is irrelevant now, but when they started to go out together she was only sixteen, and not even a streetwise sixteen. She was easily impressed by his university status. His profound dislike of her parents was based entirely on their dislike of him: they saw through him, and were suspicious of him from their first encounter. They did not, in other words, subscribe to the views held by Primrose and his dead mother that he was the centre of the universe.

The fact that the house in Roe Cross Green was so dirty and untidy that even hardened policemen were appalled, was perhaps a deep-seated rebellion against the life they were leading. Perhaps she simply gave up, aware that the only man she had ever loved or made love with was preoccupied by something else. Of course, there was no suggestion that she had any idea what he was doing to the old women who died around him – why would she have any more knowledge about death rates of elderly patients than anyone else? But she must have been aware of his obsession with work, the long hours he put in, the contempt in which he held almost everyone else. The isolation in which they lived – cut off from her family and from his – helped reinforce his view of the world, a world in which he was superior to everyone else, and intolerant of them for their 'stupidity'. Maybe she suspected something was wrong but had no idea what it was. Is that why she could no longer be bothered to even run the home along reasonably organised lines, because of an ineffable sadness about the way her life was turning out? Primrose, too, should perhaps be seen as one of Fred's victims.

As the number of deaths escalated, Shipman was running out of control. This is one way in which he behaves like a more 'typical' serial killer.

'It is characteristic of serial killers that at some point they become disorganised,' says Dr Susan Bailey. 'Some are disorganised from the beginning – they tend to come from highly dysfunctional backgrounds, they are not very bright. But others become disorganised later, as the number of crimes they are committing begins to dominate everything else, leaving them no time to run the rest of their lives effectively. Although he appears to have held everything together quite well, by the end he was drawing attention to himself.'

It was the last murder, the murder of Mrs Grundy, that finally drew attention to Fred Shipman, and he committed the forgery of her will so crudely that it is hard not to think that he wanted to be stopped. If he did not anticipate being stopped, it was an act of such supreme arrogance and greed that he really had lost all touch with reality. He murdered a wealthy widow, knowing that her daughter was a lawyer, and he forged her will, and the letters backing it up, so badly that they were bound to raise suspicions. If he hoped to get away with it, the only explanation can be that he wanted the money (about £400,000) quickly, as he may have had the intention of leaving the country rapidly (he told another GP, about six months before his arrest, that he was planning to move to France to retire 'soon'). Yet the old lady's estate was tied up in property, and it would be obvious to even the 'stupid' people Shipman despised that releasing the money would take time, time in which his forgery could be discovered.

The most obvious explanation is that he wanted to be caught, that he either knew that time was running out (he'd had warnings: Alan Massey, the Jim King medical negligence case, the previous police inquiry which he may have got wind of) or that he simply wanted to celebrate his notoriety. After all, what is the point of being the biggest serial killer ever if nobody knows about it?

Mrs Grundy's death certificate said 'old age'. It is a perfectly legitimate cause of death, but only the fool-hardy would use it. When the news of her exhumation reached the press, he posed smiling for the cameras, exuding confidence which those close to him assumed was proof of his innocence. But perhaps his confidence stemmed from relishing the prospect of being recognised for what he is: the most successful serial killer ever. After all, if he had not become greedy, and had quietly retired, nobody need ever have known about his obsession. But there is anecdotal evidence that serial killers do deliberately draw attention to themselves, either because they want to be stopped (and some, though probably not Fred Shipman, fight the impulse to kill very hard) or because they want their 'achievements' to be recognised. As they spiral out of control, they also feel a need for someone else to take over their lives, to bring some order back.

Professor Pamela Taylor believes that the final murder probably was a bid to be stopped. 'He is clearly very efficient and competent, so why call attention to his crimes unless it is part of his grandiose arrogance, which tells him there is no point at being so good at something unless somebody recognises it. Another hypothesis is that he simply got careless, particularly as the numbers were escalating. It is difficult to keep it all together, mentally, as well as the practical details. If anyone has overarching ambition, they run the risk of overstretching themselves and becoming careless.'

Perhaps, when the police appeared as he locked up his surgery on Saturday 1 August 1998, his reaction was not one of shock, but of relief.

Back in 1856 the whole of Britain was riveted by the trial of Dr William Palmer, the poisoner. People queued from 5am for places in the public gallery at the Old Bailey; the court had to be rebuilt to house all the lawyers, witnesses and spectators. When he was hanged, the rope used was sold in small pieces to the crowd, desperate for souvenirs. A gambling man all his life (it was gambling debts that led him to kill at least fourteen people, one his own wife and several of them his own children), he would have been delighted to know that £200,000 (a staggering £12 million today) changed hands in bets as to whether or not he would be acquitted.

Dr Palmer was arrogant and cavalier, and went to the dock protesting his innocence. He was only charged with one murder, but the bodies of two of his other victims had been exhumed and the prosecution were prepared to charge him with their murders if the first case failed. And, like Dr Shipman, he was only caught because with the final death he crudely forged a will leaving him £4,000 (the equivalent today of £240,000, slightly less than Shipman tried to take from Mrs Grundy's family).

Dr Palmer got away with it for as long as he did, and killed as many people as he did, for exactly the same reason that Fred Shipman was able to get away with it: he was the doctor, he prescribed the medicine, and he wrote out the death certificates. Despite great refinements in post-mortem techniques and forensic detective work in the years since Dr Palmer laced glasses of wine with strychnine, Fred Shipman still had those same major advantages when it came to keeping justice at bay. He had the trust of his victims and their families, he had the weapon within his grasp and he had the opportunity, going alone into their homes with them. Unlike Palmer, who was careless in his choice of victims, Fred Shipman specialised in elderly women, and the occasional men, who lived alone, and whose deaths, while lamented, would not be suspicious.

Professor Robert Forrest, Britain's only medically qualified forensic toxicologist (he also has a law degree) has come up with an acronym for doctors and nurses who murder those in their care: CASK, standing for Carer Assisted Serial Killings. He describes it as a 'rare, although possibly underestimated, phenomenon; the systematic infliction of injury, usually with drugs and often with a fatal outcome, to a number of patients by a member of the caring professions . . . The numbers of patients involved are not trivial. Typically between five and ten deaths are associated with each case, and the incidence appears to be of the order of one to two reported cases per million health-care workers. This implies that in Britain, cases may be seen every three to six years . . . There may be significant under-reporting of cases outside hospitals.'

From an international list of cases, which includes the English nurse Beverley Allit and the doctor John Bodkin Adams (who was acquitted in 1957 of murdering one of a series of wealthy female patients who died, leaving him money and possessions), more than 25 per cent are doctors, although the highest percentage is of nurses (45 per cent).

CASK cases do not include doctors who practise euthanasia, nor is euthanasia relevant to the Shipman case, except that there may in some of his killings have been an overlap: one or two of his victims were in pain, were very ill, may have wanted to die. It is possible that the crucial first killing was a 'mercy' killing, so that he broke the taboo of inflicting death for justifiable (at least, arguably justifiable) reasons. But the vast majority of his killings were unnecessary and involved no element of euthanasia.

Although, compared to other methods, poisoning is a relatively unusual method of killing, in CASK cases it is the most common. Professor Forrest, who knows all there is to know about poisons, believes that the choice of morphine was an intrinsic part of Shipman's urge to kill. 'You wouldn't choose it for bodies that are going to be buried – it's been found in the tissue of mummies thousands of years old. As long as there is tissue, it can be found.'

Professor Forrest concludes that there is no way of recognising potentially harmful doctors and nurses and other care workers, who may be attracted (as Shipman probably was) to a profession which gives them opportunity to harm and kill (rather than finding themselves in a position to do it by chance).

'Others in the medical profession simply have to be eternally vigilant, and prepared to think the unthinkable, because there is no way of screening out these people,' he says. 'Working in the medical profession, it is possible to deceive a lot of people for a long time.'

Because of his (fairly) clever selection of victims, Shipman made detection even harder. More than half of all people over the age of sixty-five have a long-standing illness, making the attention of the GP an unremarkable, and even welcome, occurrence. (According to a survey conducted by Age Concern, 10 per cent of all patients over the age of fifty feel they have been given inadequate treatment as a result of their age. The charity believes that the elderly are routinely discriminated against by the health services. Small wonder that in Hyde the elderly flocked to the doctor who appeared to fly in the face of this general downgrading of the elderly.)

'What we have is a doctor who is trained not to kill people, but to care for them,' says Professor Forrest. 'But all medical treatment is a form of controlled violence. It's obvious in surgery, but in medical treatment too, doctors are administering drugs all the time which are poisonous if taken wrongly.

'Why somebody moves from being a carer to a deliberate killer is extremely difficult to say, and we can only assume there is some sort of deficiency in the way they are conditioned. The ethical mores have not taken. And I guess that this sort of thing is more likely to happen when somebody is not working together with colleagues, when he doesn't have somebody around to judge him on an everyday basis. When you are put on a pedestal by the local community, you need to be reminded that you are mortal, that you are not omnipotent.

'The loss of his mother at seventeen seems to have been traumatic, but I cannot say whether that predisposed him towards killing patients. By the time you are seventeen your personality is pretty well formed.

'His pethidine addiction may well be relevant. He has an addictive personality. Traditionally, it has been nurses rather than doctors who get hooked on pethidine, because it is very effective for relieving period pains. If you develop a tolerance, you can take very large amounts. Most people cope with the stresses of medical practice without substance abuse, but doctors do have a high rate of alcoholism. The combination of the stress and the easy availability of drugs means that some doctors also become addicted.

'As a young hospital doctor he may simply have taken pethidine in order to get some sleep. He'd be doing long hours, and then going home to babies and nappies, and he might have needed something to help him sleep. Once you start, you need more and more, and you start to enjoy the sensation it produces.

'Under the conditions that prevail today, his addiction would have been treated more seriously, and he would probably have been struck off – and there are a lot of people who would be alive today if that had happened. That is when he could have been stopped. After that . . . People don't believe doctors can do this sort of thing, so he was able to carry on for a long time. But we should all be suspicious: every coroner, registrar of deaths, every person who countersigns a cremation certificate and every crematorium referee should ask themselves whether everything is as it should be, with every death. But if you ask too many questions you can upset the grieving relatives.

'He had a death rate of two and half times the average, but that is not necessarily a clue. Some doctors have practices which include lots of nursing homes, some have lots of elderly patients. Crude death rates are a poor indicator of performance, but they are an indicator. If Shipman had been a surgeon, and his death rate had been two and half times that of his colleagues, it would have been detected much earlier.'

Although Professor Forrest acknowledges that the choice of morphine left an easily detectable trail, he points out that the availability of it made it much more attractive than other virtually undetectable drugs.

As to why Shipman became a serial killer he, too, has a theory: 'I think he did it simply as a matter of convenience, getting rid of an awkward patient by killing her rather than transferring her to another GP. I think that quite a significant number of the people he killed were murdered quite simply because he did not wish to continue caring for them, for whatever reason.'

Dr Fred Shipman's crimes are going to intrigue forensic experts for many years to come. They may not have the lurid, violent fascination of some of the other famous serial killing cases (the Moors murderers, the Wests, the Yorkshire Ripper), but they are harder to understand, and defy belief more, than killings committed by misfits and madmen.

One of Shipman's colleagues summed it up: 'I didn't like him, but if you'd asked me which of my acquaintances was a serial killer, he would have been a long way down the list I would have nominated.'

The policemen who headed the case, Bernard Postles and Mike Williams, talked long into the night about what his possible motivation could be, and at the end of a long and very demanding investigation, they are no closer to an answer than anyone else.

'It's the question everyone asks: why?' says Detective Chief Superintendent Postles. 'With each killing he usually turned up on spec, but we don't know why he targeted particular people. We were constantly questioning ourselves: are we wrong? We tried to keep an open mind and be objective but it was difficult.

'We considered all the possibilities: greed, revenge, sex. Money only appeared to be the motive in the Kathleen Grundy case. There was no evidence of sexual interference with any of the victims. Clothing, apart from a rolled-up sleeve, had not been touched.

'His finances showed nothing out of the ordinary. There was no evidence of him having an affair. The only clue is in his attitude. He thinks he is superior, and wants to control the situation.'

# 16
# Conclusions

The people of Hyde, honest, hard-working, good people, are almost all enmeshed in the story of Dr Fred Shipman. They are relatives of victims, neighbours or friends of victims' families, ex-patients of his: the tentacles spread far and wide; the impact on the community is enormous. In its previous brush with notoriety, the Moors Murders, the town of Hyde was at least able to distance itself from the horrors: Brady and Hindley were in-comers, living on an overspill housing estate built by Manchester council; only the final two of their murders happened there, and the murderers' connections with the town were tenuous. The number of people who knew them locally was very limited, and the townspeople of Hyde could shudder like the rest of us, without feeling in any way part of the crimes.

The murders of Fred Shipman are very different. They were going on, with the people of Hyde as their victims, for perhaps the whole twenty-one years that Shipman practised in the town. They hit at the very heart of the community; they left nobody completely untouched.

But there is one important way in which the murders of Brady and Hindley and those of Shipman have both branded themselves on the public consciousness: they went against a very deep grain. The reason that the Moors Murders are still, so many years after the crimes, a constant subject of discussion is not because of Ian Brady, but because Myra Hindley overturned all the deeply held social stereotypes of women as the caring, nurturing sex. It was her participation, a woman's, in the killing of little children that has kept hers and Brady's names in the headlines ever since their conviction.

The murders of Fred Shipman have a similar shock value – he, too, went against all the accepted standards of his profession. He was callous, calculating and cruel. Adrian Pomfret, the ex-husband of one of the victims, Bianka Pomfret, sums it up more articulately than most: 'It's a bad do, a terrible do. I feel disgust towards him. He's a wretched human being. He's singled out elderly women who were very vulnerable, who had little support in the outside world. A guy who breaks into a bank and shoots at people to get a million pounds is an animal and should be treated as such by the law. But it is far more shocking for a man who is a GP, who under the Hippocratic oath is supposed to do his utmost to keep people alive and care for them, to kill them. He turned the Hippocratic oath into the hypocritical oath. Those women went to him like lambs to the slaughter.

'Certain people in life you are automatically wary of . . . But your local GP, no. It's very difficult to come to terms with.

'There have always been evils: genocides, war, crimes against humanity. History tells us that. I was a soldier for nine years. You expect death. You don't expect all your beliefs in the society you are brought up in, which is basically striving for ongoing improvement in civilisation, to be suddenly reversed. You don't expect that one of those people who you think of as a representative of good, a model citizen, working to achieve the good things in society, to turn out to be the opposite. He's a pillar of society, a professional person who is there to help and tend to the sick and needy, and yet he's done the reverse. You put burglar alarms in your house, your car, you warn your children not to go with strange men: you do all these things to protect them. But if somebody's sick you send them to the local family doctor for help. It should be the safest place to be. A local GP making a house-call; you should be safer in his hands than anyone else's.'

This overpowering sense of shock, and the threat to deeply held values, has unsettled the traditional, moral, old-fashioned community, where friendships and humour and mutual support are valued above all else, where sufferings and hardships are borne lightly, where the welcome (extended to Shipman as well as to others) is genuine and warm.

He has made the people of Hyde more introverted. Some have clammed up completely, devastated by the news of the many deaths, and by the media onslaught on the town. They wait for the day when normal business can be resumed, when the Shipman years can be relegated to the history books. They want no part in the gossip, the verbal inquests, the constant assessing and reassessing that goes on in the pubs, cafés, supermarkets and old folks' clubs.

Others have a natural fascination with the subject, wanting to know all they can about the murderer and his motivation. Others, wrongly, carry a guilt over what went on, never free from the thought that perhaps there was something they could have done or said which would have stopped the accelerating murder toll.

John Shaw, the gentle taxi driver, wonders if he could have halted the killings by speaking up sooner. He could not: he rightly assesses he would have been disregarded had he become involved earlier. The Massey family, the undertakers who did everything feasible to draw attention to what was happening, wonder in quiet retrospect if there was anything more they could have done to stop things sooner. There is not: they did all within their power. Councillor Joe Kitchen, unhappy with the circumstances of his mother's death, says: 'When we look back, we wonder if, had we sued him for neglect, we might have ended up saving some lives. So many people, in so many ways, end up feeling guilty for the crimes he committed – the relatives for not being more demanding and asking more questions, and so on.'

The truth is that a complaint from the Kitchen family would not have frightened Shipman into stopping, because the existing medical negligence claim against him made no difference to his behaviour.

There are many others who worked with him, or who had friends or relatives killed by him, who persecute themselves with the memories of tiny incidents or conversations which could have alerted them but which they failed to pick up on. Father Denis Maher has found himself consoling many families who believe, with hindsight, that they should have made more fuss about the suspicious circumstances their relative was found in.

'It is a terrible legacy he has given the town – so many people feel guilty, and so many families have been torn apart squabbling over missing possessions which they now believe he took,' says Father Denis.

The answer for all of them is to accept that there was nothing that they, as individuals, could do to stop the death toll earlier. They all did their best, and, for those like the Masseys and John Shaw and Dr Linda Reynolds who raised the alarm, their contribution was hugely important.

Stopping someone as well-equipped and as dedicated to killing as Fred Shipman would never have been easy. As Professor Robert Forrest points out, murderers from the medical professions are of above average intelligence.

Couple this with the availability of drugs, the excuse to be in intimate physical proximity to the victims, and in Shipman's case the selection of vulnerable, elderly people as victims, and you have a recipe for near-perfect crimes.

But there are faults to be exposed, ways in which the killing could have been stopped earlier. The manner in which society treats and undervalues the elderly is an obvious factor in all crimes affecting the very old, whether it is burglaries, thefts or, in this very unusual case, serial killing. Old ladies living alone make perfect victims: nobody to catch the killer red-handed, nobody to raise the alarm rapidly, no reason to question the death too closely because of the victims' age. Among the families of the dead there may even have been some who, subconsciously anyway, sighed with relief at the resolution of the problems of an increasingly infirm relative.

However, the population of Hyde is probably less guilty of indifference towards its elderly than most areas of the country. It is a warm, supportive and family-oriented town, with a growing elderly population. A strong sense of identity binds people together. There is an infrastructure of pensioners' clubs, sheltered housing, welcoming pubs and bingo sessions, which makes being old in this town easier than in many more affluent suburbs.

There are other questions to be answered, of a practical nature, in the bid to establish why the Shipman crimes went on for as long as they did. There is no monitoring of death rates among the patients of individual GPs, for example. The West Pennine Health Authority, which covers the Hyde area, is typical of the rest of the country: it does not have a computer system which records and cross-references the number of deaths among the patients of its 230 GPs. The authority had no way of knowing that the mortality rate among Shipman's patient list was higher than that of other doctors in the town, and there are no plans for instituting a system whereby they would know.

Similarly, all deaths are notified to registrars of births, marriages and deaths, but again there is no analysis of them by individual GP. The whole West Pennine area has a high mortality rate, even within the relatively high rate for the north-west of England: it is deemed to be a deprived area.

Instituting a computerised monitoring of the deaths within individual GP practices would be an obvious way of spotting another rogue GP like Shipman. On the other hand, the chances of there ever being another family doctor on a similarly rampant killing spree are so remote that it probably only makes sense to incorporate this analysis when statistical bases are being changed, and there are no immediate plans for this.

The strange situation of Dr Shipman having medical records of his dead patients in his garage and inside his home has already been addressed: the rules have changed, and GPs are no longer able to request the records back after they have gone to the health authority.

The procedure was that after a death, the notes were sent to the authority, who removed the patient's name from the GP's list. The notes were then either stored by the authority or by the GP, and it was up to the GP to choose. Shipman chose to have them returned to him. But this option is no longer open to GPs, and of the nineteen sets of records the police requested, fourteen were with the authority and five were on Shipman's premises. He was one of only twelve GPs, out of 104 in the Tameside area, who stored his own records.

Doctors who did store the notes of dead patients were required to do so in 'secure' accommodation. David Common, chief executive of the West Pennine Health Authority, says that in his view, storing records in cardboard boxes in a garage was not 'secure'. However, there was no duty on the health authority to check out the premises.

The other, apparently obvious, way in which Shipman's murders could have been detected earlier was through his over-prescription of morphine. The Health Authority monitors the prescribing habits of GPs, and Shipman came in for close scrutiny because he exceded his budget on a regular basis. But although he overspent on drugs, he cost the health service less than other GPs on referrals to specialists.

When inquiries were made into his prescribing, the Health Authority found nothing to worry about. Jan Forster, director of primary care for the WPHA, says: 'He was a high-cost prescriber, but the nature of his prescribing was rational. He was using a lot of hypertension drugs to reduce the incidence of heart disease. He was always very defensive and had rational arguments for the drugs he was using. His referral rates were low, so care was being provided for patients within the practice.' (In other words, he was not sending patients on to even more expensive hospital treatment.)

Nor was his prescribing of morphine out of line with other comparable GP practices.

Jan Forster says, 'What we were looking at was groups of drugs which may have been prescribed in higher than average amounts, and the opiate group (which includes morphine) did not show up.'

Morphine is covered by the Controlled Drugs Act, and anyone storing it must be on the Controlled Drugs Register, which makes them open to regular checks from the police to ensure that it is kept securely. Shipman was not on this register: he had voluntarily agreed not to keep controlled drugs after his conviction for forging prescriptions in 1976.

So the fact that he was storing morphine went unnoticed. He was allowed to prescribe it as freely as any other doctor – he was not supposed to have any in his surgery or in his medical bag.

When patients with terminal illnesses die, there is often morphine left over. The doctors and nurses in charge of their palliative care have a duty to either hand back the morphine to the Health Authority or dispose of it. Even if it is handed back, it cannot be used for another patient. Because of this, most doctors and nurses dispose of it with witnesses.

This is one area where procedures could and should be tightened up. As a result of having to look into the Shipman affair very closely, West Pennine Health Authority has sent a report to the Department of Health recommending changes that could be implemented nationally.

Another obvious area for improvement is in the monitoring of the appointment of doctors with criminal records. Although the GMC procedure is better today than it was in 1976 (Shipman would probably have been suspended from practice nowadays, and then his re-entry into the profession much more closely monitored), it remains true that health authorities do not necessarily know of the criminal records of doctors they contract to work in their area. Although Shipman's colleagues at the Donneybrook Surgery knew of his past, when he became a single-handed practitioner he did not have to inform the Health Authority. It is possible that there are other GPs practising in Britain whose health authorities have no idea of their backgrounds.

The approach to the millennium for Hyde was not a time for excitement and anticipation: it was the time of the Shipman trial, eight weeks which cast a deep, ugly shadow over the impending celebrations. People who care deeply about the town, councillors like June Evans and Joe Kitchen, the detective Stan Egerton who has made his home here for many years, the victim-support organiser Helen Ogburn, and countless more, want the town to find pride in itself again. They do not want the name of Hyde to be associated with the biggest serial killer in modern history, but they reluctantly face up to the fact that, for some time at least, that is what the rest of Britain and the rest of the world is going to remember about Hyde.

But they are hopeful, and they are right to be hopeful, that the town will recover, and that the tremendous community spirit will triumph. 'Hyde is bigger, stronger and worth more than Dr Shipman,' says Stan Egerton. 'The people here are not responsible for what happened. They will never forget it; none of us who have been involved will ever forget it. But now that the trial is over, the town can put it to rest. Hyde will recover.'

Shipman hung
himself in prison
in 2004.

Warner Books now offers an exciting range of quality titles by both established and new authors. All of the books in this series are available from:

Little, Brown and Company (UK),
P.O. Box 11,
Falmouth,
Cornwall TR10 9EN.

Fax No: 01326 569555
Telephone No: 01326 569777
E-mail: books@barni.avel.co.uk

Payments can be made as follows: cheque, postal order (payable to Little, Brown and Company) or by credit cards, Visa/Access. Do not send cash or currency. UK customers and B.F.P.O. please allow £1.00 for postage and packing for the first book, plus 50p for the second book, plus 30p for each additional book up to a maximum charge of £3.00 (7 books plus).

Overseas customers including Ireland, please allow £2.00 for the first book plus £1.00 for the second book, plus 50p for each additional book.

NAME (Block Letters) ...........................................................

..........................................................................................

ADDRESS ...........................................................................

..........................................................................................

..........................................................................................

☐ I enclose my remittance for ...........................................

☐ I wish to pay by Access/Visa Card

Number ☐☐☐☐☐☐☐☐☐☐☐☐☐☐☐☐☐

Card Expiry Date ☐☐☐☐